MEDIEVAL ENGLISH THEATRE

VOLUME THIRTY-NINE (2017)

MEDIEVAL ENGLISH THEATRE

VOLUME THIRTY-NINE (2017)

edited by

Sarah Carpenter, Gordon Kipling, and Meg Twycross

D. S. BREWER

Medieval English Theatre is an international refereed journal publishing articles on medieval and early Tudor theatre and pageantry in all its aspects (not confined to England), together with articles and records of modern survivals or equivalents. Most issues are illustrated. Contributions to be considered for future volumes are welcomed: see the end of this volume and website for further information:

<www.medievalenglishtheatre.co.uk>

First published 2018
D. S. Brewer, Cambridge

ISBN 978 1 84384 499 0

ISSN 0143–3784

D. S. Brewer is an imprint of Boydell & Brewer Ltd
PO Box 9, Woodbridge, Suffolk IP12 3DF, UK
and of Boydell & Brewer Inc.
668 Mt Hope Avenue, Rochester, NY 14620–2731, USA
website: www.boydellandbrewer.com

A catalogue record for this title is available from the British Library

Printed and bound in Great Britain by
TJ International Ltd, Padstow, Cornwall

MIX
Paper from responsible sources
FSC® C013056

MEDIEVAL ☙ ENGLISH ❧ THEATRE

VOLUME THIRTY-NINE (2017)

CONTENTS

ILLUSTRATIONS

EDITORIAL

This volume testifies to the vitality of the field of early theatre, demonstrating the eclectic range of interests *METh* engages. A group of essays approach the performance records of civic and community drama. Philip Butterworth takes us back to the founding principles of *METh* by exploring the technology of pageant-waggon maintenance and manoeuvre in the light of the Chester records – the pageant waggon being the subject of the very first volume of the journal in 1979. Similarly seeking to make sense of fragmentary record evidence, James Stokes investigates the scattered and enigmatic references to 'camping closes' and 'game places' as potential performance sites in the vicinity of Beccles in Suffolk. Jamie Beckett starts from a puzzling textual reference, the name of the Jew 'Fergus' in the lost York *Funeral of the Virgin*, pursuing local history and tradition to identify a possible hate figure. The perspective is broadened by Tom Pettitt's wide-ranging and suggestive discussion of Gladman's supposed 'Carnival' parade in Norwich in 1443, and the revealing analogues of street performance that may be found not in England but in Italy. James McBain pursues not different locations but different types of audience: examining Gascoigne's skilful play on New Comedy in the *Supposes*, he evaluates how different levels of familiarity with the genre in audiences at the Inns of Court and the University of Oxford suggest different kinds of spectator response. These last three essays all arise from papers given at the 2016 METh meeting at Canterbury, while Diana Wyatt's was delivered at the 2017 event at Glasgow. Based on a family record of a 1526 wedding, this opens up the field of household drama, with the apparently traditional mounting of a 'maske and play' as part of the celebrations. Apart from these essays, we are pleased to engage with theatrical productions of the last year, with Peter Happé's review of Elisabeth Dutton's production of the Digby MS *The Killing of the Children*, mounted on 8 February 2017 in the chapel of New College, Oxford.

The 2017 METh meeting, held in Glasgow with co-hosts Pamela King and Eila Williamson, was a special event, held to honour the life-work of Philip Butterworth, a founder member of METh. His work on the practices of early performance – technological and mechanical, magic and special effects, audiences and performance conventions – has played a key role in the development of work in early theatre over the last forty years. The topic of the meeting, 'Cultures of Performance', was chosen to reflect the broad sphere of his interests. The meeting was preceded, in what has now become a very productive tradition, by a day's symposium run by the Early English Drama and Performance Network (EEDPN) for postgraduate and early-career researchers in early theatre. This was a lively and well-attended event, with talks and workshops focused on three main areas: digital transformations and approaches, performance as research, and working with records and archives.

The packed day of the METh meeting opened and closed with personal tributes to Philip Butterworth and his work from John Marshall and Katie Normington. John Marshall, who also presented a vivid account of the varying Robin Hood celebrations mounted for 'royalty, gentry and the middling sort', and Katie Normington, who delivered an incisive overview of Philip Butterworth's own work and its implications for early theatre study. Between, two papers considered drama's engagement with topical issues: Camille Marshall discussed the stage significance of the 'mop', perhaps a doll, representing the Christ Child in the Towneley Shepherds' Plays in the light of confessional conflict around the Reformation, while Marija Krnic explored little-known records of Dalmatian saints' plays and their potential role in unifying divided social classes. Two papers addressed more elite forms of entertainment, with Sarah Carpenter introducing some newly discovered letters of playful invitation to joust from the court of Edward III, and Diana Wyatt the entertainments for the wedding of Elizabeth Nevile in 1526. Peter Happé reflected on the extraordinary versatility of the interlude form, its patrons, performers, and staging. Two papers addressed more theoretical issues playing upon early drama. Tom Pettitt introduced the concept of *interaxionality* (a counterpart to literary *intertextuality*) to explore the patterns of action that derive from one play to another, while Sarah Brazil reassessed the centrality or usefulness of the concept of *mimesis* in understanding early drama. Under the direction of Elisabeth Dutton and Olivia Robinson, the meeting joined in a reading of a new translation by Olivia Robinson and Aurélie Blanc of a convent nativity play from Huy, with the venue of the James Arnott Theatre bringing out both the sense of sacred space and the moving intimacy of the action. The session concluded with a lively Round Table touching on the previous day's EEDPN workshop (Tamara Haddad), questions of directing modern productions of medieval plays (Jodi-Anne George), the parish play recorded in the seventeenth century commonplace book of Richard Shann (Clare Egan), and the version of the York Plays performed for the Festival of Britain (Laura Rice). At the business meeting that concluded the day, the Chair of METh Society was passed from Sarah Carpenter to Clare Wright, who will lead the Society forward into the year of *METh*'s fortieth volume in 2018.

ꝏ ꝏ ꝏ ꝏ ꝏ ꝏ ꝏ

The cover design is based on the frontispiece of Wenceslaus Faber de Budweis's *Iudicium Lipsense* (Nuremberg: Friedrich Creussner, 1489–90), an almanac and prognostications for Leipzig for the year 1490. The angel is rotating the wheel of the heavens with a very practical crank handle. Unfortunately, in his anxiety to show the workings of the celestial machine (which is also a Wheel of Fortune), the artist has drawn the far down-shaft of the framework *inside* the globe it is meant to be revolving; put it on the outside, and it becomes a very practical stage machine, if one were to reduce the planets in size and weight. Mars *qui est dominus anni* is in the dominant house at the top of the wheel, and *bellum provocare velit*, which bodes especially ill for Eastern Europe. For the whole book (uncoloured), see the Münchener DigitalisierungsZentrum (MDZ) of the Bayerische StaatsBibliothek, München,[1] at <http://daten.digitale-sammlungen.de/~db/0003/bsb00033573/images/>. The image is reproduced by their kind permission.

ꝏ ꝏ ꝏ ꝏ ꝏ ꝏ ꝏ

1. Bayerische Staatsbibliothek, München, 4 Inc.s.a. 408 c, fol. 2r, urn:nbn:de:bvb:12-bsb00033573-3.

ONLINE LINKS

More and more articles these days carry lengthy and complex references to online sources. While these authenticate the writer's material, they are virtually useless to readers, who have to type them out by hand if they want to pursue them further.

This is particularly frustrating when the links are to videos or images which are, this being a journal dedicated to the theatrical arts, necessary to the writer's argument. From this issue, METh is therefore posting on its website at <www.medievalenglishtheatre.co.uk/urls.html> an active list of all the URLs referred to in the current volume, which will henceforward be only a click away. This will be particularly effective because it enables us to link to coloured images – prohibitively expensive to print, but easy to find and enlarge online. But it also gives readers a chance to link to video, which can alter and enrich their whole experience of the argument (see Tom Pettitt's article in this volume). We are aware that this is a hybrid vehicle, but we hope that it will be useful while the world makes up its mind (if it ever does) whether it prefers electronic or paper-based scholarship, or settles for a mixture of both.

PAGEANT-CARRIAGE MAINTENANCE AT CHESTER

Philip Butterworth

John Constable's famous painting, *The Hay Wain* (1821) (PLATE 1), is not only well-known for its qualities as a painting but also for its subject matter: the wain, harnessed to its three horses stands in the water of the River Stour. The driver and his companion appear to be resting on top of the wain. The most frequently recorded interpretation of the scene regards the focus to be that of 'three horses pulling a hay wain or large family cart across the river'.[1] But the spatial orientation of the wain and horses seems to be in line with the flow of the river. Access to the river looks as if it has been from the near side of the image – the Suffolk side. The ground on the far bank of the river, the Essex side, appears to be slightly higher and less negotiable. The image focuses on a seemingly stationary team in the river. Even if the painting represents a still image depicting a moving one, the direction of the team does not appear to be one of crossing the flow of the river; the horses do not seem to be pulling the wain 'across the river'. If this is the case, why is the wain in the river?

The same question may be asked of another of Constable's paintings, *Salisbury Cathedral from the Meadows* (1831) (PLATE 2), painted some ten years after *The Hay Wain*.[2] Here too, a wain, a somewhat more elaborate vehicle than that depicted in *The Hay Wain*, also appears to stand in the river (the river Nadder, a tributary of the Wiltshire Avon). There are common subject features in both paintings to condition the respective compositions. In both paintings:

1. See the following URLs for descriptions of Constable's haywain said to be travelling 'across the river', <https://en.wikipedia.org/wiki/The_Hay_Wain> [accessed 26 November 2017]; <http://www.dailymail.co.uk/travel/article-1160402/Constable-country-In-search-inspiration-The-Hay-Wain.html> [accessed 26 November 2017]; <http://www.vam.ac.uk/content/articles/s/constables-studies-for-the-hay-wain/> [accessed 26 November 2017].
2. For an analysis of the painting see <http://www.tate.org.uk/art/research-publications/the-sublime/anne-lyles-sublime-nature-john-constables-salisbury-cathedral-from-the-meadows-r1129550> [accessed 26 November 2017]. See also <https://en.wikipedia.org/wiki/Salisbury_Cathedral_from_the_Meadows> [accessed 26 November 2017]; <http://www.theguardian.com/artanddesign/2014/mar/04/constable-salisbury-cathedral-from-the-meadows-tour> [accessed 26 November 2017].

PLATE 1: John Constable *The Hay Wain* (1821)
Photo © The National Gallery London

the teams stand in line with the flow of the river; three horses pull the respective wains; two men sit on top of the wain; a man, holding a pole, stands next to a small boat or punt on the far shore; a dog stands on the near bank and focuses attention on the wain; other human figures in the foreground help to frame the narrative of the composition. Again, why is the wain in the river?

George Sturt (Bourne), writing in his classic work, *The Wheelwright's Shop* (1923), offers an authoritative wheelwright's understanding:

> Men who used carts knew something about the advantages of a little moisture for tightening wheels. Not for the horse's sake alone was it that carters would drive through a road-side pond, or choose to ford a stream rather than go over a bridge beside the ford. The wheels were better for the wetting. Very careful countryfolk – with but one cart to cherish perhaps, and that a donkey-cart – would keep a wet sack over the wheel on the sunny side for the same reason that made me, when the sun was most blazing, throw wet sacks over the water-butts in my yard, the object in my case being to keep the staves from shrinking and falling apart.[3]

Sturt's observation offers a most convincing explanation of the purpose of Constable's wains standing in the Rivers Stour and Nadder. When Sturt refers to 'moisture for tightening wheels' he indicates that the value was 'Not for the horse's sake alone'. This, of course, suggests that some benefit of the practice was afforded to the horse. A correspondence in *The Daily Telegraph* (begun 8 July 2013)[4] accepts Sturt's principal statement in respect of value to the wain but also adds understanding of the need to cool down the horses' legs and feet by standing in the water. The tenor of the newspaper exchange of views refers to this apparent knowledge being familiar to everyone.

Such familiarity is likely to have been passed down from and through agricultural practice. Strong evidence of the tradition of soaking the wheels of carts, wains, and wagons in water in order to swell and strengthen the

3. George Sturt *The Wheelwright's Shop* (Cambridge UP, 1923) 182. For precise illustrative examples of Sturt's reference to the custom of driving carts through streams, fords, or ponds, see the paintings of Myles Birket Foster (1850–1914). In Birket Foster's *Returning from Market* a cart is being driven across a ford at the side of a footbridge. In another of Birket Foster's paintings, *A Peep at the Hounds, here they come!*, a wain, pulled by three horses, appears to have just negotiated some water (possibly a ford) on a track.

4. <http://www.telegraph.co.uk/comment/letters/10165485/Constable-and-the-art-of-hay-wain-maintenance.html> [accessed 26 November 2017].

PLATE 2: John Constable *Salisbury Cathedral from the Meadows* (1831)
Photo © Tate London 2017

components and their joints is recorded in the current *Mendip Ponds Project*. This project has been concerned with conservation of the Great Crested Newt and has attempted to locate the most suitable habitats for these creatures, many of which have been identified as dew ponds.[5] In turn, a number of these ponds have been more accurately determined to be 'cart ponds'. *The Mendip Ponds Project* documentation describes these ponds:

> Cart Ponds are long narrow excavations slightly wider than a horse and cart. They are walled on both sides and usually have a base of stone slabs or cobbles, whilst the ground at either end slopes into the pool. Built during the eighteenth and nineteenth centuries, these ponds were designed primarily for livestock to drink, but secondarily to allow a cart to be pulled straight through the water, entering at one end and exiting at the other. The wooden wheels of the carts were surrounded by an iron ring [more likely to have been 'strakes'] that was in contact with the ground. During dry weather the carts were pulled through these ponds to prevent the wooden wheels shrinking away from their iron surrounds. Sixteen of the ponds in the project area are 'double-ended cart ponds'.[6]

Two modern-day examples that closely match the above description may be seen in the main street of Chipping Campden, Gloucestershire, where the feature is known as the 'cart wash', and the recently discovered version in the village of Aldfield, near Fountains Abbey, North Yorkshire.[7] Both ponds are

5. Edward Alfred Martin *Dew-ponds: History, Observation, and Experiment* (London: Werner Laurie, 1915); Walter Johnson *Folk Memory: or, The Continuity of British Archaeology* (Oxford: Clarendon Press, 1908) 295–318.
6. *The Mendip Ponds Project: A Proposal to Conserve the Great Crested Newt (Triturus cristatus) in the Mendip Hills* compiled by John Dickson, Trevor Beebee and Jasper Casey on behalf of The Reptile and Amphibian Group for Somerset, in partnership with The Mendip Hills AONB Unit and The Somerset Wildlife Trust (2014) 16. Online at <http://www.mendiphillsaonb.org.uk/wp-content/uploads/2011/08/THE_MENDIP_POND_PROJECT_PROPOSAL_Final.pdf>. See Plates 3 and 4, and the website in general <http://www.mendiphillsaonb.org.uk> for context of the project.
7. <http://www.cotswoldjournal.co.uk/news/14113360.Ancient_cart_wash_feature_in_Chipping_Campden_restored_to_its_former_glory/>. The cart pond or cart wash at Spa Ghyll Farm, Aldfield (near Fountains Abbey) was discovered by the 3D Archaeological Society, based in Harrogate. Some images of the pond may be found on their website. See also my photographs of these ponds at <http://www.medievalenglishtheatre.co.uk/urls.html>.

double-ended and stone-lined in order to permit carts to enter at one end and exit at the other. When the ponds are full they are about one metre deep at their deepest points. Here the ponds are known as 'cart washes' and this name points to the additional value of running carts through water, namely, to wash the wheels of surplus soil and mud. Although this description does not provide evidence of this practice in medieval use, the inherent principle, practice and value concerning the soaking of wheels are the same.

The Chester accounts of the Smiths, Cutlers, and Plumbers for 1560/1 record payments for the maintenance and rebuilding of their pageant carriage: 'payd the wrights for settinge the wheles viij d., & Carriage forth of the water [viij d.] \j d. ob./'.[8] In the Bowyers', Fletchers', Coopers', and Stringers' Accounts for 1571/2 payment is recorded 'for ye carynge ye welles to the water and frome & ye berygh of ye caryge viid'.[9] Further expenses are similarly recorded in the Smiths', Cutlers', and Plumbers' Accounts for 1567/8: 'to the prentis when we gat in our Cariage to drink viij d'.[10] Each of these records of payment refers to the same process of placing the wheels in water. The purpose of taking the wheels to the water was to soak them so as to expand the joints between naves, spokes, felloes, and strakes (see below). Reference to payment for 'when we gat in our Cariage to drink' does not refer to payment for drink to the 'prentice'; it refers to the process of soaking the wheels in water and is explained by the *MED* definition of *drinken*:

> *drinken* v. 4(a) To absorb (a liquid), soak up; *~in, ~up; ben dronken in*, be absorbed; also *fig.*; (b) of a liquid: to penetrate, be absorbed; soak (sth.); also *fig.*; *ben dronken in with*, be saturated with (sth.).

After spending the previous year in the 'weuers howse' (the place where the Smiths' carriage was stored), and John Joanson's 'seller' where the Coopers' carriage was stored, the respective components of the wheels apparently dried and contracted in such a way as to loosen the joints. It needs to be remembered that these Chester carriages were stored by removing their superstructures from the axletrees. In turn, the wheels were removed from the axles. Dismantling of the Chester carriages was no doubt affected by the amount of space available

8. *REED: Cheshire including Chester* edited Elizabeth Baldwin, Lawrence M. Clopper, and David Mills, 2 vols (University of Toronto Press, 2007) *1* 107; *MED setting(e)* gerund 1(a) 'The act of placing something in a place or position'.
9. *REED: Cheshire including Chester 1* 138.
10. *REED: Cheshire including Chester 1* 126.

in the cellars of individuals. However, prolonged exposure to damp earth could quite easily have encouraged rotting of carriage timbers. This is a different effect from the short-term soaking of wheels in water to create expansion of joints. Henry Best, a farmer from Elmswell in the East Riding of Yorkshire, describes in his *Farming and Account Books* (1641) methods of avoiding rot by partially taking apart his wains and carts. His motivation may not have been too dissimilar to that of the Chester guildsmen:

> Soe soone as harvest is in, our stubble led and stackes thatched, the first lette weather or vacant time that commeth, wee fetch up a payre of oxen, and sette our servants to runne the waines under the helmes: and first of all they knocke off the shelvinges, and putte the shelvinges, and loade-pinnes, and pike-stowers, of everie waine into her body; then doe they shoole [shovel] and carry away the dirte cleane from under the helmes; then do they putte on the oxen, and bringe the waines close to the ende of the helme, and there doe they dresse and make cleane the wheeles with a spade, before they runne them in, then doe they runne the first three waines in backewards with their arses first, soe that the hoppinge tree of the first standeth under the body of the seconde, and the hoppinge-tree of the seconde under the body of the third, then the fowerth and last waine wee runne her in with her nose first, bearinge her up and runninge her hoppinge tree into the body of the waine that standeth next her; then doe wee lift up the wheeles, and underpropp each wheele before and behinde with good bigge stones, to keepe them from the moysture and dampnesse of the earth; then doe wee take of [*off*] the wheeles of our two carts, and sette them close up by the bodyes of the waines, and the carts themselves wee sette them with theire bodyes sidewayes, and lette them stande upon the axletree, and leane against the side of the waines, then doe wee fetch all our longe ladders, and putte them within the braces of the inside of the helme: we runne our wheele barrowes allsoe under the bodyes of the waines. The longe helme in the stack-garth will just serve for fower waines, and under this helme doe wee lye the bodyes or wheeles of our two carts, our longe styes lye allsoe under this helme all winter, and likewise our wheele barrowes. The helme in the foregarth will doe somethinge more then shelter three waines, and under this doe wee usually thrust in our three coupes.[11]

11. *REED: Cheshire including Chester 1* 118, 126, 137–8; *Rural Economy in Yorkshire in 1641 being the Farming and Account Books of Henry Best, of Elmswell, in the East Riding of the*

Thus, the 'settinge' of the wheels in the Smiths', Cutlers', and Plumbers' Accounts for 1560/1 refers to putting the wheels back on to the axles and fixing them in place in a reversal of the process described by Best. The *MED* does not make a distinction between the *axle* and the *axletree*: *MED axel-trē* n. '1(a) The bar to which the wheels of a cart, a wagon, etc, are attached; an axletree'; *MED axel* n.2 '(a) The bar or shaft on which the wheels of a cart turn, an axle'. George Sturt, however, makes the following distinctions:

> *Arm.* The end of an axle on which the wheel runs. *Axle-Bed.* The wooden case (usually of beech) for an axle. *Axle-Blocks.* Pieces of wood on top of an axle-bed to carry the waggon or cart at a higher level. *Axle-Tree.* The whole axle, inclusive of the arms, fashioned out of one piece of timber. (This was often called 'wooden ex'.)[12]

If the wheels accounted for in the Smiths', Cutlers', and Plumbers' Accounts for 1560/1 were indeed carried, then it would seem that they had not yet been repositioned on their respective axles and could be laid flat in water. The 'water' referred to here is presumably the River Dee. If John Joanson's cellar had been

County of York edited Charles Best Robinson *Surtees Society* 33 (1857) 137; For the same account see also: *The Farming and Memorandum Books of Henry Best of Elmswell, 1642* edited by Donald Woodward (Records of Social and Economic History, NS 8; London: British Academy/Oxford UP, 1984) 143. The *MED* and the *OED* respectively identify *wain* as: *MED wain* n. 1(a) 'A two- or four-wheeled vehicle drawn by horses or by oxen, generally used for conveyance of cargo or passengers, a cart, wagon'; and *OED wain* n. 1(a) 'A large open vehicle, drawn by horses or oxen, for carrying heavy loads, esp. of agricultural produce; usually four-wheeled (but see 1b); a wagon'. Best refers to both 'waines' and 'carts' in his description, thus distinguishing between the vehicles and further implying two- and four-wheeled vehicles. The spatial sense in Best's descriptions is that the larger four-wheeled wains are first stored in position with the smaller two-wheeled carts stored up against and under the larger vehicles. Under both wains and carts are stored the 'wheele barrowes'. Best states that the 'hoppinge tree of the first standeth under the body of the seconde'. The glossary in Best's *Rural Economy of Yorkshire in 1641* describes the *hoppinge tree* as: 'The stumps in front of a waggon when the shafts have been pulled out [removed], now called waggon shears'. These 'stumps' are the side members of the horizontal frame that projects out from the turning train construction; they are more recently referred to as 'shears' or 'hounds'. The hounds are shown in FIGURE 1 of this article at number 26 in Arnold's key. James Arnold *The Farm Waggons of England and Wales* (London: John Baker, 1969; reprint 1978) 11.

12. Sturt *Wheelwright's Shop* 136 and Glossary; *REED: Cheshire including Chester 1* 142.

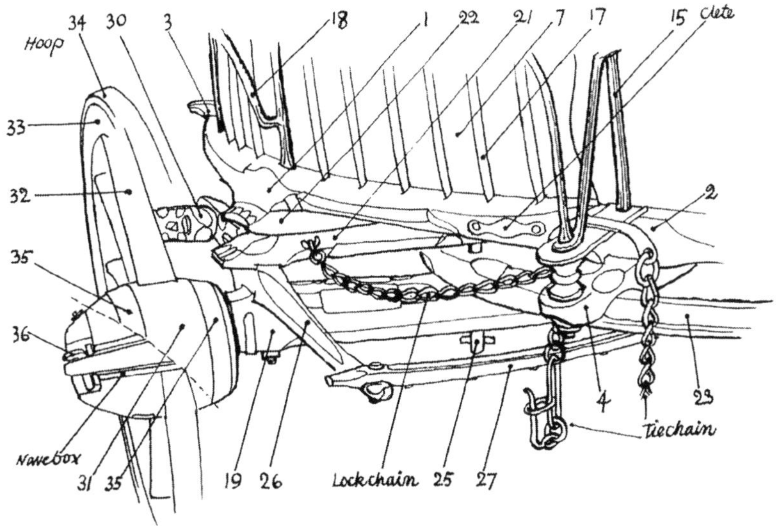

KEY

19 Axle Bed	26 Hounds	34 Strake/Tyre
23 Perch/Pole	31 Nave/Stock/Hub	35 Frett/Stock Bond
25 Perch Bolt/Pin – used with a turning train	32 Spoke	36 Lynch Pin
	33 Felloe	

FIGURE 1: Detail from James Arnold *The Farm Waggons of England and Wales* (1969) 11. Arnold included a full key to the drawing in the original publication. Here, I have only offered elements of the key that are relevant to my discussion. With some parts I have included both the medieval and more recent names.

a damp one, as cellars often are, then the need to take the wheels to the water may not have been so great.

The same purpose of soaking the wheels is recorded in payments made in the *Household Books of the Lord William Howard of Naworth Castle* in 1618: 'For drink for xj waines, iij^{s}. $iiij^{d}$'.[13] The payment shown here may indicate something

13. *Selections from The Household Books of the Lord William Howard of Naworth Castle* edited George Ornsby *Surtees Society* 68 (1878) 100; see also footnote *bush*; *REED: Coventry* 247.

of the scale of the operation which occurs among payments for provision of flour-mill equipment under the aegis of Naworth Castle. Thus the 'drink' may have been provided by the River Irthing or its tributaries, Castle Beck or Capon Clough. Like the Chester Smiths', Cutlers', and Plumbers' Accounts for 1567/8 cited above, this payment is also described as 'drink' to the vehicles. Just as the Chester carriages had been laid-up for almost a year, so too had William Howard's wains been effectively mothballed over winter. The need 'for drink' came after lengthy periods of inactivity and concomitant drying out.

On all wains, waggons, and carts the wear and tear produced by the wheel and axle engagement was considerable. The same appears to be the case with pageant carriages at Chester and other pageants at York and Coventry. Sturt describes the sideways forces that act upon a waggon and its wheels when pulled by a horse:

> The loaded body of a cart or waggon, swinging to the horse's stride, becomes a sort of battering-ram into the wheels, this side and then that. It slides to and fro, on well-greased arms, right into the nave of each wheel. Now the off-side wheel gets a ramming, and promptly throws the weight back to the near side. And so it goes on with every horse, all day long. The wheels have to stand not only the downward weight of the load; a perpetual thrust against them at the centre is no less inevitable.[14]

Pageant carriages at Chester were not pulled by horses but pulled/pushed and generally manhandled into position by 'potters of the charych' – putters of the carriage.[15] However, the same lateral displacement of carriage superstructure and wheels must have put considerable pressure on wheel-naves through changes of direction and manipulation around street corners. This pressure would conceivably have been greater when, as must often have been the case, the superstructure was higher, and the carriage operated under possible windy conditions. It needs to be stated that there is no evidence of Chester carriages possessing pivoting front axles i.e. the front wheels were not permitted to turn into the body of the carriage as a means of turning in a new direction. Indeed, there would be little purpose to be fulfilled in using pivoting front axles unless

14. Sturt *Wheelwright's Shop* 93.

15. *REED: Cheshire including Chester 1* 92, 95, 96, 118, 123–4, 126, 138, 140, 142, 164, 166–7.

there was a means of directing and controlling their use.[16] A partial means of controlling the turning train is offered by the philanthropist, Henry Eustasius Strickland in his A *General View of the Agriculture of the East-Riding of Yorkshire* (1812) when he writes:

> Little can be said in favour of the waggons which are in general use here; they are high, narrow, and long; an inconvenient form for the purposes for which they are intended, that of carrying a top-load, particularly in such parts of the country as are irregular; and they have but one peculiarity in their construction which seems worthy of more general adoption. This is a strong chain on each side of the waggon, of which one end is fixed to the back of the fore-axeltree, and the other to the under-side of the body, of such a length as just to prevent the opposite wheel from locking against the side of the waggon in turning; by which means the body may be set much lower between the wheels, without being weakened by cutting the side to admit the wheel, (as is sometimes done,) and the waggon may be turned within a much smaller space.[17]

16. There is no guild evidence of the use of pivoting front axles on pageant vehicles at any of the locations around the country where they were employed. This is not to say that such axle configurations did not exist, but they did not determine the design and construction of English pageant vehicles. The parallel shafts connected to a pivoting front axle within which a horse could be placed was the principal means of controlling the turning train on wains. Since the Chester carriages were not pulled by horses, another sort of device would have been necessary to control pivoting front axles if they had been involved. There is no evidence of the use of such devices. Although farm, brewery, and mercantile waggons with turning trains have been used in modern productions and been capable of manipulation after removal of the shafts, this has made for makeshift methods of controlling the turning train on vehicles that were not designed and constructed to be operated without shafts. For discussion of evidence relating to pivoting front axles see Marjorie Nice Boyer 'Medieval Pivoted Axles' *Technology and Culture 1: 2* (1960) 128–38; A. Rupert Hall 'More on Medieval Pivoted Axles' *Technology and Culture 2: 1* (1961) 17–22; Alan H. Nelson 'Six-wheeled Carts: An Underview' *Technology and Culture 13: 3* (1972) 391–416; John Marshall '"The Manner of these Playes": The Chester Pageant Carriages and the Places where they Played' in *Staging the Chester Cycle* edited David Mills (Leeds Texts and Monographs NS 9; University of Leeds School of English, 1985) 17–48, at 26.
17. H.E. Strickland A *General View of the Agriculture of the East-Riding of Yorkshire* (York: Thomas Wilson, 1812) 82.

Clearly, the design and development of the turning train on farm waggons had not been fully mastered by the end of the eighteenth century.[18] However, use of chains, later known as 'lock chains', on either side of the waggon to prevent the front wheels turning into the body remained until the demise of such waggons in the twentieth century.

Samuel Smiles, writing in the *Quarterly Review* of waggons that did not make use of pivoting front axles, states:

> it is difficult for us to understand how a four-wheeled plaustrum, without a perch, was ever coaxed round a curve – how it turned nobody knows – and with the rude wheels keyed on to the axles, as was generally the case in baggage-waggons, and without grease, the friction must have been so enormous.[19]

Smiles' reference to a 'plaustrum, without a perch' focuses on the ability to steer the waggon without a turning train. The 'perch' or 'pole' (as Sturt terms it) was the

> long beam which, in timber-carriage and farm-waggon, joined together the two under parts, viz. the fore-carriage and the hind-carriage. The fore-carriage, with its round-pin (*q.v.*) going down through the front end of the pole, could pivot round on it.[20]

18. The same solution to the problem of fore-wheels turning into the sides of waggons is referred to by George Bellas in a letter to the editors of *Museum Rusticum et Commerciale: or Select Papers on Agriculture, Commerce, Arts, and Manufactures, drawn from experience, and Communicated by Gentlemen engaged in these Pursuits* (London: R. Davis, J. Newbery, L. Davis and C. Reymers, 1764) 479:

    > This I have done by two chains, about two feet in length each, to be fixed at one end by a pin about three quarters of an inch diameter, through the fore bed, about one foot behind the upper pillow, and key'd; the other through the under pillow, by a pin about one foot in length, and a nut, to screw it to what length may be necessary: these chains, on each side one, to hang loose when the waggon is drawn in aright line; but upon the turn to check it just before it locks.

19. Samuel Smiles 'The Lives of British Engineers' *The Quarterly Review 114* (October 1863) 289–331, at 313; *MED perche* n.2 1(a) 'A rod, pole, staff; a fixed horizontal rod for hanging cloth, clothing, armor, cord, etc.; a fuller's rod; a pole supporting vines; a rod supporting the body of a cart above the axletree'.
20. Sturt *Wheelwright's Shop* 220.

An extended perch can be seen protruding from the rear of the underside of Constable's haywain. Given that there is no evidence of the use of turning trains on the pageant carriages at Chester some sort of leverage/dragging force was necessary to convey the Chester carriages into their altered direction.[21] The answer to Smiles' dilemma appears to have been partially accommodated at York by use of long poles referred to as 'pottyng stangs'; at Newcastle payment is recorded for 'two Spares for Stanges' and at Norwich '4 men for ther labowrs wayhtyng upon ye Pageante wit<u>h</u> Lewers [*levers*]' are recorded for the presumed same purpose of levering pageant vehicles into a new direction.[22] The technique of levering the carriages was presumably to place the tip of the pole on the ground under the vehicle on either side of the wheels with the pole wedged against the underside of the carriage and to push the upper section of the pole upwards to create the necessary 'lift' and 'drag'. Greater effectiveness of this method might have been achieved by timed co-ordination of the effort of the 'putters'. Such synchronised effort could be organised in such a way as to enable the 'putters' to lever in the same direction or to lever in opposing directions from the respective ends of the carriage. Each lift could only move the carriage by a few inches at a time and the poles or 'stangs' would need to be repositioned for the next lift. Depending on the severity of the turning arc the putters might simply realign the carriage by dragging the front wheels into their new direction or, in the case of a right-angled bend, work on both front and rear wheels by pulling them in clockwise (right-hand bend) or anticlockwise (left-hand bend) direction at the same time. If dragging the front wheels was the conventional way of turning the carriage into a new direction, then some method of facilitating this procedure would seem to have been desirable and necessary. One means of creating a new alignment might have been by placing wet or greased boards in front of the front wheels and then pulling the wheels on to the boards so that the carriage could be pulled or pushed in order to slide

21. Philip Butterworth 'The York Mercers' Pageant Vehicle, 1433–1467: Wheels, Steering, and Control' *METh 1: 2* (1979) 72–81, at 76 and note 43; Marshall '"The Manner of these Playes"' 25.

22. *REED: York* edited Alexandra F. Johnston and Margaret Rogerson, 2 vols (University of Toronto Press, 1979) *1* 96; *REED: Newcastle* edited J.J. Anderson (University of Toronto Press, 1982) 29; *REED: Norwich 1540–1642* edited David Galloway (University of Toronto Press, 1984) 340; *MED stang* n.1; for *lewer* see Robert Forby *The Vocabulary of East Anglia* 2 vols (London: J.B. Nichols, 1830) *2* 194; Walter Rye *A Glossary of Words used in East Anglia: Founded on that of Forby, with Numerous Corrections and Additions* (English Dialect Society; London: 1895) 127.

sideways over the boards. Such boards would be rapidly put in place when the carriage arrived at a given point and quickly removed by the putters when the new orientation had been achieved. The carriage would thus pivot on the rear wheels. Another potential method of turning the carriage, employing the same principle of sliding the carriage into position, might have been one implied by payments for rushes, packthread, and grease in the records at Coventry. Rushes, tied into bundles by the packthread and greased, may well have permitted a sliding/dragging action when placed under the front wheels in the form of a carpet.[23] However, there are no such records for the use of rushes at Chester. This technique of sliding the vehicles is magnificently demonstrated in the Gion Matsuri-Yamaboko Parade in Kyoto, Japan. The *Matsuri Times* describes:

> Turning the yamaboko festival floats. The wheels of *hoko* and *hikiyama* are fixed to rotate only in [a] straight direction thus turning a heavy float during the parade poses quite a challenge. At the crossroads where the procession turns, huge crowds gather to observe the spectacle. This process is called *tsujimawashi*. Bamboo stalks are laid on the ground in a circular shape and poured with water to make them slippery. The float is pulled so that the front wheels are placed over bamboo and the whole group turns the front of the vehicle sideways. It usually takes several tries to turn the float by 90 degrees.

Long poles ('pottyng stangs' at York) used as levers complement the bamboo stalks in sliding/levering the floats. The road surface is of smooth tarmacadam. Wheels on the larger floats are some 6–7 feet in diameter. Again, on the larger floats there are some hundred 'putters' both pulling and braking the float by pulling on long ropes. The whole operation is smooth enough for many people to remain on the float while the manoeuvre takes place.[24]

It is for these reasons of realigning the Chester carriages that the accuracy of the description offered by David Rogers in his *Breviaries* of 'these pagiantes' being of 'vj wheeles' (1609) is brought into question. Such questioning is made more permissible because of Rogers' later description (c.1624) that specifies the pageants were built 'vpon 4 wheeles'. The contradiction implicit in these

23. *REED: Coventry* 204, 206, 209, 224, 230, 237. See Marshall '"The Manner of these Playes"' 26; see also Albert C. Leighton *Transport & Communication in Early Medieval Europe AD 500–1100* (Newton Abbot: David & Charles, 1972) 74–5.

24. For film of this impressive technique, see <https://www.youtube.com/watch?v=BGjRyilJelY> [accessed 5 December 2017].

statements has been considered elsewhere.[25] The introduction to *REED: Cheshire including Chester* suitably warns that

> it is tempting perhaps to dismiss parts of the Rogers' descriptions on the grounds that they were written down some thirty-five years after the last performance, whereas the contemporary guild accounts and the texts may reflect more closely the actual conditions of performance.[26]

Thus, blanket acceptance of Rogers' accounts should not inhibit appropriate analysis when set against primary evidence of a different nature in guild accounts. There is no evidence in any of the Chester guild accounts of six-wheeled carriages. Dragging a six-wheeled carriage into a new alignment, assuming that the wheels were all of the same size, from the front of the carriage would require the front four wheels to be slightly lifted off the ground in order to pivot on the rear wheels. Manipulation of the carriage from behind would similarly involve lifting the rear four wheels in order to pivot on the front two wheels. Another inhibiting condition to weaken the case for six-wheeled carriages arises from their overall sizes; these have been estimated to be from '4 or 5ft wide by 8 to 10ft long'.[27] Positioning of three wheels along an estimated carriage length of '8 to 10ft' would have been unnecessary and impractical. Four points of contact with the ground provided by four wheels, whether the carriage was in motion or stationary, would provide a much more stable platform on which to play, particularly if the ground was uneven.

The relative intractability of wheels held on an axle that could not permit lateral turning is referred to by Edward Burt in his *Letters from a Gentleman in*

25. For Rogers' *Breviaries* see *REED: Cheshire including Chester 1* 326–32 at 332, 438–42 at 485; Nelson 'Six-wheeled Carts: An Underview' 391–416; Marshall '"The Manner of these Playes"' 17–48. Nelson arrives at the conclusion that the two accounts by Rogers cancel out each other in terms of their contradictory statements about '4' and '6' wheels: 'We must finally concede that the unanimous weight of unambiguous evidence speaks against the possibility that the English Corpus Christi pageants were ever mounted on six-wheeled carts' (416); whereas Marshall suggests, 'It would appear, then, that the Chester pageant carriages possessed certainly four and possibly, in some instances, six wheels attached to two or three fixed axles' (26).
26. *REED: Cheshire including Chester* xxxix.
27. Philip Butterworth *Staging Conventions in Medieval English Theatre* (Cambridge UP, 2014) 34–8. A number of more modern farm, brewery, and mercantile wagons used in modern productions tend to be slightly larger at 12′ by 6′ but they still have only four wheels.

the North of Scotland to his Friend in London (1754) when he describes the similar turning requirements of two-wheeled carts:

> When the Carter has had Occasion to turn about one Sort of these Carts in a narrow place, I have seen him take up the Cart, Wheels and all, and walk round with it, while the poor little Horse has been struggling to keep himself from being thrown.[28]

Block-wheel carts, where wheels were fixed to the axle, consisted of planks of solid timber and were even less easy to manipulate. Such carts were the kind to be found all over Europe before (and after) the reintroduction of spoked wheels:

> THE Wheels, when new, are about a Foot and half high, but are soon worn very small: They are made of three pieces of Plank, pinned together at the Edges like the Head of a Butter Firkin, and the Axeltree goes round with the Wheel, which having some Part of the Circumference with the Grain, and other Parts not, it wears unequally, and in a little Time is rather angular than round, which causes a disagreeable Noise, as it moves upon the Stones.[29]

28. Edward Burt *Letters from a Gentleman in the North of Scotland to his Friend in London* (London: S. Birt, 1754) 88–9; H. Swainson Cowper 'Some Old-fashioned Contrivances in Lakeland' *The Reliquary and Illustrated Archaeologist* 4 (Jan 1898) 15–28, at 20–2.
29. Burt *Letters from a Gentleman* 89. The noise produced by these carts is similarly referred to by Alfred C. Haddon *The Study of Man* (London: Bliss, Sands, 1898) 189–90:

> The 'groaning cart,' or as the Spaniards poetically term it, the 'singing cart,' 'Carro que canta,' may still be heard in the picturesque parts of Cantabrian and Atlantic coasts; but it is probably doomed to disappear, as carts of the same shape but with an iron hub in the wheels, with felloes, with the axle fastened to the floor of the vehicle, and which do not squeak, are silently but surely replacing them. The friction of the axle against the wedges in the floor of the waggon which keep it in its place, produces the squeaking or jarring sound which from time to time sounds like a tune or its octave; this is useful as a warning to prevent two carts from meeting in a narrow street, and also serves for the recognition of an approaching waggon. In the towns the creaking of carts is forbidden, so the drivers grease the axles with tallow, soap, or bacon, but as soon as they have passed the last house of the town they remove the tallow and put resin [*rosin* not *resin*] and water on the axle to make it groan again, so great is the pleasure they take in it.

See also Hans Gadow *In Northern Spain* (London: Adam and Charles Black, 1897) 273: 'Except in some of the towns, where law compels the use of grease, the axles are never

The difficulty of turning spoked four-wheeled vehicles, without pivoting front axles, was even more evident for vehicles with solid wheels. H. Swainson Cowper in his 'Some Old-fashioned Contrivances in Lakeland' alludes to this difficulty when he writes: 'cart-wheels on this principle were naturally very awkward; for as they did not revolve separately, it was advisable, if not necessary, in turning a corner to make a great sweep round, instead of a sharp turn'.[30]

It is not clear whether the players at Chester travelled on the carriages while they were in motion between performance stations. However, one can quite easily imagine that the putters might have wished that the players should walk in procession, ahead of or behind the carriage, in order to lessen the overall weight of it, thus making their task of realigning it that much easier. The wheels would, no doubt, resist the pressure to move sideways and be dragged into their new orientation. Because pageant vehicles at Chester, Coventry, and York were of the type of design where the wheels revolved upon the axles this would inevitably put considerable strain on the connection of axle and nave. The most vulnerable part of this connection would inevitably have been the inside of the nave, later termed 'the box',[31] which contained the 'bushes'.[32] Evidence for this condition is borne out by records of payments to repairs and maintenance of their respective parts. These wheels consisted of naves, spokes, felloes, and strakes.[33]

lubricated, with the result that a heavily laden cart makes the most awful squeaking, squealing, creaking, croaking, howling noise'. The attendant noise created by this kind of wheels is referred to in *Jacob's Well, An English Treatise on the Cleansing of Man's Conscience* edited Arthur Brandeis *EETS OS 115* (1900) 260: 'As a carte-qweel, drye & vngrecyd, cryeth lowdest of oþere qwelys'.

30. Swainson Cowper 'Some Old-fashioned Contrivances in Lakeland' 22; E.B. Taylor 'On the Origin of the Plough, and Wheel-Carriage' *The Journal of the Anthropological Institute of Great Britain and Ireland 10* (1881) 74–84, at 81.

31. Sturt *Wheelwright's Shop* 123.

32. *OED bush* n.3 1: 'The metal lining of the axle-hole of a wheel; hence, the metal (or wooden) case in which the journal of a shaft revolves'.

33. *REED: Cheshire including Chester* 92, 96, 106–7, 118, 138, 140, 142, 164, 166; *REED: York* 95–6, 97, 99–100, 288, 294, 302, 309. See *REED: Coventry* edited R.W. Ingram (University of Toronto Press, 1981) *Index* for 'pageant wagons: building and repair, cart nails, coterells, nails, soap for wheels, spokes'; *MED strāke* n.2 1(a) 'One of the separate pieces of iron together forming a band used to secure the felloes of a cartwheel to each other, a strake; *cart~*; *~nail*, a nail for fastening strakes'. At Coventry, strakes appear to have been called 'iron bondes' and strake nails 'spykyngs': see *REED: Coventry* 52;

John Fitzherbert in *The Boke of Hvsbandrie* (1523) details 'The necessary thynges that longeth to a plough/ cart/ or wayne':

> This wayne is made of dyuers peces y^t woll haue a great reparacion: that is to say they wheles/ & those be made of nathes spokes fellies & doules/ and they must be well fettred with wode or yron. And if they be yron bou̲nden they are moche the better/ & though they be the derer at the first/ yet at length they be better chepe: for a peyre of whelys yron bounde woll weare seuyn or eyght peyre of other whelys/ & they go rounde and light after oxen or horses to drawe. Howbeit on mares [marshy] ground and soft ground the other whelys be better: bycause they be broder on the soule/ and woll nat go so depe. They must haue an axyltre clout with eight wayne cloutes of yron/ two lynpines of yron in the axyltre endes/ two axil pynnes of yron/ or els of tough harde wode. The body of the wayn of oke/ the staues/ the nethar rathes/ the ouer rathes/ the crosse somer/ the keys and pycstaues ... Also a cart made of asshe bycause it is light and lyke stoffe to it/ as is to a wayne/ and also a cart sadell/ bacbandes/ belly bandes/ and a cart ladder behynde whan he shall cary outher corne or kyddes or such other.[34]

Fitzherbert's description of the constructional elements of the English wain is probably the most detailed and complete one of its time. The edition referred

226 for 'Carte nayl̲e̲s̲ for the whell̲e̲s̲'; 241 for 'Cart nayle'; 156 for 'gret naylys to the Whelles'; see also 245 for 'greate nayles'. For identification of these differently named nails see James E. Thorold Rogers *A History of Agriculture and Prices in England* 7 vols (Oxford: Clarendon Press, 1866–1902) *1* 544–5. Rogers identifies strake nails, cart nails and great nails as the same items; see also Rogers *A History of Agriculture and Prices 3* 544 col. 1, 545 col. 1, 548 col. 1, 563 col. 4, 566 col. 3, 567 col. 1.

34. Fitzherbert's identity is uncertain. The *Oxford Dictionary of National Biography* claims that he is 'John' Fitzherbert, the brother of Sir Anthony Fitzherbert, a judge and legal writer, whereas Walter W. Skeat reasons that the author is Sir Anthony Fitzherbert. The *Short-Title Catalogue* also atributes the work to John Fitzherbert: see 'Fitzherbert, Sir Anthony' at <http://www.oxforddnb.com>; *The Book of Husbandry by Master Fitzherbert* edited Walter W. Skeat (The English Dialect Society; London: Trübner, 1881) vii–xviii; *A Short-Title Catalogue of Books Printed in England, Scotland, & Ireland and of English Books Printed Abroad 1475–1640* compiled A.W. Pollard and G.R. Redgrave (London: The Bibliographical Society, 1926; revised W.A. Jackson, F.S. Ferguson and Katherine F. Pantzer, 1986).

to here is of 1523.[35] The description offered by Fitzherbert is not only a valuable one in determining constructional features of carts and wains but also one that may be used to compare with the recorded properties of pageant carriages at Chester. The wheels of the wain consist of 'nathes spokes fellies & doules'. The 'nathe' also went under the name of 'nave', 'hub' and 'stock' and was the central turned block of wood with its core drilled out by an auger to accept the end of the axeltree. Mortice holes were cut around the edge of the nave to accept the ends of the spokes. The spokes could be fashioned by turning them on a pole-lathe or paring them into shape with a draw-knife. The other ends of the spokes were fitted into mortises cut into the felloes. These were curved pieces of wood joined together to create the effective rim of the wheel. The means of joining the felloes to each other was by the use of dowels, or round pegs, cut and shaped to fit into round holes drilled into the ends of adjacent felloes. The dowels were hammered halfway into each felloe and thus joined. There were two main benefits to be derived from this practice: one was to locate the felloes in respect of each other and the second was to hold the felloes together.[36] There are no references to the use of 'douels' in the Chester records but they do occur at York in the Bakers' Account Books for 1555: 'Item payd ffor Dowlyng off the pagand qwellys and other thynges A bowt it iij s viij d'.[37] In the *Cursor Mundi* the four wheels on a wain are likened to the Evangelists, Matthew, Mark, Luke, and John. Here, 'þe quelis ar ioyned *with* mani a dowle'.[38] The Later Version of the Wycliffite Bible refers to the wheels of a 'char':

> Sotheli the wheelis weren siche, whiche maner wheelis ben wont to be maad in a chare; and the extrees, and the naue stockis, and the spokis, and dowlis of the wheelis, alle thingis weren ȝotun.[39]

35. John Fitzherbert *Here begynneth a newe tracte or treatyse moost profytable for all husbande men: and very frutefull for all other persons to rede* (*the boke of husbandrie*) (London: Rycharde Pynson, 1523) fols iii^{v}–iiii^{r}.

36. See Sturt *Wheelwright's Shop* 106; this is the principle upon which IKEA flat-packed furniture is partially constructed with fluted dowels.

37. *REED: York* 322.

38. *Cursor Mundi Part 4* edited Richard Morris *EETS OS* 66 (1877) 1218 line 21270 (Fairfax).

39. *The Holy Bible: containing the Old and New Testaments, with the Apocryphal books, in the earliest English versions made from the Latin Vulgate by John Wycliffe and his followers* edited Josiah Forshall and Sir Frederic Madden, 4 vols (Oxford UP, 1850) 2 181, 33; *MED char*

Use of dowells to locate and join two adjacent felloes to each other was clearly a fundamental part of English wheel construction from the fifteenth century to the present day. An earlier English practice of connecting adjacent felloes to strengthen wheel construction appears to have been through the use of *groporum* or 'gropes'. These were seemingly small plates of iron which were nailed (with grope nails)[40] to straddle the inside faces of two adjacent felloes. They performed the same function as dowels in strengthening the connection between two felloes. They could be used in conjunction with dowels or in place of them.[41]

By way of illustration Fitzherbert only refers to the accoutrements of one 'axyltre' and not two. Thus, it may be inferred that the description: 'an axyltre clout with eight wayne cloutes of yron/ two lynpines of yron in the axyltre endes/ two axil pynnes of yron' refers to the furnishing of one 'axyltre' with the implication that the other one is commensurately completed. The wheels 'must be wel fettred with wode or yron'. If the wheels are 'yron bounden they are moche the better' and 'woll weare seuyn or eyght' times longer than 'other whelys'. The purpose of Fitzherbert's description is to establish and explain the required parts of a wain. Thus the account presents some knowledgeable authority. The requirement of 'an axyltre clout with eight wayne cloutes of yron' suggests that four clouts were located on each axle arm of the axletree. This implies two clouts underneath the axle arm and two on top. 'Clouts' were

n.2 1. 'A wheeled vehicle, such as (a) a carriage or coach; 2. A cart or wagon'; *OED yoten* 'Cast'.

40. *Calendar of Letter-Books Preserved among the Archives of the Corporation of the City of London at the Guildhall, Letter-Book C. Circa A. D. 1291–1309* edited Reginald R. Sharpe (London: John Edward Francis, 1901) 88–9; the *OED* defines *grope* n.2 as 'A kind of nail'. It cites a quotation from 1411 of '50 grope & 1 c clout nails' by Rogers *History of Agriculture 3* 546 (see note 33). Rogers offers the following explanation of the nature of 'gropes': 'Gropes appear to be pieces of iron binding together the inner joint of the fitting, and grope-nails to have been used for fastening these to the wood. The price at which the last-named parts of a cart-wheel are purchased indicates that they were slight'; Rogers *1* 544. R.E. Latham in his *Revised Medieval Latin Word-List from British and Irish Sources* (London: British Academy, 1965) lists '*grop/a, -um* 1273, 1425, †*grospa* 1377, *grapa* 1248, 1325, *grabba* 1446, *grippa* 1270, 1371, iron clamp (esp. for mending cart-wheels); *-o*, to clamp (cart-wheels) 1267, 1308; compare *2 crabba*'.

41. Rogers' explanation does not appear to be incorrect but it is not specific enough to provide full details. Nor is the definition offered by Latham a full one, although the specific reference to 'clamping' combined with Rogers' description of *gropes* as 'pieces of iron' point to their identity and function.

iron plates shaped and nailed around the end of the round axle to protect it from continuous friction from the inside of the nave. The *MED* defines *clout* n.1 as '2(a) A metal plate or shield to prevent excessive wear, as on an axeltree [*axel-tre~*] or on the moldboard of a plow [*molde-bred~*, etc.]; (b) *~nail*, a nail with a flat head'. The purpose of the flat head was to allow the wheel to roll over the head without interference. Sturt, in his glossarial explanation of *clout* amplifies the *MED* definition when he describes it as:

> An iron plate let into the arm of a wooden axle (on the underside) … Lying flush with the wood, and requiring to be very smooth and exact, the clout was fastened with special countersunk nails called clout-nails.[42]

Clouts were primarily, but not exclusively, nailed to the underside of the axletree arm as it entered the box of the nave – the weight of the carriage pressing down on the axle. At Chester in the Smiths', Cutlers', and Plumbers' Accounts for 1571/2, payment is recorded for '6 Cart clouts & nayles vij d'. Different conjectured permutations for the distribution of these clouts to four wheels is possible.[43]

Fitzherbert also itemises two forms of pins to the axletree: one item consists of 'two axyll pynnes of yron/ or els of tough harde wode' and the other refers to 'two lynpinnes of yron in the axyltre-endes'. Effectively, these lynch pins are the means of stopping the wheel running off the axletree arm.[44] The two 'axyll pynnes of yron' are used to fix the axletree to the body of the wain. Their use is also recorded at Chester in the carriages of the Coopers (see above) and the Smiths. In the Smiths', Cutlers', and Plumbers' Accounts for 1571/2 payment is recorded for 'pinns for the Axtrees ij d'.[45]

42. Sturt *Wheelwright's Shop* 214.
43. Marshall '"The Manner of these Playes"' 24. Marshall suggests that the reference to '6 Cart Clouts & nayles' helps to promote the case for a six-wheeled pageant: see *MED axel-trē* n. 2 *~clout*, *~hop*, 'a band or hoop about the axletree'. This definition requires the 'clout' or 'hop' to encircle the axletree arm as a band. Presumably, more than one clout would have been needed to complete such a band around the axletree arm. A record in the Smiths' accounts at Coventry records payment: 'for ij tre hopps to ye paient whelles 4d'; *REED: Coventry* 20, 152; *REED: Cheshire including Chester 1* 142; *REED: Kent 1* 110.
44. *MED lin-pin* n. 'A linchpin'; *OED linch-pin* n. 'A pin passed through the end of an axle-tree to keep the wheel in its place'.
45. *REED: Cheshire including Chester 1* 142.

Fitzherbert's itemised description prefigures the records of such components in the Smiths' and Coopers' pageant carriages at Chester. Here, evidence of revolving spoked wheels on axles is provided by some ancillary requirements in guild accounts. Payments for 'frettes' and 'ffreytyng', 'clouts & nayles', 'for ieren & byndyng of a welle', and taking 'our Cariage to drink', each represent components and processes that explain the construction of the spoked wheel. Some other payments that do not present such strong evidence of spoked-wheel construction refer to the wright and his skill and use of soap, grease and tallow as lubricants.[46]

Another important feature of the wheels described by Fitzherbert was that of 'binding' them with iron:

> And if they be yron bou<u>n</u>den they are moche the better/ and though they be the derer at the first/ yet at length they be better chepe: for a peyre of whelys yron bounde woll weare seuyn or eyght peyre of other whelys.[47]

The means of binding wheels at this time was not by use of a continuous iron hoop or tyre but by 'strakes'. These were iron bars that could be bent around the circumference of the wheel and nailed on to the felloes with large-headed nails known as 'strake nails', 'cart nails', or 'great nails'.[48] As a further means of strengthening the binding, strakes were required to straddle the felloe joints. Sturt writes:

> A strake was an iron shoe, nailed across one joint only, where two felloes met. Each joint had its strake. If there were six felloes, there were six joints and six strakes. But the strakes were never joined. They did not even quite meet.[49]

46. *REED: Cheshire including Chester 1* 92, 96, 107, 138, 142; *REED: Coventry* 41, 51, 92, 150, 153, 161, 163, 165, 167, 175, 177, 179, 183, 185, 191, 197, 202, 241.
47. *MED binden* v. 3(c) 'to "bind" (a wheel) with a rim, a barrel with hoops'; *REED: Cheshire including Chester* 138; *MED dressen* v. 4 'To mend or repair'; *Testamenta Eboracensia* transcribed Lewis Baker (no named editor) *Surtees Society* 4 (1836) 417: John Sandford of Tikhill left in his will (1429): 'a pare of cart wheles new bonden'; Rogers *A History of Agriculture and Prices* 3 544 col. 3, 549 col. 3, 554 col. 4, 561 col. 2, 567 col. 3, 569 col. 1, 580 col. 1, 581 col. 2; Ornsby *The Household Books of the Lord William Howard* 38; *REED: Coventry* 63, 95, 193, 235.
48. Sturt *Wheelwright's Shop* 123.
49. Sturt *Wheelwright's Shop* 146.

Presumably the reason why strakes, when nailed in position, did 'not even quite meet' was to accommodate any expansion through heat. If the ends of the strakes were permitted to expand into each other they would create a buckling of the strakes and loosening of the nailed construction. Even so, there is evidence of strakes being cut too short to fulfil their intended purpose.[50]

50. *Calendar of Letter-Books* C 88–9. The statute delivered here concerns a complaint delivered by ironmongers of the city that the length of imported strakes was too short. This deficiency was determined by measuring the imported strakes against a standard of three iron rods of 'accustomed length'. This being the case, the length of the strakes must have been set against wheels of a recognised and measured circumference, otherwise they could not have been deemed to be too long or too short. The account reads:

> On the grievous complaint made by ironmongers of the City of London to Elyas Russell, then Mayor of London, and to the Aldermen of smiths of the Wealds (*de Waldis*) and other merchants bringing strakes of wheels (*feruras rotarum*) for carts to the City of London of much shorter length than they were accustomed to be, to the grievous loss and scandal of the whole trade of ironmongers of the City aforesaid, and demanding a remedy for the premises, an inquisition was held by lawful and trustworthy men, who presented three iron rods of just and of old accustomed length of strakes, and also of the length and breadth of skids (*groporum*) for the wheels of carts, which rods [were] marked with the mark of the Chamber of the Guildhall, London; whereof one remains in the aforesaid Chamber, and another rod was delivered to John Dode and Robert de Padingtone, ironmongers of Chepe, on Monday next before the Feast of Purification of the Blessed Mary [2 Feb.], 29 Edward I. [A. D. 1300–1]; and the third rod was delivered on the Monday aforesaid to John de Wymondham, ironmonger of Bridge. The said John, Robert, and John swore upon the Holy Gospels that from day to day they would warn all merchants bringing such iron rims (*ferramenta*) to the City of London, as well from the Wealds as elsewhere, to bring thenceforth no such iron rims unless they be of the length and breadth aforesaid, upon pain of forfeiting the said rims; and that such rims as should be found contrary to the assize aforesaid after the Feast of Easter next would be altogether forfeited, &c.

In this account Sharpe translates *groporum* as 'skids'. This appears to be an incorrect translation. However, it is the case that 'skids' or 'skid-pans' were used as a braking device on carts and wagons. A cart thus made use of two skids as recorded in H.T. Riley *Memorials of London and London Life in the 13th, 14th, and 15th Centuries* (London: Longmans, Green, 1868): 'one pair of iron skids, value 6s 6d' (49). See note 37 above and *drug-bat* in Sturt *Wheelwright's Shop* Glossary 216. Given that Rogers accounts for payment of 'grope … nails' (note 39 above), it is unlikely that such nails were used on skids or drugbats. Grope nails were presumably intended to nail gropes in place by straddling the inside faces of two adjacent felloes. A note in Riley's *Memorials* also connects *gropi* with skids: 'Properly, the iron grooves, or hooks, at the end of a skid, for stopping a cart' (49). Although Riley's description may be a correct one to describe skids, *gropi* were not skids.

The bending of strakes was conducted when they were hot and capable of being hammered into the convex shape of the felloes and nailed in place.[51] This process is often referred to as 'binding', 'tiring', or 'shoeing' the wheels.[52] Development of the technique to weld or 'shut' a longer iron bar to form a continuous iron band around the wheel had not taken place by the late sixteenth century. It was not until the nineteenth century that this practice became more commonplace.[53]

The constant and intrinsic design problem with the spoked-wheel/axle arrangement not only caused inevitable wear and tear through friction but also through being jolted as the carriage progressed. The nave, in particular, was subject to considerable pressure and the means by which the nave was strengthened was by *fretting*.

The Chester Cordwainers' and Shoemakers' Accounts for 1549/50 list: 'It*em* peyd ffor ffreytyng of the weyles xvj d'.[54] Similarly, the 1560/1 Smiths', Cutlers', and Plumbers' Accounts, record payment 'for frettinge the wheles & nayles xviij d'.[55] In the 1571/2 Bowyers', Fletchers', Coopers', and Stringers' Accounts payment is recorded 'more for frettes & for axeltre penes viii d'.[56] The *MED* and the *OED* offer the following definitions of *freten* and *fret* (from the French *frette*):

> *MED*: *freten* v.3 (a) To bind or fasten (something), fasten (things together), tie or wrap (something with a thong, strap, etc.), tie (in a bundle), lace (voiders into the joints of armor); to fasten (a cord, etc.), to tie (a cord in knots); (b) *fig.* ppl. bound (by rules); constrained; *fretted in fere*, in packs.
>
> *OED*: *fret*, v.3 To bind (properly, with a hoop or ring).

Randle Cotgrave in his *Dictionarie of the French and English Tongues* defines *frete* as 'A Verrill; the yron band, or hoope that keeps a wooden toole from

51. Sturt *Wheelwright's Shop* 148.
52. *OED tire*, n. 2; *OED shoe*, v. 3.
53. Sturt *Wheelwright's Shop* 123.
54. *REED: Cheshire including Chester* 92.
55. *REED: Cheshire including Chester* 107.
56. *REED: Cheshire including Chester* 138; *MED axel-trē* n.2: '~*pin*, a pin or nail for fastening the axletree to the cart or wagon'.

riuing'. The *Verrill* is a 'ferrule'.[57] Later seventeenth-century examples of frets are specifically recorded as reinforcing metal bands around naves. The function of the fret was the same as that of the verrill round the top of a chisel handle, to prevent the bound part from splitting or fracturing when hit with a mallet: Randle Holme states that 'The Frets … of a Wheel … are Iron Hoops about the Nave' and Darlington in *The Folk-Speech of South Cheshire* defines the *fret* as: 'the belt of iron which goes round the nave of a wheel. Also called Clam'.[58] If these examples of the word *fret* are semantically the same as in the earlier sixteenth-century ones, then 'ffreytyng' is the process by which iron bands were fastened tightly around the inside and outside rims of the nave to enable it to withstand the normal pressures of its use. Further nineteenth-century evidence of the technique of 'binding' the nave corroborates the process of fixing metal bands on either side of the spokes as they enter the nave.[59]

The above examples of the verb *to fret*, taken from the seventeenth and nineteenth centuries, refer to 'Iron Hoops about the Nave' and 'the belt of iron which goes round the nave of a wheel'. The 'hoops' and 'belt of iron' referred to in these examples do not refer to continuous hoops or belts. Indeed, the technique of welding to create an unbroken band is not recorded until the late seventeenth century. The earliest *OED* reference to the noun *weld* is 1831. The earliest *OED* reference to the verb *weld* is 1678 [1677] from Joseph Moxon's *Mechanick Exercises, or the Doctrine of Handy-Works*.[60] However, the function of the 'frets' could still be partially achieved by bands of iron whose ends are brought together around the nave and nailed in position without being welded. A stronger band or 'bond' might have been achieved if the ends of the band had been allowed to overlap in such a way as to be riveted through the overlapping ends of the band. Any projections produced by the rivets on the inside of the

57. Randle Cotgrave *A Dictionarie of the French and English Tongues* (London: Adam Islip, 1611). French *frette* comes from OF *ferret*, from Latin *ferrum*, 'iron'. *Ferrule* comes from Latin *viriola*, a bracelet, altered through false etymology from *ferrum*. Cotgrave was also a Chester man.

58. *OED fret* n.5; Randle Holme *An Accademie of Armory or A Store House of Armory & Blazon* (Chester: printed by the author, 1688) 332; Thomas Darlington *The Folk-Speech of South Cheshire* (The English Dialect Society; London: Trübner, 1887) 194.

59. Sturt *Wheelwright's Shop* 117, 131, 182; *fretting* does thus not refer to binding the wheel as Marshall describes it: see Marshall '"The Manner of these Playes"' 26.

60. Joseph Moxon *Mechanick Exercises, or the Doctrine of Handy-Works* (London: Joseph Moxon, 1677) 8–9.

band would, no doubt, bite into the wood of the nave. Any projected rivet heads on the outside of the band would not adversely interfere with its function.

At Coventry, payment is also recorded in the 1565 Drapers Accounts for frets: 'Itm payde for vj fretts to the wheles ij s' and 'Itm payd for nayles to Sett on the fretts wall v d'.[61] Here, payment is recorded for 'vj fretts' to be shared over a presumed maximum of four wheels. Thus, more than one fret per nave seems likely for some wheels. Some four years later at Coventry another payment is made for a fret: 'Itm a freat of Iron for one of the whells viij d'.[62]

The activity of 'clouting' seems less likely to equate with 'ffreytyng' since the process of 'ffreytyng' would have been to the wheels and not the axle. But if clouts were used on the axletree arm without similar metal protection on the inside of the box then the clouts themselves would have worn the inside of the box. If clouts existed on the arm of the axletree then these must have come into contact with a metal interior to the box. Hence, the proliferation of records of payment for grease and soap to lubricate the axle arms and boxes.[63]

Sturt, with considerable clarity, explains the importance of the relationship between the 'stock' (nave, hub), the cast-iron 'box' in the stock, the 'stock-bonds' (the bands or 'frets' around the nave), and the necessary 'wedges' to keep the wheel running accurately on the axle. Sturt offers a possible solution to the tightening of a 'stock-bond' by use of wedges hammered into the end grain of the nave. The technique is offered in relation to a stock-bond that has been welded. However, it is quite possible that the same process could be conducted with a riveted stock-bond:

> 'Boxing' a wheel, or 'boxing it on,' meant wedging into the stock that cast-iron 'box' which was to run on the axle; inserting, if you like, the central iron socket into the wood-work. When a wheel, with this 'box' fixed into it, was slipped on to the projecting 'arm' or axle-end, it became part of the cart. The cart (or waggon) at last had a wheel to run on.
>
> Not an easy job was this boxing. It began with chiselling or gouging out the whole of the middle of the stock. A tool called a 'router' was used for this in after years, but I think not in those more distant days I am dealing with now. Rather, the central auger-hole was enlarged with the buzz. A wide gouge then shaped the hole roughly, and finally it was made

61. *REED: Coventry* 230.

62. *REED: Coventry* 250.

63. *REED: Cheshire including Chester 1* 142.

> a little too large for the box, which could so be shifted to one side or to the other of it.
>
> For, as the wheel, with this box in it, would have to pivot round on the axle-arm, it was most important to have the pivoting true. It would never do to have the wheel wobbling from side to side. Presumably it would have to keep in the deep ruts of a country lane; and how could it do that if the box was out of place? Or how, again, could the upper edge of the wheel be prevented from rubbing into the cart, if the revolving box sent it periodically straddling out at the ground? Plainly, the box must be tested before it was fixed; it must be put in loose first, and only tightened, wedged up on this side or that, according as trial directed.
>
> Very ingenious and pleasing was the 'swinging' of a wheel for this purpose. The axle-arm was provisionally screwed on to the workman's bench, high enough to let the wheel lifted on to it swing round and round clear of the ground. Then, so as just to touch the tyre with one corner, a small block of wood was placed on the ground, and the wheel was spun round to see what would happen. Now the block was knocked away; now the wheel swung away from it altogether; and any such case was a hint for a wedge to be put in, the wheelwright knew where.
>
> The wedges (hand chopped, out of heart of oak) were not themselves allowed to touch the box. Truly, that brittle cast-iron might easily have snapped, if jarred too closely by such a sledge-hammering as the wedges were subjected to. A place having been started by a broad iron wedge (knocked in and then knocked out again) the oak wedge was driven into the elm itself, splitting it open slightly. (There was no danger of splitting dry elm too far). The iron stock-bond prevented the stock from opening outwards at all; only by spreading inwards, towards the cast-iron box, could the elm make way for this oaken wedge. But this was exactly what was wanted. Until the box was fixed immovable, in its right place, wedge after wedge was driven in; and when at last the wedges came to be chiselled off they fitted so tight that no division could be seen between them and the stock; a difference between oak grain and elm grain alone showed where they were.[64]

Sturt refers to the 'box' as one made of 'brittle cast-iron' and he warns about cracking the box when sledge-hammering the wedges into the nave. Thus,

64. Sturt *Wheelwright's Shop* 129–31.

the question that needs to be posed is: did the Chester Smiths' and Coopers' carriages make use of cast-iron boxes?

The earliest *OED* reference to *cast iron* is one of 1665. There are no references to *cast iron* in the *MED*. Similarly, there are no *MED* references to the process of welding. It seems that the medieval 'box' consisted of 'bushes' of iron that were hammered into round collars but were not welded or 'shut'. 'Shutting' or 'shooting' is the process of welding a metal joint. Randle Holme refers to 'bushes' as 'The Bushes are irons within the hole of the Nave to keep it from wearing'.[65] Given that Holme refers to 'irons', in the plural, 'within the hole of the Nave' one implication from this description is that there was more than one piece of iron in the hole of the nave. A further implication is that two semicircular plates (in section) were made to butt up against each other to form a cylindrical lining.

Although the earliest *OED* reference to *cast iron* is from 1665, it is not the earliest one to refer to the process of casting iron. Other terms exist that refer to casting iron.[66] The process of founding metals by running them hot into a mould is recorded from the fourteenth century and iron founders are also recorded from the fourteenth century.[67]

It has often been the case that military solutions to problems and obstacles in war have led to significant inventions. Cannon that could be moved on wheels were some of the earliest examples of the use of bushed wheels. Scottish records in *A Collection of Inventories and other Records of the Royal Wardrobe and Jewelhouse; and of the Artillery and Munitioun in some of the Royal Castles* refer to the use of brass bushes in cannon wheels in the year 1566:

> Item ane pair of new cannone quheillis [*wheels*] buschit with brass nocht [*not*] shod
>
> Ane uther cannon of fonte [*cast iron*] callit thrawin mowth markit with the porkpik [*porcupine*] montit [*mounted*] upoun ane new stok weill garnist with yron werk hir auld aixrie [*axletree*] on schod [*unshod*] with

65. Holme *An Accademie of Armory* 332.

66. See *MED yēten* v.3, 7b '(a) To melt (metal), refine; also *fig.*; melt down (a metal object) for recasting; *ppl. yoten*, molten, refined; *yoten werk*, ?the craft of founding; (b) to cast (metal); form (a metal object) by casting, found'.

67. *MED yētere* n. '(a) A smelter or founder of metal; also one who casts metals'.

ane pair of auld rottin quheillis weill garnist with yron werk & bousches of fonte.[68]

The name 'thrawin mowth' seems a very suitable nickname given to a cannon by its gunners. The *OED* glosses the term as: 'crabbed, ill-tempered, snarling'.[69] And 'bousches of fonte' refers to bushes of cast iron. *Font* (n.2) is defined by the *OED* as '1.a. The action or process of casting or founding and 1.b. Cast iron'. Randle Cotgrave in his *Dictionarie of the French and English Tongues* (1611) defines *fonte* as 'A melting, founding, or casting of mettalls'.

Whether the wheels of Chester carriages of the 1560s were furnished with cast-iron bushes is unclear. Clearly, the process of casting iron was not unknown in the 1560s. Equally, use of cast-iron bushes in naves was also not unknown. In fact, the 1571/2 Smiths', Cutlers', and Plumbers' Accounts demonstrate that their carriage was almost certainly furnished with metal bushes, given that there is payment made for the use of clouts. The 1560/1 and the 1567/8 Smiths', Cutlers', and Plumbers' Accounts respectively record payment for 'gray sope for the wheles iij d' and 'a pound of grey sope iij d'.[70] The 1571/2 Smiths', Cutlers', and Plumbers' *Accounts* also record that more was spent 'in gresenge of

68. *A Collection of Inventories and other Records of the Royal Wardrobe and Jewelhouse; and of the artillery and Munitioun in some Royal Castles 1488–1606* edited Thomas Thomson (Edinburgh: no publisher, 1815) 168, 250.

69. *OED* sv *thrawn* adj. SPECIAL USES *thrawn-mowit*; *Dictionary of the Scots Language*: *Thraw(i)n*, A. adj. 1. d 'Tuo great cannonis, thraw mow (PITSC[OTTIE] *1* 331/3 thrawin mouth) and hir marrow'.

70. *REED: Cheshire including Chester* 107, 126; John Stow in his 1603 edition of *A Survay of London* offers the following description: 'I haue not read or heard of Sope making in this Cittie till within this fourscore yeares, that *Iohn Lame* dwelling in Grassestreete, set vp a boyling house for this Cittie, of former time, was serued of white Sope in hard Cakes (called Castellsope, and other) from beyond the seas, and of gray sope, speckled with white, verie sweete and good, from Bristow, solde here for a pennie the pound, and neuer aboue pennie farthing, and blacke sope for a halfe pennie the pounde'; *A Survay of London* (London: John Windet, 1603) 253. This description does not appear in Stow's 1598 edition. Black soap was used to lubricate moving parts and white soap was used for washing purposes; see *Dictionarium Rusticum, Urbanicum & Botanicum: or, a Dictionary of Husbandry, Gardening, Trade, Commerce, and all sorts of Country-Affairs* 2 vols (London: James and John Knapton, Arthur Bettesworth, R. Robinson, Jer. Batley, J. Taylor, and Thomas Astley, 1726), *II* sv *soap*: 'black soap, 'tis made with strong *Lye* as aforesaid, and Whale or Fish-Oil, commonly called Train-Oil, and 'tis brought to a due consistency by convenient boiling'; *MED sope* n. 2 (b); *MED blak* adj. 4 (c); Nicholas Breton *The Court and Country* (London: John Wright, 1618) sig. D4v; Rogers *A History of Agriculture and*

the caryghe \welles/', and in the same accounts payment is recorded 'for Tallow for wheles ij d'. Such payments for soap, grease, and tallow support my assertion about the function of clouts on axles and metal cylindrical boxes in naves. The separate payments at Chester 'ffor ffreytyng of the weyles', 'frettes', 'Cart clouts & nayles', 'drink' to 'our Cariage', 'pinns for the Axtrees', and 'for ieren & byndyng of a welle', each contribute cumulative evidence for the construction and use of iron-bound spoked wheels on the Smiths' and Coopers' pageant carriages.[71]

The working problems associated with the act of turning pageant carriages into new alignments in the streets of Chester permits understanding of the wheel arrangements of the carriages of the Smiths and Coopers. These are not the same kind of wheels as those depicted in the illustration opposite the title page of the *Chester Mysteries* by J.H. Markland (1818).[72] Here, the wheels are imagined as block-wheel in construction. Traditionally, spoked wheels have been made of elm for naves, oak for spokes, and ash, elm, oak, or beech for felloes. Each of these timbers presents different characteristics in respect of moisture content and properties of strength, rigidity, flexibility, and durability. Wheelwrights know of these characteristics; they know of the ways in which timber behaves under different conditions and how it might fulfil its required tasks; they know what happens when timbers are soaked in water. As Sturt, writing of wheelwrights in the early nineteenth century, says:

> Well experienced in all wheels, and understanding what was sure to be wanted for waggon or cart in years to come, these men required no telling what to do. They knew well enough. All the wheel-making lore of the country-side for generations guided their judgement.[73]

University of Leeds

Prices 1 466–7; *3* 556 col. 4, 559 col. 1, 565 col. 2, 569 col. 4, 572 col 3; *REED: Kent 1* 118, 125, 142.

71. *REED: Cheshire including Chester* 92, 107, 126, 138.

72. *Chester Mysteries* edited J.H. Markland (London: Roxburghe Club, 1818) frontispiece.

73. R.G. Bateson *Timber Drying and the Behaviour of Seasoned Timber in Use* (London: Crosby Lockwood, 1952); Sturt *Wheelwright's Shop* 44–9.

CARNEVALE IN NORWICH, 1443: Gladman's Parade and its Continental Connections

Tom Pettitt

Most of my contributions to the field of Medieval Theatre have focused on the three-way relationships between drama, folk custom and pageantry, and what follows will be no exception. This is a field in which it is necessary to supplement the limited texts and records surviving from the period itself by recourse to later (nineteenth, twentieth century), derivative or analogous folk traditions on which we are better informed – a procedure I have previously deployed extensively if cautiously, and this 'regressive' approach will figure here too. But it will be somewhat overshadowed on this occasion by a 'comparative', transnational one, since whatever their (considerable) interest and significance in their own right, continental European traditions of drama, custom and pageantry are potentially useful as further supplementing the insular evidence for a given feature.

In this regard my point of departure is the assumption that before Britain became an island in the early modern period, England was home to a local *oikotype* of Pan-European traditions, so that, to put it bluntly, anything *they* had, *we had too*: if the French had *farces* and *sotties*, so did we; if the Dutch had *abele spelen* and *rederejkers*, so did we; if the Germans had *Fastnachtspiele*, so did we. And if, at first sight, we *didn't*, this must be the result of different procedures of record-*making*, or different patterns of record *survival*, or different degrees of record *accessibility* (including strategies of record *publication*), or different perspectives of *scholarly enquiry*.

Carnival/Shrovetide

This does not always work. Although the French had well-documented nuptial *charivaris* in the Later Middle Ages, and the Italians the analogous *mattinata*, the English had nothing of the kind. But this was not insular exceptionalism – it just made us part of a European *charivari*-free zone which also included northern Germany and Scandinavia.[1]

1. Tom Pettitt 'Nuptial Pageantry in Medieval Culture and Folk Custom: in Quest of the English *charivari*' *Medium Ævum Quotidianum* 52 (2005) 89–115; online at <https://www.

A particular challenge is the season of Carnival, which in Europe is so full of spectacular festive customs that among the unwary the term has come to mean 'festival' in general (particularly if it is subversive and upside-downy). For carnival in the strict sense, the festive period immediately before the beginning of Lent, the current English term is *Shrovetide*, which sounds altogether more respectable. But the spirit of 'no sex please, we're British' is emphatically post-medieval, and in earlier times it was also called, more frankly, *Gut-tide*,[2] as well as the calendar-oriented *fast-in-gong* or *fastens-eve*, this last equivalent to the Danish *fastelavn*, and the High German *Fastnacht*. In other words, as with *carm-entrant* and *carne-vale*, the festival was defined in relation to the period of fasting it ushered in (the now current English *Lent* reflecting, it seems, the noticeable lengthening of daylight hours through the seven-week period it lasts). But if England also had a *Fastnacht*, a Carnival season, where are its Carnival customs; its *Fastnachtspiele*? If they had them, we had them.

In the case specifically of *Fastnachtspiele* it does seem that discrepant Anglo-American scholarly perspectives are part of the problem, in the shape of a characteristic focus on genre which can obscure or confuse other perspectives, as noted in another connection by John Marshall.[3] In this case the alternative perspective called for is contextual, for quite a number of late medieval plays conventionally treated generically as moralities, or interludes (or moral interludes) were evidently designed for and performed under the auspices of the *fastens-eve* revels of domestic or institutional households, and so qualify by at least some definitions as *Fastnachtspiele*, as I have argued in the case of the morality *Mankind* and as Leif Søndergaard has suggested for *Dame Siriz*[4] – two items one would perhaps not place in the same category from conventional, generic, perspectives.

And as a necessary precondition for such a context-based category there is, just, enough medieval evidence to document that substantial English households

academia.edu/4018274/Nuptial_Pageantry_in_Medieval_Culture_and_Folk_Custom_in_Quest_of_the_English_charivari>.

2. Thomas Middleton *The Family of Love* 4. i. 48 in *Works* edited A.H. Bullen, 8 vols (London: John Nimmo, 1885) 3 71.
3. John Marshall, review of *REED: Shropshire* edited Alan B. Somerset, in *Speculum 72: 1* (1997) 223–6, at 226.
4. Tom Pettitt '*Mankind*: an English *Fastnachtspiel*?' in *Festive Drama* edited Meg Twycross (Cambridge: D.S. Brewer, 1996) 190–202; Leif Søndergaard 'Two Carnival Plays from Late-Medieval Denmark' in *Festive Drama* 203–22.

(including the royal court) and English institutions (including colleges and law schools), like their continental analogues, operated with an *extended* season of winter revels persisting beyond New Year, through alternative conclusions to the Christmas season such as Twelfth Night and Candlemas, and ending at Carnival, which saw a culminating burst of festivity with accompanying customary performances.

Most of the evidence available at the time for this household/institutional, indoor, carnival and its interludes is reviewed in my *Mankind* article. The challenge of the English Carnival resides rather in the lack of evidence of Shrovetide activity analogous to the outdoor customs, performed under community (civic; guild) auspices, in the form of parades, pageantry, and perambulations, which is probably what most people mean by 'carnival', and which looms so large in the immediately pre-Lenten celebrations of many European societies and their New World diaspora, from the Nuremburg *Schembartlauf*, through the multiple processions of the *reynages* analysed in Emmanuel Le Roy Ladurie's celebrated study of *Le Carnaval de Romans*,[5] to those nearly naked ladies on the floats of the Rio samba schools.

Street Carnival in Late Medieval England

In the quest for English *oikotypes* of such continental carnival pageantry, the egg-and-spoon races of fully clad village wives of my Essex childhood hardly qualify, and surviving medieval documentation remains exceedingly disappointing. A sweep of *REED* volumes (alongside providing further documentation of indoor feasting) serves to confirm the picture established by Ronald Hutton: that outdoor Shrovetide activities were largely confined to intercommunity football, archery contests, horse-racing, cock-fighting and cock-threshing (plus an occasional dancing bear).[6]

There are sporadic items prompting curiosity, but which ultimately fall short of what is needed, for example the custom of 'going a-hoodiwinking' in Herefordshire,[7] which on reflection must be a synonym for mumming (i.e. a

5. Emmanuel Le Roy Ladurie *Le Carnaval de Romans* (Paris: Gallimard, 1979); *Carnival in Romans* translated Mary Feeney (London: Penguin, 1981).

6. Ronald Hutton *The Stations of the Sun: A History of the Ritual Year* (Oxford UP, 2006; reprinted 2007) chapter 15, 'Shrovetide' (151–68).

7. In 1589: *REED: Herefordshire, Worcestershire* edited David N. Klausner (University of Toronto Press, 1990) 15 (Introduction), 66 (the record), 210 (translation), 274 (notes).

house-visit custom of disguised figures), or the cross-dressed couples dancing in the churchyard (but not, it seems, parading) in the depraved depths of darkest Sussex,[8] or the 1653 confession of a Thomas Gill of Bruton, Somerset, 'that Tuesday night beinge Shroue Tuesday he with others ... did throwe many great stones at many doors' – thus far just a macho version of the 'Lent Crocking' of later tradition – but then: 'he saw ffiue men with visages (*i.e. masks*) and beating a brass pan[, who] went vp and downe the Streetes'. This is technically a carnival procession in the sense of a procession at Shrovetide, but later that night 'the Bar of Richard Illinges doore was beaten out' – doubtless meaning (as already suggested by the rough music of beating pans), that we are in the presence of some kind of castigation or mischief custom, that is, an aggressive, malevolent house-visit, the connection with Shrovetide perhaps opportunistic rather than organic.[9]

NORWICH 1443

This dearth of documentation for early English carnival pageantry confers particular significance on the celebrated account of events in Norwich in 1443, quoted here from Hudson and Tingey's *Records of the City of Norwich*, the source for most scholarly discussion:

> John Gladman of Norwich ... of disporte as is and ever hath ben accustomed in ony Cite or Burgh thrugh al this reame on fastyngong tuesday made a disporte wt his neighburghs having his hors trapped with tyneseyle and otherwyse dysgysyn things crowned as King of Kristmesse in token that all merthe shuld end with ye twelve monthes of ye yer, afore hym eche moneth disgysd after ye seson yerof, and Lenten cladde in white with redde herrings skinnes and his hors trapped with oyster shelles after him in token yt sadnesse and abstinence of merth shulde

8. In 1620/1: *REED: Sussex* edited Cameron Louis (University of Toronto Press, 2000) 180 (the record), 287 (notes, suggesting the Shrovetide connection).

9. *REED: Somerset including Bath* edited James Stokes and Robert J. Alexander, 2 vols (Toronto University Press, 1996) 2 637–8. Compare *REED: Herefordshire, Worcestershire* 312, conversely, for a castigatory 'colestaff riding' in Worcestershire in 1572/3 whose date suggests it occurred at Shrovetide. Castigatory customs were basically occasional, prompted by a situation or an event independently of season, but could be saved up to take advantage of the time and mood of a major seasonal festival.

> followe and an holy tyme; and so rode in diuerse stretes of ye Cite w^t other peple w^t hym disgysed making merthe and disporte and pleyes.[10]

This has everything one might hope for by way of documenting carnival parades in late medieval English cities:

1. an explicit association with *mardi gras* itself – 'fastyngong tuesday';
2. figures representative of the antagonistic seasons whose calendrical border was crossed at Shrovetide, that is

   > Carnival – here understood as the persistence of Christmas – appropriately in the guise of a mock king, perhaps a variant of the ubiquitous lord of misrule,

   and

   > Lent – also appropriately decorated with the fish and shellfish characteristic of Lenten diet;
3. a spectacular horseback parade through the streets which included, perhaps at stations along the way, some kind of performance presumably involving Christmas and Lent and their relationship – which would qualify the custom (in the systematic terminology dear to German scholarship) not merely as a *Prozessionsspiel* (to be watched as it paraded past) but as an *Umzugsspiel* (a perambulation pausing for a more elaborate, perhaps dramatic, display before audiences at one or more stations);[11]
4. finally, as a bonus, the confident assertion that this was a custom not unique to Norwich, but observed 'in ony Cite or Burgh thrugh al this reame'.

And if REED has not yet found evidence of it in *any* of the other cities or boroughs of the realm surveyed thus far (and I shall be delighted to be told I have missed something), it is natural to invoke those factors with regard to record-keeping, survival and accessibility, and scholarly perspective, noted earlier. The importance of perspective (medieval and modern) is illustrated in relation to

10. *The Records of the City of Norwich* edited W. Hudson and J.C. Tingey, 2 vols (Norwich and London: Jarrold, 1906) *1* 345–6; see <https://archive.org/details/recordsofcityofn01norwuoft>. My transcript (for future reference) retains the punctuation of the text as here published.

11. For the distinction, see Leopold Schmidt *Das deutsche Volksschauspiel. Ein Handbuch* (Berlin: Erich Schmidt, 1962) 36–41.

one of the customs noted above, for while we might dismiss the ubiquitous Shrovetide cock-fighting as a sport irrelevant for street pageantry, Ronald Hutton quotes the reminiscences of the seventeenth-century antiquarian John Aubrey of the practice in his schooldays, an account which atypically extends into the aftermath of the combats, when the owner of the champion cock would parade 'through the streets in triumph decked with ribbons, all his school fellows following with a drum and a fiddle' on their way to feast at their master's house.[12] While customary parades (and perambulations) can be undertaken for their own sake, and so productive of documentation, they can also be auxiliary, essentially a means (if concurrently demonstrative and spectacular) of getting to and/or from the venue for some customary activity or other, and so often unnoticed or taken for granted.[13]

Thus encouraged, we *could* play the transnational card, and seek authentication of the Norwich account in continental evidence, and will in due course do so, but not before confronting problems, both contextual and textual, seriously undermining its documentary credentials.

Contextual Aspects

The simplest and most basic problem with regard to context is that Gladman's parade did not occur and could not have occurred 'on fastyngong Tuesday' in 1443, which was 5 March. The parade was in some way related to a riot in Norwich which provoked a royal inquisition, and that inquisition delivered its verdict several days before Shrove Tuesday, on 28 February. It furthermore indicated that Gladman's parade occurred between 22 and 25 of January (almost six weeks before Shrovetide).[14] We who have asserted or assumed otherwise[15]

12. Hutton *Stations of the Sun* 153–4.
13. We shall encounter the same phenomenon again later in connection with Shrovetide archery contests.
14. The discussion of the historical context that follows is largely based on Norman P. Tanner *The Church in Late Medieval Norwich, 1370–1532* (Toronto: Pontifical Institute of Medieval Studies, 1984) 146–52.
15. Ian Lancashire *Dramatic Texts and Records of Britain: A Chronological Topography to 1558* (Cambridge UP, 1985) 236; Thomas Pettitt '"Here Comes I, Jack Straw": English Folk Drama and Social Revolt' *Folklore* 95: *1* (1984) 3–20, at 5; most recently Claire Sponsler *The Queen's Dumbshows: John Lydgate and the Making of Early Theater* (Philadelphia: University of Pennsylvania Press, 2014) 205.

have been misled by the text's perhaps deliberately ambiguous formulation (to which we will return).

This contextual problem is also literally *con-textual* in that the account just quoted is not the only documentation, and not necessarily the most reliable, for the events concerned. Indeed this account of the parade is itself often (as above) cited out of its own textual context, lacking adjacent passages revelatory of its true status. The full statement actually begins, 'And wher that it was so that on John Gladman of Norwich ...', revealing the whole description of the parade as an adverbial clause syntactically prefatory to (and rhetorically pre-emptive of) the immediately ensuing main clause, which complains that notwithstanding Gladman's wholly innocuous activity, certain ill-disposed persons

> ... caused the seid meir and comonalte and the said John Gladman to ben indited of that, that thei shuld an ymagined to a made a comon rysyng and a corouned the said John Gladman as kyng w^{t} coron ceptre and diademe.[16]

The 'King of Christmas' scenario is in other words designed to counter and refute an *alternative* (and prior) account, a con-text, according to which the parade was an insurrectionary demonstration, and Gladman's crown a challenge to established royal authority. Furthermore the full text of that antagonistic account, here merely summarised by the opposition side, is also available, and merits more serious attention than it has as yet received.[17]

These very disparate witnesses to the event represent the respective views of the two sides in a long-running dispute over rights and resources between on the one hand the City of Norwich, as represented by the mayor, most of the council, and many common citizens, and on the other the powerful Cathedral Priory, seconded by neighbouring monastic institutions, regional magnates and a faction within the city oligarchy. It culminated on 25 January 1443 when a crowd of commoners initiated a siege of the Priory, trying in vain to break down its gates. When after a few days order was restored, the Crown instigated the formal inquisition just mentioned, at which the alternative account effectively became the official view. It places the parade in the run-up to the riot, asserting

16. *Records of the City of Norwich* 346.

17. Its relative neglect is doubtless due partly to its comparative colourlessness, but it may also have played a role that the *Records of the City of Norwich* supplied (340) only a partial and somewhat misleading translation of the Latin original (remarked on by Tanner *Church in Late Medieval Norwich* 151, note, with which I concur).

that, having on 22 January decided on action, the Mayor and commons of the city:

> arranged for John Gladman of the said city, merchant, to ride in the city on a horse, like a crowned king, with a sceptre and sword carried before him by three unknown men;[18] and [*three named artisans*] and twenty-four other persons to likewise ride on horseback, before the said John Gladman, with a crown upon their arms and carrying bows and arrows, as if they were valets of the crown of the lord king; and a hundred other unknown persons, some on horseback and some on foot, to follow the same John Gladman, carrying bows and arrows and swords. They went around urging people in the city to come together and to make an insurrection and riots there.

This riding might feasibly have been on the same day, 22 January, or at any time in the interim before, but quite separately from, the actual insurrection on 25 January, when (still according to this account), by ringing the bells of the city, the conspirators summoned some three thousand armed men 'to come together in bands and to make a violent insurrection throughout the entire city', who thereupon marched on the Priory.[19]

This account was part of the presentment of the jury delivered at the royal inquisition on 28 February 1443, and although doubtless designed to further the views of one party, it was formulated little more than a month after the events concerned, and at least has the virtue of compatibility with contemporary procedures (which do not need transnational documentation). Symptomatic is the alleged ringing of the church bells to summon the insurgents, which has not been fully understood, perhaps because something has been lost in translation from the Latin original. In historian Norman Tanner's translation of the passage concerned (not cited directly in the quotation above), the bells of the city were 'rung in turn'. Hudson and Tingey in *Records of the City of Norwich* offer similarly 'struck … in turn', but evidently conscious of a difficulty they supply in a note

18. The third man presumably bore the diadem which is mentioned alongside the sword and sceptre in the city's summary of the accusation, quoted above, but for some reason forgotten here.
19. Tanner *Church in Late Medieval Norwich* 149–50, Tanner's own translation of the Latin original.

the original Latin: *campanas vice versa pulsarunt.*[20] 'Vice versa' surely indicates that rather than 'in turn' the bells were rung *out of turn* (in relation to a regular chime or peal); in the idiom of the time they were rung 'awkward' – or as we would say, 'jangled'. This was the normal form of alarm (the French *tocsin*), also referred to as making the bells 'ring "awake!"' by which the members of a community were informed of an immediate, acute threat, and upon which able-bodied men should at once muster in arms at their designated assembly points (exactly what was claimed to have happened in Norwich), forming bands under the command of their constables. And this would not have been the first or the last occasion on which this official procedure was deployed to rouse the community in favour of an enterprise that was retrospectively deemed illegitimate in the eyes of higher authority – and thus effectively a revolt or insurrection. A century later in the aftermath of the 1549 Western Rebellion, parish churches in the region would be stripped of their bells precisely because they had been (mis)used for this purpose.[21]

Also standard procedure in an urban context at an earlier stage of a crisis was a mounted parade through the streets alerting citizens to an emerging contingency (say an anticipated French or Scottish invasion) and requiring the community, literally, to be on guard. It was also designed to be a demonstration (both inwards and outwards) of strength and resolution, and a means of checking the citizenry's state of readiness. Most major cities in England had such a 'marching watch', and although it was most familiar in the annual exercise, which in a period of sustained peace might modulate into just another form of civic pageantry, at its core the mayor, sheriffs, and other officials, accompanied by substantial units of armed men – including men with bows – put on a serious show of force.[22]

20. Tanner *Church in Late Medieval Norwich* 150; Hudson and Tingey *Records of the City of Norwich* 340 and note 8.

21. For this and other details evoked here see my '"Folk Allegory" in the Idiom of John Ball' in *Essays on Medieval and Renaissance Culture in honour of André Lascombes* edited Michel Bitot, Roberta Mullini, and Peter Happé (Tours: Université Francois Rabelais, 1996) 55–68, at 68; 'Approaching Medieval Disorder: Folk Routes' in *Voix (et voies) du désordre au Moyen-Âge* edited Tatjana Silec (Paris: Publications de l'Association de Médiévistes Anglicistes de l'Enseignement Supérieur, 2013) 5–49, at 34 and note 80.

22. Most studied (typically in the context of the pageantry) is the London Midsummer Watch, for which see Anne Lancashire *London Civic Theatre: City Drama and Pageantry from Roman Times to 1558* (Cambridge UP, 2002) 50–2, 'The Midsummer Watch: Beginnings'; Sheila Lindenbaum 'Ceremony and Oligarchy: The London Midsummer Watch' in *City and*

Much of the opposition account of the Gladman parade just cited is eminently compatible with a marching watch (in what was at this time the kingdom's second largest city) – from the number of participants, through the mixture of marchers and riders, to the variety of arms on display. Even some of the more provocative aspects of the parade, as reported by the opposition, could result from putting a political 'spin' on a more innocuous reality: in a regular marching watch the mayor would be in regalia, accompanied by figures displaying his insignia (including a sword) and substantial groups would be in livery marked by the symbol of the guild they represented or of the city itself. All that was needed for a rebranding as something insurrectionary at the hands of a hostile jury was to give the whole business a rather more regal appearance (implying a coronation procession, or the triumphal entry of a rival monarch) largely by reference to crowns: those displayed on the arms of some of the marchers, one on the head of Gladman. Altogether, if the present enquiry were an historical exercise trying to determine 'what actually happened'[23] this is one of the more promising scenarios for the Norwich parade: the city staged a marching watch which its opponents presented to higher authority as an insurrectionary demonstration.[24]

Alternative scenarios for some more or less innocuous customary activity susceptible to both aggressive enhancement and negative spin might be suggested by the circumstance that the main figure in the parade was John Gladman, rather than the mayor himself. Incidentally the extraordinary appropriateness of the name – which would do very well as a pseudonym for a festive lord of misrule (or a rebel leader invoking carnivalesque subversion) – does seem to be pure coincidence: the same John Gladman is mentioned in

Spectacle in Medieval Europe edited Barbara A. Hanawalt and Kathryn L. Reason *Medieval Studies* 6 (Minneapolis and London: University of Minnesota, 1994) 171–88. For other cities the realities behind the pageantry are sporadically discernible in Robert Withington *English Pageantry* 2 vols (Cambridge, Mass: Harvard University Press, 1918) 43–6.

23. For a sustained attempt (by a real historian) to pin down exactly what happened by comparing the rival accounts within the local social context, see Philippa C. Maddern *Violence and Social Order: East Anglia 1422–1442* (Oxford: Clarendon Press, 1992) 196–205.

24. Indeed it has been suggested that Jack Cade's parade through the capital during the 1450 revolt was deliberately imitative of the London Marching Watch (on which I, however, have reservations); see Alexander L. Kaufman *Historical Literature of the Jack Cade Rebellion* (Aldershot: Ashgate, 2009) chapter 3, 'Jack Cade's Carnivalesque Midsummer Celebration'.

Norwich documents not directly related to the parade, and indeed there are several people with this surname living in Norwich at the present time.

That independent documentation is mostly in relation to Gladman's membership of Norwich's powerful 'Bachery Guild', which in turn was alleged to have had a hand in the troubles of 1443.[25] And for late medieval guilds, craft or devotional, public parading through their home city was second only to seasonal feasting as a not merely characteristic but definitive activity, and near-contemporary evidence for the deployment of guild pageantry in the service of political ends is provided by the resistance of cities in northern Flanders to Burgundian hegemony.[26] In such guild parades the guild master (or a temporary festive surrogate) would figure prominently, and members would be in livery, including the guild's insignia on the cap or coat. And protest aside there would be a distinctly martial aspect if the parading were in connection with an archery contest (which, we have seen, could occur at Shrovetide), and this in turn could take the form of a 'popinjay shoot' – the target a model bird (or sometimes a live bird tethered by a string). There are European instances (a kind of adult analogue of Aubrey's schoolboy cock-fighting) where the members parade from their guild hall to the venue, each carrying his bow, with last year's winner in the place of honour, which on the way back is assumed by the new winner.[27] Such parades would not merely *look* military, but *were* military, for the whole point of the custom was to train the citizen militia.[28]

Textual Aspects

But whatever it was Gladman and his supporters thought they were doing, the opposition's interpretation of it as insurrectionary prevailed, the city and its

25. Tanner *Church in Late Medieval Norwich* 78; Tanner notes that, perhaps significantly, 'No more is heard of it after 1443'. For the role of guilds in Norwich civic life at this period, see Ben R. McCree 'Religious Guilds and Civic Order: The Case of Norwich in the Late Middle Ages' *Speculum* 67: *1* (1992) 69–97, which touches on Gladman and the events of 1433 in passing.
26. Peter Arnade 'The Public World of Revolt and Submission' in *Realms of Ritual: Burgundian Ceremony and Civic Life in Late Medieval Ghent* (Ithaca: Cornell University Press, 1996) chapter 4 (95–126).
27. Anu Mänd 'Shooting the Bird and the *Maigraf* festival in Medieval Livonian Towns' *Medium Ævum Quotidianum* 38 (1998) 46–65; see also Peter Arnade 'Shooting Confraternities and the Circulation of Prestige', chapter 3 of *Realms of Ritual.*
28. For an illustration see Arnade 'Shooting Confraternities' 69, fig. 7.

officers subjected to severe (if financial rather than capital) penalties. The city's refutation, vastly more interesting for the study of Shrovetide pageantry, was not, however, presented in connection with this investigation in the immediate aftermath of the events, but no less than five years later, in 1448, in support of an application for mitigation of those penalties. Together with the blatant discrepancy with regard to the date of the parade, this delay must mean the city account carries less authority (with regard to what actually happened) than the assertions of the opposition.[29] This uncertainty is reinforced by the textual evidence, which suggests the authors were struggling to achieve retrospectively a plausible construction of the original parade, whatever it actually was, as something customary and therefore innocuous, unrelated to the disturbances.

In the upshot, wisely avoiding anything remotely provocative, the city council opted to claim that Gladman and his company were performing an innocuous, widespread, custom, devoid even of military, let alone insurrectionary overtones, marking the transition from an extended Christmas season to Lent. But the effort required is eloquently reflected both in the discrepancies between the no less than three distinct drafts surviving in the city archives (now curated by the Norfolk Record Office), and in the alterations to each of them individually, in the form of deletions (of letters, words and phrases – some still legible, some just blotches) and interlinear additions.

In what follows these three variants will be identified by an elaboration of the numbers assigned to the documents of which they are a part in the Norfolk Record Office online Catalogue, respectively 9c2A,[30] 9c2B,[31] and 9c3.[32] Although the Catalogue suggests that 9c3 is an 'earlier, rough draft' of the

29. Tanner *Church in Late Medieval Norwich* 148 – this is presumably why Tanner provides a full text of the inquest verdict but only a (somewhat garbled) summary of the city's defence.

30. City of Norwich Records, case 9, shelf c, no. 2, <http://nrocat.norfolk.gov.uk/DServe/DServe.exe?dsqServer=NCC3CL01&dsqIni=Dserve.ini&dsqApp=Archive&dsqCmd=Show.tcl&dsqDb=Catalog&dsqPos=0&dsqSearch=%28%28text%29%3D%27john%20gladman%27%29> (one of two documents under this entry).

31. City of Norwich Records, case 9, shelf c, no. <http://nrocat.norfolk.gov.uk/DServe/DServe.exe?dsqServer=NCC3CL01&dsqIni=Dserve.ini&dsqApp=Archive&dsqCmd=Show.tcl&dsqDb=Catalog&dsqPos=0&dsqSearch=%28%28text%29%3D%27john%20gladman%27%29> (second of two documents under this entry).

32. City of Norwich Records, case 9, shelf c, no. 3, <http://nrocat.norfolk.gov.uk/DServe/dserve.exe?dsqServer=NCC3CL01&dsqIni=dserve.ini&dsqApp=Archive&dsqDb=Catalog&dsqCmd=show.tcl&dsqSearch=(RefNo==%27NCR%2F9%2F19%27)>.

two documents in 9c2, the latter are also referred to as 'draft copies', and no attempt will be made here to distinguish an 'original' or 'final' version: they are taken to represent three parallel attempts at drafting a reconstruction. The text quoted above from the *Records of the City of Norwich* seems to be a critical edition correcting errors and conflating more than one original (the Catalogue entry for 9c2 suggests these were 9c2 and 9c4). It is disconcerting, however, that the *Records* text includes a short phrase (noted in passing shortly) found in none of the archive drafts – but the existence of a fourth version with yet more variations would merely add to the sense of hesitancy and uncertainty already reflected in the three studied here.[33]

Some earlier discussions of Gladman's parade have been alert to the existence of multiple drafts, and have even noted variations,[34] but this seems to be the first time all three have been subjected to sustained comparative analysis. It is undertaken on the basis of transcriptions made by Professor Joanna Dutka in preparation for her edition of *REED: Norwich to 1540*, and generously placed at the disposal of this study.[35]

As will by now be apparent, the authors confronted their first major challenge in the inescapable discrepancy between the calendrical auspices of the custom adduced, Shrovetide, and the actual occasion of the performance several weeks earlier. This may be why they opted for a syntax which, abetted by the absence of punctuation throughout all three drafts, achieved a convenient ambiguity. Thus 9c2A asserts that Gladman, in a manner

> ... as is and euer hath been acustomed in eny Cite or burgh thurgh al this reame on fastyngong tuessday made a disporte ....

33. Following its recent revision the NRO catalogue no longer confuses the situation further by erroneously but consistently dating these documents to the 1430s.

34. Alan H. Nelson *The Medieval English Stage* (Chicago UP, 1974) 122–3; Chris Humphrey '"To Make a New King": Seasonal Drama and Local Politics in Norwich, 1443' *METh 17* (1995) 29–41, revised as 'Seasonal drama and local politics in Norwich, 1443' in Humphrey's *The Politics of Carnival: Festive Misrule in Medieval England* (Manchester University Press, 2001) 63–82.

35. This discussion and its results are accordingly provisional awaiting Professor Dutka's more informed and competent analysis in the context of other late medieval Norwich records. As a matter of courtesy I have refrained from quoting all three versions in their entirety. Quotation is also with the blessing, for which much thanks, of the Norfolk Record Office (communication of 9 January 2015).

A pause (which we would signal with a comma) is clearly necessary somewhere, but there are two legitimate options, offering significantly alternative meanings. Inserting a pause after 'reame'

> ... as is and euer hath been acustomed in eny Cite or burgh thurgh al this reame, on fastyngong tuessday made a disporte ...

would give us a Gladman who on Shrove Tuesday performed a disport also customary elsewhere; while waiting with the pause until after 'tuessday'

> ... as is and euer hath been acustomed in eny Cite or burgh thurgh al this reame on fastyngong tuessday, made a disporte ...

would have him make a disport which elsewhere is customary on Shrove Tuesday, without specifying exactly when he did it in Norwich in the year concerned. The *Records of the City of Norwich* does from time to time supply punctuation in its edition of the account, but not at this point, with the consequence that any scholar who *does* insert a comma is making a decision on what it means (with consequences for subsequent discussion). Thus those who punctuate to produce an explicit assertion that the Norwich parade occurred on Shrove Tuesday[36] make the account say something it doesn't, and may destroy a deliberate syntactic ambiguity (*amphibology*) designed to say something in an eminently deniable manner – a strategy not unknown in delicate situations, witness the instruction, *Eduardum occidere nolite timere bonum est*, sent to his keepers by the king's enemies in Marlowe's *Edward II*.[37]

The other drafts seem intent on clouding the issue further with variant formulations and supplementary specifications. 9c2B follows the above as far as 'on fastyngonge', but inserts interlinear additions (signalled by <...>), almost in the manner of a gloss, to specify the occasion as 'on fastyngonge <a> tuesdaye <in ye ende of Krystemasse & by fore candelmesse>'. The inserted 'a' is an astute obfuscation exploiting the circumstance that Shrovetide is a movable feast, linked to the date of Easter, so that while always on 'a Tuesday', 'fastyngonge' can occur within a range of dates in February or March (and who can be expected to remember when that was five years ago?). The further

36. William Tydeman *The Theatre in the Middle Ages* (Cambridge UP, 1978) 19, perhaps following E.K. Chambers *The Medieval Stage* 2 vols (1903; reprinted London: Oxford UP, 1967) *1* 261 note 4.

37. <https://en.wikipedia.org/wiki/Syntactic_ambiguity>.

specification, however, is blatantly misleading, since while it might have been forgotten that in 1433 Shrove Tuesday (5 March) was over a month later than Candlemas (2 February), as a matter of ecclesiastical arithmetic Shrove Tuesday could *never* occur 'before Candlemas'.[38] This may be the closest we come to a smoking gun indicating the presence of deliberate fabrication. Meanwhile 'yn ye ende of Krystemasse' usefully shifts the focus from the awkward Shrovetide to the more plausible Christmas, which was closer in calendrical terms, already signalled by the presence of a Christmas King, and which in some contexts actually did end at Candlemas.

Perhaps reluctant to protest this much, 9c3 is altogether more diplomatic. It has already paused over the confident declaration of the others that this parade 'is & euer hath been' customary in English cities, writing but then deleting 'is and euer' to leave the modest remark that the parade 'hath ben acustomed'. Then in specifying the date it lacks or omits the ultimately damaging reference to Candlemas, and thinks very hard about the rest. Evidently agreeing that the vagueness of 'a tuesday' is preferable it too inserts an 'a', but forgets to stop and rather draws attention to itself by ending up with '<a tues> Tuesday'. This is now a Tuesday not merely 'in ye ende of Krystemasse' as with 9c2B, but 'in the *last* ende of Christemesse' (my italics: the word is part of the drafted text, not an interlineation), as if trying to stretch Christmas without quite reaching Shrovetide. But the latter itself effectively disappears, for having accidentally (or) on purpose replaced 'fastyngonge' by 'fastyngend', which technically should mean Easter, the end of Lent, it deletes this, and so ends up saying merely it happened 'on a tuesday in the last ende of Christemesse' – the most cautious formulation of all and the least incompatible with the undeniable facts.[39]

The three descriptions of the parade itself display similar discrepancies, perhaps suggesting that the custom invoked was not a vivid living memory for the authors. At the beginning, while all three versions agree that Gladman made a 'disporte', only two (9c2A and 9c2B) specify that it was 'with his neighbours', while at the end, although all three state that he and other disguised people (in

38. Arcane discrepancies with the now current Gregorian calendar are not relevant here. Shrove Tuesday was and is defined in relation to Easter Sunday which in turn was defined in relation to the spring equinox, and under the then current Julian calendar this was arbitrarily fixed as 21 March, whatever the astronomical realities. Easter Sunday could at the earliest fall on 22 March, Shrove Tuesday accordingly at the earliest on 3 February.

39. This would identify the date of Gladman's ride as 22 January 1443, the only Tuesday in the range 22–25 January specified by the opposing faction.

addition to those described in the interim) made 'mirth and disports and plays', only two (but not the same two – 9c2B and 9c3) add that to do so they 'rode in diverse streets of the city'. The third (9c2A), however, writes at an earlier point (having described only part of Gladman's appearance) 'and so rode to his neghburs houses' only to cross it out to make room for further description: it was presumably intended to feature in the final statement, but in referring to houses rather than streets suggests a perambulation with house-visits rather than a parade.

The core of the account concerns the major symbolic figures in the parade: the King of Christmas, Lent, and the figures representing the Twelve Months. Least stable between the three drafts is the description of the Christmas figure. All agree that he is 'crowned as King of Christmas', but only 9c2B provides a coherent elaboration to the effect that his horse was trapped with tin foil (*Records of the City of Norwich* reads 'tinsel') and 'other wyse dysgysy thynggis'. 9c3 omits the reference to the horse, so that it is apparently Gladman himself who is thus decorated, while 9c2A achieves the same as 9c2B but only after two false starts. First it elaborates the statement about the horse's decoration with details unique to this version, 'with smale bladders puddynges and lynkes'. This is, however, crossed out, and the draft continues with the riding to neighbours' houses already discussed – evidently premature as this too is erased and the 'tinfoil ...' business inserted.

This version (9c2A) is also idiosyncratic with regard to Lent, who is not merely not described but not mentioned at all – although several (now illegible) words have been written and then erased at the point we would expect something. The other two are almost identical, and adequately represented by the *Records of the City of Norwich* text quoted above, except that while the latter and 9c2B agree in having Lent 'clad in white with red herrings' skins', 9c3 perhaps more plausibly has him 'clad in whyte & [*and*] redherynges skynnys' – that is, in the skins of both white and red (respectively pickled; smoked) herring, both being major Lenten foodstuffs in this period.[40]

There is also some awkwardness in the commentary on these two figures. The presence of Lent is quite properly explained as 'in token that sadness should follow and a holy time' (9c2B and 3; 9c2A omits; it is here *Records of the City of Norwich* adds a phrase: 'and abstinence of merth'). But this is anticipated with a similar interpretation of the Christmas figure, 'in token that all mirth(s) that

40. Among many standard references see Eileen Power *Medieval English Nunneries c.1275 to 1535* (Cambridge UP, 1922; digital reprint 2010) 139.

season should end' (9c2B and 3; 9c2A garbles) – which is less logical, unless the drafters at this point were envisaging a parade involving only a representative of Christmas-Carnival who is taking his leave of the community (which is not, as we shall see, out of the question).

Implications

Contextual and textual problems conspire to suggest that the City of Norwich's 1448 apologia is singularly unconvincing as documentation that John Gladman led a customary Christmas and Lent parade through the streets of the city on Shrove Tuesday, 1443, or even indeed that this is what he and his fellows performed during the run-up to the riot of 25 January. Sandra Billington suggests the city representatives 'tried to rewrite the events of January 1443, reinterpreting the icons of their procession',[41] but even this may be too generous.

Such considerations complicate, to the extent of vitiating, the standing of these events in Norwich in early 1443 as instances of what I have termed 'interaxionality' between seasonal custom and social revolt. Both custom and revolt, like stage plays and pageantry, are forms of Performance Culture, between which, analogously to the intertextuality of verbal culture, units or aspects of action can be transferred, taking with them connotations that can infuse their new host.[42] If Gladman's parade was indeed, as the city authorities asserted, a widespread seasonal custom, but was nonetheless also, as the city's opponents insisted, an overt and essentially insurrectionary demonstration, it would rank alongside more celebrated instances of interaxionality between custom and revolt which have been alleged in connection with the English Peasant Risings of 1381 (Jack Straw) and 1450 (Jack Cade), not to mention Leroy Ladurie's notoriously exploding Carnival at Romans in 1579.[43]

41. Sandra Billington *Mock Kings in Medieval Society and Renaissance Drama* (Oxford: Clarendon Press, 1991) 19–20.

42. The concept is introduced, checked against alternative approaches, and applied in my 'Staging Intrusions: Interaction and Interaxionality in Medieval English Theatre' in *Medieval Theatre Performance: Actors, Dancers, Automata and their Audiences* edited Philip Butterworth and Katie Normington (Cambridge: D.S. Brewer, 2017) 52–75.

43. These instances are critically examined in my 'Approaching Medieval Disorder: Folk Routes' in *Voix (et voies) du désordre au Moyen-Âge. Volume issu du colloque du Centre d'études médiévales anglaises de Paris-Sorbonne, 22–23 mars 2012* edited Tatjana Silec (Paris: Publications de l'Association de Médiévistes Anglicistes de l'Enseignement

But this would require constructing a scenario for the events in 1443 by arbitrarily selecting and combining aspects from both accounts into conformity with some notion of how things ought to have been. For instance William Tydeman writes that a '"mockery king" ritual was being enacted at Norwich in 1443 when a riot took place during a ride by the "kyng of Crestmesse" with a crown and sceptre'[44] – which takes the 'King of Christmas' from the city's account, the 'sceptre' from the city's summary of the alternative which it is refuting, and adds a riot which does not take place 'during' the parade in either account. Similarly Anthony Gash asserts that

> ... we have evidence for the symbolic contrast between Christmas and Lent being used for political purposes by discontented artisans in fifteenth-century Norwich. ... John Gladman, ... dressed as the King of Christmas, and other artisans, also in masquerade, led a revolt of the citizens ...[45]

which effectively takes the content of the parade from the City account (which denied it had any link to the unrest) and inserts it into the motivation of the revolt as alleged by the city's enemies (who said the parade had a very different content, where a King of Christmas would have no place). Claire Sponsler describes Gladman's parade as comprising Christmas and Lent figures (from the defence) plus three men carrying crown, sceptre, and sword (from the accusation which the defence denied) and as riding to the priory to initiate the attack.[46] This is not a simple philological question: the images of the Norwich events thus constructed can provide the point of departure for elaborate subsequent analysis and interpretation.

Supérieur, 2013) 5–49, author's draft accessible online at <https://www.academia.edu/11641587/Approaching_Medieval_Disorder_Folk_Routes>.

44. Tydeman *Theatre in the Middle Ages* 19.

45. Anthony Gash 'Carnival Against Lent: The Ambivalence of Medieval Drama' in *Medieval Literature: Criticism, Ideology and History* edited David Aers (Brighton: Harvester, 1986) 74–98, at 85. Gash is the source for a similar hybrid account in Kathleen M. Ashley's 'Introduction' to *Mankind* edited Kathleen M. Ashley and Gerard NeCastro (Kalamazoo: Medieval Institute Publications, 2010), online at <http://d.lib.rochester.edu/teams/publication/ashley-and-necastro-mankind>.

46. Sponsler *The Queen's Dumbshows* 205. This last item, asserted by neither statement, is also introduced by Nelson *Medieval English Stage* 123.

All of which suggests that, rather than attempting to establish what really happened, a more appropriate, if more modest, goal would be to explore the thinking behind, and so possible models for, the city representatives' achievement of their retrospective reconstruction.

TRANSNATIONAL PERSPECTIVES

The Combat between Carnival and Lent

On the assumption that the Norwich apologists would be unlikely to invoke an activity 'accustomed in ony Cite or Burgh thrugh al this reame', if there were none such, but faced with the absence of English corroboration, we may turn, on this revised understanding of what is at stake, to potential European evidence, and a promising candidate is near at hand in Pieter Bruegel the Elder's celebrated painting representing 'The Combat between Carnival and Lent' (1559; PLATE 1).[47] As persuasively demonstrated by Claude Gaignebet in a groundbreaking study,[48] whatever *else* it aims at by way of allegory and symbolism (the topic of most interpretations), Bruegel's picture represents, within a circular, calendrical framework, realistic vignettes of customary activities (for which it therefore constitutes documentation) marking the extended period between Christmas and Easter:

to the left
(anticlockwise from the top),
on the side of the square dominated by taverns:
the pastimes, parades and folk plays
of the festive season from Twelfth Night to Fat Tuesday;

to the right
(anticlockwise from the bottom),
on the side of the square in the shadow of a church:
the religious observances and charitable practices
of the Lenten season from Ash Wednesday to Easter Sunday.

47. Kunsthistorisches Museum, Vienna, full reproduction (copyrighted) online at <http://www.khm.at/de/object/320722549d/>. Reproduced frequently online and in most standard works, for example Bruegel *The Paintings* edited F. Grossman (London: Phaidon, 1966) plates 6–12.

48. Claude Gaignebet 'Le combat de Carnaval et de Carême de P. Bruegel' *Annales* E.S.C. *27* (1972) 313–45.

PLATE 1: Pieter Bruegel the Elder *Strijd tussen Carnaval en Vasten* ('The Combat between Carnival and Lent'), 1559: Kunsthistorisches Museum, Vienna. © KHM-Museumsverband.

In the middle foreground, prominently and exactly at the point of transition between these antithetical phases, Bruegel depicts the impending collision, in what is effectively a mock tournament, of two processions comprising suitably clad and accoutred figures accompanying principals respectively representing Carnival and Lent.

This encounter has been characterised by various commentators as 'a representation of an old play, popular in many countries',[49] and depicting 'an important event in community life in early modern Europe'.[50] The scene, Arthur Haberlandt noted in an influential study, reflects a 'directly observed folk custom'.[51] It is therefore tempting to suggest that just such a joust figured among the 'disporte and pleys' in the Shrovetide parade of Christmas and Lent figures through 'diuerse stretes of ye Cite' in the custom invoked in the Norwich defence. But the match is less than perfect, and the juxtaposition directly misleading if the authority of Bruegel is invoked to assert a performance of this kind was customary in England in the later Middle Ages.

Least problematic, ironically, is the most overt discrepancy between the two sources, the Norwich attribution to Christmas of the antagonistic role in relation to Lent that Bruegel, with greater calendrical plausibility, assigns to Carnival. As already noted in passing, Christmas could be and sometimes was perceived and treated as lasting until the beginning of Lent,[52] qualifying a Christmas figure as a party to the encounter, and this is sometimes reflected in seasonal custom and ceremony, if not street pageantry. A mid-fifteenth-century Swedish Shrovetide interlude, *Julens och Fastans Träta*, comprises an altercation between figures representing Yule and Lent, most likely prefatory to a fight,[53]

49. Grossman *Bruegel* 190.

50. Wikipedia at <https://en.wikipedia.org/wiki/The_Fight_Between_Carnival_and_Lent>.

51. Arthur Haberlandt 'Das Faschingsbild des Peter Bruegel d. A' *Zeitschrift fur Volkskunde NS* 5 (1933): 237–49, at 239.

52. Samuel Kinser has suggested that this phenomenon is found 'especially in mountainous areas where winter's weather exempted people from work but not pleasure', which would not apply to Norfolk; Samuel Kinser *Rabelais's Carnival: Text, Context, Metatext* (Chicago UP, 1990) 50.

53. Translated and analysed in Leif Søndergaard and Tom Pettitt 'The Flyting of Yule and Lent: A Medieval Swedish Shrovetide Interlude' *Early Drama, Art and Music Review 16: 1* (Autumn 1993) 1–11; reprinted in *The Dramatic Tradition of the Middle Ages* edited Clifford Davidson (AMS Studies in the Middle Ages 26; New York: AMS Press, 2005) 297–307; see also Leif Søndergaard 'La lutte de Carnaval contre Carême – un jeu de carnaval suédois dans la tradition européene' in *Théâtre et spectacle, hier et aujourd'hui.*

while an early-sixteenth-century English *carole* seems to provide a speech for a Christmas Lord as he takes leave of a household at the approach of Lent (perhaps in a ceremony in which both figures were personified):

> *Now haue gud day, now haue gud day!*
> *I am Crystmas, and now I go my way.*
> 1. Here haue I dwellyd with more and lasse
> From Halowtyde till Candylmas …
> 3.3 Me thynke I here, Lent doth call
> *Now haue gud day!*[54]

But with regard to the validity of Bruegel's picture as evidence for this kind of encounter in customary street pageantry, there is a salutary disillusionment in the (for me, belated) appreciation that while Gaignebet's study *does* assert and document that the activities, respectively carnivalesque and Lenten, depicted on each side of the picture, represent contemporary social reality, that is not the case with the aggressive encounter between Carnival and Lent and their trains which gives the picture its name,[55] and indeed recent contributions from within Bruegel studies reflect a growing scepticism in this regard.[56]

It has furthermore been suggested that for this part of the panorama Bruegel was inspired by a quite different custom with the same choreography of colliding parades, the Battle between Winter and Summer (which could also

moyen âge et renaissance edited Michèle Populer (Paris: Éditions du CTHS, 1991) 227–43.

54. *The Early English Carols* edited R.L. Greene (Oxford: Clarendon Press, 2nd edition 1977) no. 141. The figure will sometimes be referred to as 'Christmas-Carnival' in what follows.

55. The title was conferred by a contemporary and close associate of Bruegel.

56. Gaignebet 'Carnaval et de Carême' 316: 'En dépit des affirmations réitérées des commentateurs nous montrerons que ce tableau doit très peu à une forme littéraire ou cérémonielle'. Walter S. Gibson *Bruegel* (London: Thames & Hudson, 1977) 79: 'It is not clear whether similar confrontations between Carnival and Lent were actually staged during the carnival season'; Katrien Lichtert 'The Artist, the City and the Urban Theatre: Pieter Bruegel's "Battle between Shrovetide and Lent" Reconsidered' in *Portraits of the City. Representing Urban Space in Later Medieval and Early Modern Europe* edited Katrien Lichtert and others (Turnhout: Brepols, 2014) 83–97, at 90; online at <https://www.academia.edu/10177065/The_Artist_the_City_and_the_Urban_Theatre_Pieter_Bruegel_the_Elders_Battle_between_Shrovetide_and_Lent_1559_Reconsidered>.

be performed at Shrovetide).[57] Or alternatively he might have been inspired by existing pictorial representations of the theme, in which case the question is shifted to whether *they* reflect customary Carnival vs Lent pageantry.[58] Perhaps the most realistic pictorial antecedent is the tournament represented at the bottom of the January page in the celebrated early-sixteenth-century *Breviarium Grimani* (another Flemish production) depicting an engagement between two spear-and-shield wielding figures, each sitting on a barrel fixed to a sledge or hurdle and pulled towards each other across an icy surface by a group of helpers. But as the association with January suggests there seems to be no connection with Shrovetide, the two sides are thematically indistinguishable, and the whole looks more like a sport than a custom.[59] While adamant that 'it would be a mistake to see (in the encounter of the two main figures in Bruegel's picture) … a true realistic representation of a scene performed in a carnival play', Hanns Swarzenski suggests that in Bruegel's likely immediate source of inspiration, an etching by Franz Hogenberg,[60] 'an actual Carnival pageant seems to be depicted'. However, what might be considered its most realistic feature, the fisticuffs between the women pulling the respective carts, was, according to Swarzenski, itself an established pictorial theme.[61] This in turn

57. Elke M. Schutt-Kehm *Pieter Bruegels d. A. 'Kampf des Karnavals gegen die Fasten' als Quelle volkskundlicher Forschung* (Artes populares 7; Frankfurt am Main: Peter Lang, 1983) 115. Standard accounts of this custom include Waldemar Liungman *Der Kampf zwischen Sommer und Winter* (FFC 130; Helsinki: Finnish Academy of Sciences, 1941) and Hans Moser 'Zur Geschichte des Winter- und Sommer-Kampfspiels' *Bayerischer Heimatschutz* 29 (1933) 33–45.

58. Alternative pictorial representations are surveyed by Schutt-Kehm *'Kampf'* 111–14; Siegfried Wagner *Der Kampf der Fasten Gegen die Fastnacht. Studien zu Form, Funktion und Entwicklung des Systems von Fastnacht und Fasten im Spätmittelalter und der Frühen Neuzeit* (Munich: tuduv, 1986) 45–6, and most comprehensively Hanns (*sic*) Swarzenski 'The Battle between Carnival and Lent' *Bulletin of the Museum of Fine Arts (Boston)* 49: *1* (1951) 1–11.

59. Invoked by Haberlandt 'Das Faschingsbild des Peter Bruegel d. A' 239–40 (who claims to detect carnival features in the garb and accoutrements of participants – hard to determine this on the basis of the reproduction online at <http://www.ottodoenneweg.de/files/be70e9f3943b58522392c8e8e7518311-6.html>.

60. 'Den vetten Fastelavont met alle syn gasten compt hier bestriden die mager Vasten': etching with explanatory text. Published 1558 (a year ahead of Bruegel) by Hieronymous Cock, online reproduction at <http://www.metmuseum.org/collection/the-collection-online/search/408590>.

61. Swarzenski 'Battle between Carnival and Lent' 2 and 3 note 1.

draws attention to the purely practical aspect of envisaging what would have happened had Bruegel's (or Hogenberg's) figures, armed as they are, actually achieved the kind of contact typical of a tournament: the impracticability is highlighted in derivative paintings which focus on this central encounter, and bring the contestants within striking distance of each other.[62]

Pictorial evidence proving inadequate or at best inconclusive, Bruegel's relevance will depend on other varieties of documentation. And while the conflict between Carnival and Lent is very well documented and has been intensely researched as a powerful and widespread *topos* in late medieval literature and culture, including formal dramatic productions and indoor customs performed at Carnival time,[63] there is desperately little evidence for it, even in continental Europe, under the auspices of customary street pageantry.

Easily the closest to Bruegel's depiction is a folk tradition from the Italian West coast provinces of Lazio (centred on Rome) and Campania (centred on Naples), observed until about 1900,[64] where the two figures have their own, separate, processions, each represented by an effigy and paraded in a cart. The procession of Carnival (a pot-bellied, red-faced man decorated with sausages) sets off from the centre of the city or village; that of Lent (an emaciated old

62. With the same title, but generally assigned to the 'school' or 'circle' of Bruegel the Younger. Among many variants, see for example Boston Museum of Fine Arts, <http://www.mfa.org/collections/object/combat-between-carnival-and-lent-33366>. Swarzenski examines this painting in the context of the whole sequence of depictions from pre-Bruegel to post-Bruegel in 'Battle between Carnival and Lent'.

63. In addition to studies already invoked above in connection with Bruegel (notably Gaignebet, Schutt-Kehm; Wagner), major surveys include Martine Grinberg and Sam Kinser 'Combats de Carnaval et de Carême: Trajets d'une metaphore' *Annales E.S.C. 38: 1* (1983) 65–98; Eva Kimminich 'The Way of Vice and Virtue in European Carnival Plays: The Battle of Carnival and Lent: Textuality and Popular Culture' *Fifteenth-Century Studies 15* (1989) 183–208.

64. The main authorities are Nicola Borrelli *Tradizioni aurunche* (Rome: L. Proja, 1937) 46 (for the region) and Gaetano Amalfi *Tradizioni ed Usi della Penisola Sorrentina* (Palermo: Carlo Clausen, 1890) chapter 2, 'Feste, Fiori e Frutta', online at <https://issuu.com/mimmocinque/docs/curiositpopola08pitruoft>, 37–42 for the Sorrento region. Their descriptions (summarised in my main text) are reproduced in Paolo Toschi *Le origini del teatro italiano* (Torino: Boringhieri, 1955; reprinted 1969) 159–60, and there are French summaries and extracts in Arnold van Gennep *Manuel de folklore français contemporain* (Paris: Picard, 1937–58), revised reprint as *Le Folklore français* 4 vols (Paris: Robert Laffont, 1998–99) *1* section 1, 'Cycle de Carnaval-Carême' §3, 'Les personifications du Carnaval et du Carême' 790–840, at 802.

woman dressed in rags decorated with vegetables) sets off from the country outside. The two processions meet and confront each other at a city gate, or by the first house of the village, but there is no direct conflict, as the issue between them is decided by the intervention of a third figure representing Death, who slays Carnival with his scythe. Carnival is burnt, and Lent makes a triumphal entry into the City (but will in turn be immolated at a later date).[65]

With regard to historical documentation there is another, in some ways closer, Italian parallel in the mock tournament staged in an urban landscape similar to Bruegel's (the square in front of Bologna cathedral) at Shrovetide 1506, between two groups of soldiers, led, respectively, by figures representing Carnival (a fat man on a fat horse) and Lent (an old woman on a thin horse) – who themselves engaged in less military grappling. But this was evidently a one-off event, arranged by the city's prince, and not a customary show: it does not seem to have been repeated in later years.[66]

Invoking this instance at the opening of their comprehensive and sophisticated exploration of the Carnival vs Lent *topos*, Martine Grinberg and Sam Kinser seem to suggest that the encounter was also manifested in a parallel tradition of Shrovetide pageantry persisting into recent times:

> La confrontation entre Carnaval et Carême est un élément essentiel de certains carnavals urbains à partir du xve siècle et surtout au xvie siècle. Sans pouvoir affirmer qu'elle fut générale, cette représentation se retrouve aussi bien en France qu'en Allemagne, en Angleterre qu'en Italie, sous des formes spécifiques. Ces affrontements se perpétuent également dans des carnavals, urbains et ruraux, jusqu'au xxe siècle.[67]

65. There may have been something similar at Metz, where effigies representing Carnival and Lent were burnt in succession (van Gennep 835). He also makes a reference to some kind of folk version of the Carnival vs Lent combat at Venès (Lauragais), but without elaborating (791–2).

66. Summarised in French in Grinberg and Kinser 'Combats de Carnaval et de Carême' 65, the full Italian text of the record (a letter from a spectator) is provided in Toschi *Origini del teatro italiano* 152. Also discussed by Wagner *Der Kampf* 47–8.

67. Grinberg and Kinser 'Combats de Carnaval et de Carême' 65 (translated Pettitt): 'The confrontation between Carnival and Lent is an essential element in some urban carnivals starting with the fifteenth century and above all in the sixteenth. While not in a position to assert it became universal, this exhibition is to be found as much in France as in Germany, in England as in Italy, in different forms. Furthermore these confrontations persisted in carnivals, urban as rural, up to the twentieth century'.

It would be very convenient (and this paper would be a good deal shorter) if this were indeed the case, but no documentation is offered, the study moving quickly on to its main focus, the theme's literary and dramatic manifestations. Revisiting the topic a few years later Kinser repeats the assertion (if with a shifted emphasis):

> although personifying Carnival and Lent and juxtaposing them in combat was a literary tradition dating from the thirteenth century, it was not a parade performed in the streets until the fifteenth or sixteenth century,[68]

and now supplements the Bologna tournament with a Shrovetide performance at Zittau in eastern Germany in 1505 comprising a combat between figures representing Sausage and Herring,[69] and a 1599 Valencia pageant featuring Carnival (performed by the playwright Lope de Vega) on a mule decked with rabbits and poultry, and Lent (performed by a court Fool) on a mule decked with various kinds of fish and wearing a hat fringed with eels and sardines. Having paraded on they rode around a little until both fell off their mounts, an ensuing skirmish therefore carried out by cavaliers in their respective trains.[70] But as Kinser indicates, this too was very much a contrived pageant (including a speech written by de Vega), for a particular occasion (celebrating an upcoming royal wedding) rather than a regular custom. Meanwhile the Zittau performance seems closer to the literary (albeit dramatic) tradition, and the source suggests performance under school auspices, the Sausage performed by a deputy teacher (*Schulcollaborator*).[71] Kinser states that the battle ended with the Sausage figure being 'thrown into the river' suggesting an outdoor, public performance, but the original (*Röhrtrog*) may suggest rather a trough, water tank, or cistern.[72]

68. Samuel Kinser *Rabelais's Carnival: Text, Context, Metatext* (Berkeley, Los Angeles, Oxford: University of California Press, 1990) 51.
69. Kinser *Rabelais's Carnival* 53.
70. Kinser *Rabelais's Carnival* 53–4.
71. Wagner *Der Kampf* 48. Wilhelm Creizenach *Geschichte des Neueren Dramas Vol. 1: Mittelalter und Frührenaissance* (Halle: M. Niemeyer 1893, 2nd edition 1911; reprinted New York: Benjamin Blom, 1965) 462. Creizenach also mentions other early instances which do not seem to be customary parades.
72. It is revealing that this is the only instance of a combat between Carnival and Lent in Hans Moser's comprehensive survey of urban Carnival customs in the later middle ages, 'Städtische Fasnacht des Mittelalters', in *Masken Zwischen Spiel und Ernst* [edited Hermann Bausinger and others] (Beiträge des Tübinger Arbeitskreises für

The food symbolism on display here reappears in the well-documented carnival festivities at Metz in the early sixteenth century. In 1521 this included a dancing combat between two groups (of women) respectively led by Carnival (*Charnage*; decorated with sausages and puddings) and Lent (*Caresme*; decorated with herrings and *bicquehoulz* – probably shellfish). But here too this was an innovation, which does not seem to have become a regular tradition.[73]

Jean-Claude Aubailly in his authoritative *Le Théâtre Médiévale, profane et comique* juxtaposes Bruegel's depiction with 'nombreux jeux dramatiques, exécutés vraisemblement sur la place publique le jour du Mardi gras', but as usual the examples offered are scripted, dramatic set pieces suitable for a scaffold stage, rather than customary parades.[74] Arthur Haberlandt cites a reference in Sebastian Franck's homiletic *Weltbuch* of 1534 to figures dressed as kings (*künig*) in carnival revels, but there are more than one, and they figure among many guises rather than specifically as 'carnival kings', in the context of generally milling about in costume rather than a formal parade.[75] On balance, it seems right to agree with Ethan Matt Kavaler (if I read him aright) following his survey of the evidence, that while tournaments were traditional in the Low Countries and elsewhere at Carnival time, and while some were 'mock' tournaments to entertain rather than actual sporting contests, and others more ceremonial markings of seasonal transitions (like Winter to Summer), tournaments between Carnival and Lent (unlike those between Summer and Winter) were sporadic, one-off occasions under particular circumstances, to which Bruegel's picture is a kind of analogue in the visual arts.[76]

But if students of the literary and pictorial renditions of the Carnival vs Lent theme in general and of Bruegel's picture in particular have a hard time pinning down analogous customs, conversely, for students of Shrovetide customs, like Marjoke de Roos, Bruegel's picture itself is the most striking evidence for the whole idea of perceiving (and thus representing) Shrovetide as a stand-off

Fastnachtforschung; Tübingen: Tübinger Vereinigung für Volkskunde, 1967) 135–202, at 183.

73. Martine Grinberg 'Carnaval et societé urbaine, xive–xvie siècle. Le royaume dans la ville' *Ethnologie française* 4: 3 (1974) 215–44, at 231. It is not specified, but they might well have approached each other in opposing parades.

74. Jean-Claude Aubailly *Le Théâtre Médiévale, profane et comique* (Paris: Larousse, 1975) 95.

75. Haberlandt 'Das Faschingsbild' 238.

76. Ethan Matt Kavaler *Pieter Bruegel: Parables of Order and Enterprise* (Cambridge UP, 1999) 130.

between the two seasons.[77] In his standard survey of German folk drama, Leopold Schmidt's statements on Carnival vs Lent customs repeatedly appeal to Bruegel's picture as the major instance.[78] The argument is clearly in danger of becoming circular, the pictures explained in terms of the European customs, the customs documented by the pictures.

And the circularity is reproduced on the transnational axis: it almost seems that the best available evidence for Bruegel's indebtedness to custom is that same account of Gladman's parade of Christmas and Lent in Norwich in 1443 whose authenticity we seek to document by appeal to Bruegel. Symptomatically, perhaps, when in the course of their literary explorations Grinberg and Kinser briefly revert to the theme of carnival customs, it is precisely and solely the Norwich account to which they refer for evidence.[79]

This line of enquiry therefore proves to be something (pun intended) of a red herring, and for more than one reason – which actually means that the damage is limited. For the Gladman parade, as described in the account quoted, symbolises not a *confrontation* between Christmas-Carnival and Lent, but the inevitable *succession* of the one by the other, 'in token y^{t} sadnesse and abstinence of merth shulde followe and an holy tyme' (rather as in the English *carole* quoted above). This discrepancy in symbolism is confirmed by a significant and signifying feature still somewhat neglected in the analysis of pageantry, their disparate choreographies. For whereas in Bruegel's picture (and Hogenberg's), as in the Italian evidence (and as in the Summer vs Winter custom Bruegel may have used as a model) two separate parades advance towards each other in evident anticipation of a collision, in the Norwich record the two figures advance in calendrical order in the same direction in the same parade ('Christmas … and Lenten … after him').[80]

77. Marjoke de Roos 'Battles and Bottles: Shrovetide Performances in the Low Countries (c.1350 – c.1550)' in *Festive Drama* edited Twycross 167–79, at 173.

78. Leopold Schmidt *Das deutsche Volksschauspiel. Ein Handbuch* (Munich: Erich Schmidt Verlag, 1962) 38, 47, 171.

79. Grinberg and Kinser 'Combats de Carnaval et de Carême' 4–5 and 97 note 12. There is some discrepancy here (as also at note 14) between the content of the main text and the endnote, suggesting that one has been revised without the other being brought into line. The Norwich account remains the prime evidence in Kinser's later discussion in his *Rabelais's Carnival* (50).

80. Incidentally this 'after him' is delayed so long in the sentence its antecedent could erroneously be taken to be 'horse', leading to the notion that the Lent figure is not on this horse but walking ahead of it, as suggested by Sponsler *The Queen's Dumbshows* 205.

This does not rule out a combat in connection with the 'disporte and pleyes ... in diuerse stretes of ye Cite', but this would be achieved by an elaboration of the parade choreography (distinct from Bruegel's tournament mode) with the Christmas and Lent figures, on arrival at a given station, breaking out of the line (which would probably process into a circle and halt, to establish a performance space) before squaring up to each other for the combat. This was doubtless the procedure annually deployed at Norwich at this period a few months later in the more convincingly documented St George's Day parade, when St George and the Dragon processed in line among the guildsmen, but on arrival at the designated venue engaged in combat (thereafter presumably getting back into line for the return procession).[81] But this does not seem likely in the Gladman procession, where the presence of figures representing the twelve months also suggests a sequential, rather than a confrontational, choreography and symbolism (discussed at length below).

The Death of Carnival

Had we been sufficiently attentive to notice that the Norwich refutation opted for a Carnival parade whose central aspect was not a combat but the departure of Carnival, our quest for authenticating European analogues would have been less complicated, and the temptation to invoke Bruegel less seductive, the more so if it were in the absence of a figure representing Lent (as in one of the Norwich drafts).

French folk tradition of the nineteenth century in particular had a widespread customary observance of parading a figure representing Carnival through the community, and indeed pausing for 'disports' along the way – more specifically a mock trial, and, some time subsequently, an execution, usually in the form of immolation. The latter is facilitated by carnival being represented by a straw effigy (or, occasionally, by a straw-clad man who extricates himself adroitly as the fire is applied). Ejection into a river was also an option.[82] There are analogous performances in Italian folk tradition,[83] and by a fortunate chance

81. E.K. Chambers *The Medieval Stage* 2 vols (London: Oxford UP, 1903; reprinted 1967) *1* 222.

82. See the extensive survey in Arnold van Gennep *Le Folklore français 1: 1* 'Cycle de Carnaval-Carême' §3: 'Les personifications du Carnaval et du Carême', 790–840; there are some lengthier accounts of local traditions at 827–9.

83. Toschi *Le origini del teatro italiano* chapter VII #3, 'Il processo e la condanna di Carnevale nel folklore italiano contemporaneo' (232–6).

(due to polemics between local factions), valuable evidence of such customs in the mid sixteenth century is available from the German region of Westphalia (abutting on to Belgium and Holland). Particularly striking is the documentation from the city of Münster, where Carnival was personified by an effigy of linen clothes stuffed with hay and straw, also referred to as the Fool (*Morio*, *Geck*) or Doctor. He was apparently constructed at, or quietly taken to, a village outside the city, whither the brothers of the Münster St Anne's guild rode out to fetch him on the Thursday before Shrove Sunday. They paraded him back into the city and around its streets in a cart, ending up at the Market Square, of which they made three circuits. It is not entirely clear whether the figure presided over the festivities from a position in the marketplace (rather than residing at the guild's hall), but a week later, on the Thursday after Shrovetide (the day after Ash Wednesday), he was again paraded through the city, only now booed and hissed at as responsible for all the sins and excesses of the past week; back in the market square he is tried, condemned, and immolated.[84]

Discrepancies in relation to Norwich 1433 include the mode of transport – the French Carnival figure only rarely paraded on horseback, and usually in a cart[85] – and of course the mood of the occasion: in Norwich evidently a regretful farewell; in French folk tradition the expulsion of a figure (now, at the approach of Lent) perceived as reprobate – indeed there are substantial overlaps with analogous Shrovetide customs in which the figure expelled was rather Winter or Death.[86]

84. N. Humburg *Städtisches Fastnachtsbrauchtum in West- und Ostfalen. Die Entwicklung vom Mittelalter bis ins 19. Jahrhundert* (Münster: Volkskundliche Kommission für Westfalen, 1976), online at <http://www.lwl.org/voko-download/BilderNEU/422_005Humburg.pdf>, provides a description and analysis (24–6) on the basis of two local chronicles written respectively in 1573 and c.1601 (full texts of relevant passages at 230–41). He also provides a review of the custom over a longer period in this region (109–14) backed by local records (335–42). The custom does not seem to figure prominently in later German folk tradition, which evidently prefers scapegoating and expelling Winter or Death in such carnival processions (on which see note 82).

85. Van Gennep *Folklore français 1: 1* 823–4.

86. For these see for example Robert Pearson Flaherty '*Todaustragen*: The Ritual Expulsion of Death at Mid-Lent – History and Scholarship' *Folklore 103* (1992) 40–55 and Waldemar Liungman *Traditionswanderungen Rhein-Jenissei Eine Untersuchung über das Winter- und Todaustragen und einige hierhergehorige Bräuche* 2 vols (FFC 129 and 131; Helsinki: Finnish Academy of Sciences, 1941 and 1945).

However, in some local traditions the execution was followed by a further parade mimicking a funeral procession, with appropriate expressions of grief,[87] and in Italy at least the custom has in places persisted to the present.[88] But even here Carnival would most likely be represented as a tattered hunchback or beggar, not a crowned king as in Norwich.[89] Oddly, there are a number of references to a carnival mock ruler, typically elected from within a youth-guild, who presides over the festival, sometimes indeed a king (*Re*), precisely in the manner of a Christmas Lord of Misrule.[90] Logically he would be the most appropriate candidate to represent Carnival to figure in these end-of-carnival pageants, but that does not seem to have been the case. This ignominy was most often, as we have seen, reserved for an effigy, but in one case, at least (in central Italy) the latter was 'crowned as a king' (*coronato da re*).[91]

Analogous customary activity involving the parade of a figure representing Lent was more common at mid-Lent or later, so the two rarely appeared together[92] – although a female figure in attendance, normally represented as Carnival's widow, could occasionally also be construed as Lent[93] – and as at Norwich the Lent figure was usually decorated with fish.[94] Perhaps the closest approach to the Norwich account from this direction is the (critical) depiction of German carnival customs in the anti-Catholic polemic, *Regnum Papisticum*

87. Van Gennep *Folklore français 1: 1* 795; Toschi *Origini del teatro italiano* chapter 9, 'La morte di Carnevale' # 1, 'Il transporto e il pianto funebre'.
88. For a video of a Sicilian local tradition, see <https://www.youtube.com/watch?v=x1w-w7Kh2i8>.
89. Van Gennep *Folklore français 1: 1* 792–808.
90. Toschi *Origini del teatro italiano* chapter 5 #2, 'Il Carnevale come Re e come persona viva'; Humburg *Städtisches Fastnachtsbrauchtum* 274–5 (early city records).
91. Toschi *Origini del teatro italiano* 235.
92. For an isolated instance, where Lent figures among the judges condemning Carnival, see van Gennep *Folklore français 1: 1* 827. To the extent that these customs involving a Lent figure symbolised the end of Lent, thus paralleling customs marking the end of Carnival, there is an English analogue in the otherwise odd-looking London procession in March 1553 in which a dying 'Jack of Lent' (the season evidently male in England) is treated by a physician and shriven by a priest. And since the procession also includes a Lord of Misrule (who will have reigned during the preceding Christmas-Carnival season), this almost qualifies as a calendrically staggered variant of the Norwich parade. *The Diary of Henry Machyn* edited J. Gough Nichols (London: J.B. Nichols, 1848) 33.
93. Van Gennep *Folklore français 1: 1* 835.
94. Van Gennep *Folklore français 1: 1* 836.

of 1553 by Thomas Kirchmair (under the pseudonym Naogeorgus; Latin original 1553, German translation 1555), where there are public parades by groups representing both the end of Carnival and the beginning of Lent. Since they occur on Ash Wednesday, Carnival is not represented in person, but his mourning followers go around with lanterns (in broad daylight) trying to find where he has disappeared to; meanwhile another group parades with a herring tied to a pole, shouting that puddings must now make way for fish. It is neither stated nor excluded that they are part of the same parade, but it is also said (of the Lent group or both) that they performed entertainments and foolish songs (*ludos, et carmina risu; lecheliche spil / Mit ungezierten gsengen*).[95]

The Twelve Months

In what may be a further instance of the distortion induced by the juxtaposition with Bruegel's Combat of Carnival and Lent, most discussion of the Norwich account, including this one thus far, give very little attention to twelve of its fourteen identifiable characters. Amid all the uncertainty and confusion of the Norwich drafts exculpating Gladman's parade, the far and away most stable part is actually the statement that the twelve months of the year paraded ahead of Gladman, each month guised in accordance with its season. It is common to all three versions, with only minor variations in formulation (none with substantive repercussions) and only one small erasure and correction (in 9c2A) in the course of drafting. The neglect may also be due to factors other than Bruegel. While the theme is probably just as common in literature and art (for example in those Burgundian Books of Hours from just this period, and as the Labours of the Months)[96] it lent itself much less readily than Carnival vs Lent

95. Thomas Naogeorg *Sämtliche Werke* edited Hans-Gert Roloff (Berlin: De Gruyter, 2014–15) 6: *1* (2015) *Regnum Papisticum Lateinische Fassung von 1553* (Latin edition, 1553) lines 309–12 (the Carnival group) and 313–16 (the Lent group), 6: *2* (2015) *Deutsche Fassung von 1555* (German edition, 1555), *Das Päpstisch Reych* translated Burkhard Waldis, Book 4 lines 19–26 (Carnival Group) and 26–35 (Lent group). In Anglophone scholarship, prior to this recent scholarly edition, the work has normally been quoted from *The Popish Kingdome, or reigne of Antichrist, written in Latine verse by Thomas Naogeorgus, and englyshed by Barnabe Googe* (London: Henrie Denham for Richard Watkins, 1570; facsimile reprint edited Robert Charles Hope (London: Chiswick Press, 1880), here 49a (lines not numbered) – it should not, of course, be deployed as documentation for English customs.

96. For some instances see Toschi *Origini del teatro italiano* 613–15.

to powerful elaboration in late medieval culture or to powerful sub-Bakhtinian analysis in latter-day Medieval Studies.

It may also be relevant that in the *Records of the City of Norwich*, the authority usually cited, the editors have inserted a comma which temporarily garbles the sense: Gladman was

> crowned as King of Kristmesse in token that all merthe shuld end with ye twelve monthes of ye yer, afore hym eche moneth disgysd after ye seson yerof.

Thus punctuated the passage could be construed as an invocation of the year-goes-around *topos*[97] rather than, as it should (with the comma after 'all merthe shuld end'), as initiating a specification of the Norwich order of march, in which Gladman as King of Christmas had 'afore him' twelve figures[98] representing the months of the year, just as 'after him' came the figure of Lent.

But for whatever reason it happened, this focus on Christmas/Carnival and Lent has misdirected contextual, historical, and transnational exploration, for if the reconstruction of Gladman's parade in the City defence is perceived rather as a procession of the Twelve Months, with significant but auxiliary figures in attendance, then it is possible to identify immediately a customary tradition with which it may be usefully juxtaposed. That tradition is documented, however, not in England or Germany or France,[99] but in Italy (which also

97. As indeed understood by Kinser *Rabelais's Carnival* 50.

98. If each had a torchbearer, as happened in maskings, this would correspond to the 24 men ahead of Gladman in the parade as described by the city's opponents. (Alternatively, if the months were mounted – as in current traditions discussed below – each horse would need a groom to keep it steady during performance.)

99. There is no reference in the standard surveys, respectively Schmidt *Das deutsche Volksschauspiel*; van Gennep *Le Folklore français*. It would be wrong not to mention, but disruptive to invoke, the striking but presumably fortuitous parallels between the Norwich account and the masque performed at Knowsley House (the seat of the Earls of Derby), on Twelfth Night 1641. It dramatised the end of Christmas partly by the demise of a representative figure (an ailing old man – who is told he will be buried at Candlemas), partly by the routing of his retinue of plump 'Gambolls' and 'Festivalls' by a troupe of 'leane ghostlike apparisions' representing the Friday fast-days which are forerunners of 'hungry lentt'. But then the scenery changes to reveal a temple, which itself opens to reveal New Year and figures representing the twelve months, each of which in turn (starting with January) gives a short speech offering blessings characteristic of its season to the host. The full text, with a detailed headnote, is available in

provided the closest analogues to Carnival and Lent street parades plus an instance of Carnival versus Lent tournament), and as recorded from recent folk tradition rather than in late medieval texts and documents. But it may be hoped that historical extrapolation will be more feasible in a country where long-term continuity in customary activities (and in record-making and record-keeping institutions) has been less disrupted by say the Reformation, Industrialisation, or other sociocultural upheavals.

In the nineteenth and early twentieth centuries the Parade of the Twelve Months (*I Mesi*) seems to have been widespread in many regions of both northern and southern Italy, with performance invariably at Shrovetide and most often annually.[100] Performers could be mounted (horses or donkeys) or on foot, or some the one and some the other, and the auspices are a perambulation of the community, with halts at a limited number of suitable stations (squares; crossroads) for a performance. The parade is often accompanied by musicians, and on arrival at a venue performers ride or march into a circle which when completed (as postulated above for Norwich) forms the performance area.

The core of a given performance is a speech-sequence or *Reihenspiel*, in which each Month in turn offers a description of his (or occasionally her) qualities,[101] appropriate for the month concerned. More often than not those speeches are in verse, and can be sung to a traditional melody, and it is here that a historical perspective may be introduced, for while the custom as performance is documented only since the nineteenth century, the verses sung in a number of local traditions can be traced back, via an oral tradition which has introduced a good deal of variation, to a song composed in the fourteenth century.[102]

The words uttered by the individual month can also refer to his appearance or objects he carries, both suitable to the time of year concerned: we may remember that in the Norwich account each month was said to be 'disgysd

REED: Lancashire edited David George (University of Toronto Press, 1991) Appendix 4 (252–66).

100. This introductory statement is based on the survey in Toschi *Le origini del teatro italiano* chapter 14 #5, 'Le rappresentazioni dei mesi e delle stagioni' (612–38), the discussion of the customs (after a review of the literary topos), starting at 620. Toschi notes (638) an isolated instance in southern France.

101. In the sense that a male performer can be dressed as a female.

102. Toschi *Origini del teatro italiano* 615–19; 631–8, and for a direct juxtaposition of the medieval text with a folk performance, 624–5.

after ye seson yerof'. For example, in a local tradition from the Terra di Lavoro region in Piedmonte, as recorded in the interwar period, and much cited in scholarship:

January	carries a pruning knife and sweets
February	has a whip topped with evergreens
March	is dressed as a peasant with a yellow jacket
April	is in summer clothes and carrying a bouquet of flowers
May	is similar, but displaying rings and jewellery[103]
June	is dressed as a reaper carrying a sickle
July	carries a few ears of corn
August	is jaundiced (presumably reflecting local realities), and carries a live chicken
September	is in shirtsleeves, carries a basket of fruits
October	is very similar
November	is dressed in black with gold stripes and ribbons, carrying ears of wheat
December	like November, but carrying a doll and a bottle of wine.[104]

Reference in the speeches is otherwise mainly to the prevailing weather and to agricultural activities, although February can be given to remark that he is 'short', and August, as we have seen, tends to be ailing. Most figures are also generously beribboned, and several of them, in the course of their speeches, offer (or throw) sweets or fruits to the spectators.

Transcribed in local dialect, the speeches are a linguistic challenge, but there follows an attempt to give the gist of a couple of the months from the same local tradition:[105]

103. April and May perhaps female figures, but the source is not explicit.

104. Toschi *Origini del teatro italiano* 620–3. The original account was by Nicola Borrelli, 'I Mesi' *Il Folklore Italiano 1* (1925), subsequently reproduced in the same author's *Tradizioni aurunche* (Rome: Proia, 1937); reprint edited Gaetano Tamborrino Orsini (Perugia: Centro studi Minturnae, 1984).

105. Antonio Martone 'Canti popolari di Terra di Lavoro: i Mesi' *Il Sidicino* 8 (August 2011), online at <http://www.erchempertoteano.it/Teano/Tradizioni/Canti_pop/Canti_pop017.htm> (lacks pagination), after a useful introduction provides the original, dialect text as published by Borrelli (preceding note), followed by a translation into standard Italian. I have also taken advantage of the parallel-text French translation in *Le Théâtre Populaire Européen* edited Leopold Schmidt (Paris: Maisonneuve et Larose, 1965) 3 42–9.

APRILE	APRIL
Io songo Abbrile cu' la lapa spèrta,	I am April with the swarming bees,
vèsto la terra e gli àrbori a la 'gnura.	I clothe the earth and the naked trees.
Ogni augello fa lu suo versetto,	Each bird makes his verses
he releases some birds to fly away	
pe' ne cuprì' montagne co' valluni.	to fill the mountains and valleys.
Lu speziale fa la sua rezzètta	The apothecary writes his prescription
pe' guaragnà' patacche e ducatuni.	to win half and whole ducats.
Io songo Abbrile e so' bel giovinetto,	I am April and a likely lad
a Maggio ròno chistu ramogliètto.	To May I give this sprig.
offers flowers to May	
MAGGIO	MAY
Io songo Maggio e so' maggior di tutti,	I am May and maybe[106] best of all,
Maggior di tutti quanti 'st'àuti Misi.	better than these other months.
D'oro e d'argento li guarnisco tutti,	I garnish everything with gold and silver,
pure li ciucci stanno allegramente!	and even the asses are cheerful!
Sunate chitarre e ogni strumento,	Guitars and all other instruments play
pe' fa' star lor signori allegramente.	to make their lords be jocund.
Io me ne parto cu le bone spese,	I go my way when things are cheap,
rimano 'n fiore tutti 'st'àuti mesi	and leave a flower to all these other months.

This sequence is prefaced by a Presentation which is the task of the supernumerary figures, one of whom tends to be the leader of the troupe in the figure of New Year (*Cappo d'Anno*), the other (in English terms) a clown or Fool, a variant (in local terms) on *Pulcinella*. To the extent the latter is sometimes construed as representing Carnival we come disconcertingly close to the Norwich account.[107] There is also a local tradition in which the parade is led by a king (*il Re*) wearing a crown and carrying a staff of office, but he does not seem to personify Carneval.[108]

106. Attempting to reproduce the original's evidently intended pun on 'May' (*Maggio*) and 'greater' (*maggior*).

107. Toschi *Origini del teatro italiano* 212–18.

108. Toschi *Origini del teatro italiano* 627 and compare 629; *Cappo d'Anno* might also be interpreted as Chief or King (not to mention 'Captain') of the Year.

As a rule Lent does not seem to appear in these Twelve Months parades, but there is actually one local tradition in which March claims to represent *la Quaresima* (and its verses are clearly descended from the medieval ballad).[109] Interestingly these Italian folk traditions also share a calendrical ambiguity with the constructed Norwich custom. Performance is at Carnival, which is manifestly perceived as the beginning of a new annual (perhaps specifically agricultural) cycle, and so an appropriate context for a Twelve Months custom, but the speeches derive from a (more literary?) tradition which sees the New Year as starting with January. In conformity with the latter the local tradition quoted from above has January begin his speech, 'I am January, the first to come in …' (as he indeed is), and this is common, but there were also local traditions in which the sequence began with February or March (in which Shrovetide fell).[110] It would have been interesting to hear how the Norwich image-builders envisaged the sequence of the months in their construction.

Finally, the Italian custom of *I Mesi* offers not merely a persuasive analogue to the Norwich parade but also the opportunity of seeing the memories or imaginations of the Norwich councillors literally come to life, as in some localities (typically small, remote towns), the tradition has continued to the present or been revived by local enthusiasts, sometimes with scholarly assistance. While much is made of preserving or at least recording the immaterial heritage of the given region,[111] encouraging tourism is very likely a factor, and certainly a result. Which has its advantages, for recordings of recent performances uploaded onto YouTube usefully supplement more institutional resources such as the website of the Italian Folk Archives,[112] currently under construction, but with pages on two local traditions.

Particularly well documented is the tradition in the small town of Bagnoli del Trigno in Isernia Province (Molise Region), for which the Italian Folk Archives provide a substantial description, the full text of the speeches, and

109. Toschi *Origini del teatro italiano* 626.

110. Toschi *Origini del teatro italiano* 626.

111. For an instance of engagement by a local historian see Pasquale Capuano (another fortuitously appropriate name) 'La cavalcata dei 12 Mesi' *Macerata Campania* (n.d.), <http://www.omniamaceratacampania.it/index.php?option=com_content&task=view&id=67&Itemid=51>.

112. Istituto Centrale per la Demoetnoantropologia/Museo Nazionale delle Arti e Tradizioni Popolari, <http://www.idea.mat.beniculturali.it>.

several pictures from recent performances.[113] This can be usefully supplemented by local tourism websites,[114] educational blogs,[115] and several YouTube videos.[116] However, this is a revival of a defunct tradition, and in the process[117] it seems that an original performance mode in which the speeches were sung or declaimed has been replaced by what those involved thought of as a more viable carnival mode, comprising symbolic figures on floats, drawn by tractors, with the verse for each month written on a piece of cardboard on the float concerned.[118]

Closer to the traditional performance mode just described (and so to the Norwich account) is the tradition at Cercepiccola (Campobasso Province; Molise Region), in which the figures perambulate on, and speak from, horse- (or donkey-)back.[119] The mounts are, like their riders, richly decorated. Its main idiosyncrasy lies in an intermittent, rather than annual incidence, and in the number of supernumerary figures. In addition to a master of ceremonies and two Pulcinellas, they encompass the Grandfather (= Time) and the Father (= the

113. 'Carnevale a Bagnoli del Trigno', <http://www.idea.mat.beniculturali.it/feste-e-tradizioni/molise/item/216-carnevale-a-bagnoli-del-trigno>.

114. E.g. agnoli del Trigno 'Il Carnevale dei 12 Mesi' *Isernia Turismo*, <http://www.iserniaturismo.it/modules/smartsection/item.php?itemid=285> (with a version in English); 'Carnevale dei mesi dell'anno 2016, Bagnoli Del Trigno *Folclore*, <http://www.folclore.it/It/Eventi/Italia/Molise/Isernia/Bagnoli-Del-Trigno/Carnevale-dei-mesi-dell'anno.html>.

115. 'Carnevale in Molise – Carnival in Molise' (college teaching materials, 2007/8), <http://www.slideshare.net/athens/carnevale-in-molise-carnival-in-molise>.

116. <https://www.youtube.com/watch?v=izS4pzzzApQ>; <https://www.youtube.com/watch?v=FGfEjkw1TvQ>.

117. Well documented in Giovanni Mascia 'Il Carnevale dei Mesi a Bagnoli del Trigno' *L'Arcoloaio: Rivista Molisana di Tradizioni Popolare e Scienze Umane 1* (1996) 9–24; online at <https://www.academia.edu/7475473/Il_carnevale_dei_Mesi_a_Bagnoli_del_Trigno._Relazione_di_presentazione_del_volume_di_Mauro_Gioielli_23_febbraio_1995_>.

118. Actually a procedure not altogether alien to late medieval and Renaissance pageantry.

119. The Italian Folklore Archive's site at <http://www.idea.mat.beniculturali.it/feste-e-tradizioni/molise/item/219-carnevale-a-cercepiccola> has some illustrations, but in this instance more informative is 'Il carnevale di Cercepiccola' (12 April, 209), on the regional culture site ArcheoMolise, <http://www.archeomolise.it/antropologia/10158-il-carnevale-di-cercepiccola.html> (includes full text and transcriptions from local newspaper accounts); see also <http://www.slideshare.net/athens/carnevale-in-molise-carnival-in-molise> (college teaching materials, 2007/8). I have not had access to Simonetta Tassinari *Il Carnevale a Cercepiccola: I Mesi* (Campobasso: Edizioni Enne, 1988).

Year) of the Months, two paupers (rag-collectors), plus characters representing the four seasons (their speeches interspersed between those of the Months at appropriate places): even the musicians have self-presentational speeches. And most speeches include both spoken and sung verse. This may explain why each perambulation encompasses performances at only four stations.

Among currently active local traditions, perhaps the closest to the kind of custom envisioned at Norwich (and accessible on some useful YouTube videos) is that of Riesi (Caltanissetta Province) on Sicily.[120] A video of the 1992 performance shows the arrival of the cavalcade at a station (<https://youtu.be/8enTFdebgTw?t=2>; the irritating music has been added later) and the speeches of the individual riders (with interesting variations on how to use a horse as a stage):

1.	Presenter	0.39	<https://youtu.be/8enTFdebgTw?t=39>
2.	'Cappo d'anno'	1.45	<https://youtu.be/8enTFdebgTw?t=105>
3.	February	3.26	<https://youtu.be/8enTFdebgTw?t=206>
4.	March	4.28	<https://youtu.be/8enTFdebgTw?t=268>
5.	'April' (female)	5.35	<https://youtu.be/8enTFdebgTw?t=335>
6.	May	7.08	<https://youtu.be/8enTFdebgTw?t=428>
7.	'June'	8.20	<https://youtu.be/8enTFdebgTw?t=500>
8.	'July'	10.31	<https://youtu.be/8enTFdebgTw?t=631>
9.	'August'	11.43	<https://youtu.be/8enTFdebgTw?t=703>
10.	'September'	13.08	<https://youtu.be/8enTFdebgTw?t=788>
11.	'October'	15.03	<https://youtu.be/8enTFdebgTw?t=903>
12.	'November'	16.50	<https://youtu.be/8enTFdebgTw?t=1010>
13.	'December'	18.22	<https://youtu.be/8enTFdebgTw?t=1102>
14.	January?[121]	20.20	<https://youtu.be/8enTFdebgTw?t=1220>

120. For a popular account see Giuseppe Calascibetta, 'La tradizione dei Tredici Cavalieri', *I percorsi della cultura* (12 Feb., 2013), online at <http://ipercorsidellacultura.blogspot.dk/2013/02/la-tradizione-dei-tredici-cavalieri-la.html>.

121. Although the event is locally known (see preceding note) as 'The Thirteen Horsemen' (with reference to the months and a Presenter), here there are quite clearly fourteen. My command of the local dialect is limited, but where the name of a figure is in inverted commas in my description it is because I have heard it used in that figure's speech. I assume the performance deploys separate figures for the Presenter and *Cappo d'Anno* (New Year), in which case the last month to speak is January (not identified above as his opening lines are cut from the recording), with February the first month of an annual cycle that begins at Shrovetide.

(One also notes with interest some instances of 'Prompting in Full View of the Audience'.) The speeches here are a little longer than elsewhere, as they include (incorporating another carnival tradition) satirical commentary on recent events.

These explorations have effectively encompassed two avenues of approach to John Gladman's Norwich procession of 1443, respectively national (insular) and transnational, each with subsidiary investigations. Quite independently of continental connections (but with repercussions for their direction and implications), the familiar text describing the event proved to be three texts, which had both a literal con-text in the form of an alternative account, and a context in local events and the ambient calendar. Analysis of all this material suggests that the spectacle of the King of Christmas, Lent, and figures representing the Twelve Months, all guised to suit their identity, parading through the streets of Norwich during Shrovetide 1433, never happened. It certainly didn't happen on Shrove Tuesday, and what exactly happened (in late January of that year) was very likely something quite different: most plausibly some kind of demonstrative parade, in response to a political crisis, by civic and guild representatives, cloned on, if not technically qualified as, a Marching Watch. But for the historian of customary performance, as opposed to *histoire événementielle*, identifying what really happened is less important that identifying the model on which the Norwich authorities retrospectively sought to reconstruct the event into something customary rather than insurrectionary.

Despite the discrepancy in dates, they opted (at the cost of severe drafting problems) for a Shrovetide parade of a kind common, they asserted, in other English cities, and which might indeed also have occurred at Norwich in happier times. Of this custom there is to date no English evidence whatsoever (but nor is there anything that would rule it out), hence the appeal to transnational evidence in the hope it may provide documentation for a pan-European tradition which for some reason escaped English record-making procedures. This investigation, in turn, required three attempts to establish any significant documentary basis for discussion.

1. The pursuit of customary street pageantry involving a conflict between a festive, Christmas/Carnival figure and one representing Lenten austerity, inspired by Pieter Bruegel the Elder's celebrated painting on this theme, was largely fruitless: the painting, it transpires, was not based on such a custom, for which, despite the strength of the *topos* in literature and formal drama, there is desperately little evidence.

2. A more modest quest for customary parades marking and lamenting (as does the parade in the Norwich account) the passing of Carnival, found rather more evidence, in both historical records and later folk tradition, and in several areas (Germany, France, Italy), but the match was imperfect, not least the discrepancy between the usually humble or wretched status of the Carnival figure in the customs, and the regal 'King of Christmas' at Norwich. Nonetheless there were tantalising signs of a King (of Carnival) and even a Lent figure in some local traditions.
3. The previous two searches (and it seems all other discussion of the Gladman parade) having completely ignored them, a third was undertaken in quest of Shrovetide parades involving figures representing the twelve months of the year. Precisely this is to be found in the widespread Italian custom of *I Mesi*, in which figures, often mounted, in appropriate guise, and accompanied by supernumeraries (Time; New Year; Pulcinella), perambulate a community and at designated stations present a show in which each Month steps forward to describe his qualities. There were also signs that one or other of the accompanying figures might be construed as Carnival.

This whole exercise was undertaken with a view to exploring whether there were indeed such Shrovetide customs, as described at Norwich (whether Gladman's was one such or not) in late medieval England. The result must be declared as inconclusive, for although there is a fairly close match between the (imagined) Gladman parade and *I Mesi* (and while the latter has quite probably late medieval antecedents), the lack of anything similar in intermediate regions (Germany, France, the Netherlands) allows the alternative speculation that the reconstruction was modelled on an Italian, rather than an English, tradition. But this surely, would have been a risky ploy in an appeal to the Crown?

In the process an important lesson has been learnt regarding the transnational approaches to medieval drama: it is a two-way street. Vagaries of record production, preservation, and accessibility can also mean that England can offer documentation of continental traditions for which there is none, or which is confined to recent folk custom. And indeed, as we have seen: Gladman's parade is regularly appealed to as evidence for the Shrovetide custom on which Bruegel is alleged to have based *The Combat of Carnival and Lent*. Gladman's parade is among the best evidence we have for late medieval street pageantry marking the end of Carnival. Gladman's parade is the *only* evidence we have for a premodern customary parade of the Twelve Months – to the extent they haven't already, Italian scholars will welcome it with delight: should we tell them it never really happened?

Centre for Medieval Literature and Institut for Kulturvidenskaber
University of Southern Denmark

THE BECCLES GAME PLACE AND LOCAL DRAMA IN EARLY NORTH-EAST SUFFOLK[1]

James Stokes

Like a number of other Suffolk communities, the town of Beccles, in north-east Suffolk, had a dedicated outdoor recreational site, which Beccles called The Game Place. Records also show that Beccles had its own local players, and other performers, during the late medieval and early modern periods. However, based on the fragmentary nature of the records, it is not possible to confirm or to deny a connection between The Game Place and the players. This lack of clarity concerning the playing tradition in Beccles is typical of the difficulty with Suffolk in general. Parish and civic records copiously confirm that villages and towns in every corner of the county staged plays. Early Suffolk also had innumerable dedicated outdoor recreational sites, called by various names and used for various diversions including, in one verifiable instance, the staging of plays (see below). Those sites turn up in communities great and small in every part of the county; indeed, no other region of England approaches Suffolk in its number of dedicated playing sites. Further, the great majority of surviving play texts from the late medieval period have certain, if confounding, connections with Suffolk. As John Coldewey has observed, of the 'thirty-five vernacular English play texts and fragments [that] survive from the late middle ages', many derive from East Anglia – and many of those from Suffolk.[2] But while all these evidences indicate the presence of an extraordinarily rich playing tradition, the tradition itself remains obscure, and largely disconnected from the culture that created it. The dots strenuously resist connecting. This study, focusing as it does on one small town resting in a part of a county that was rich in parish drama, hopes to offer a few brush strokes to one corner of what turns out to be a very complex, and largely unfinished, picture of local drama in early Suffolk.

1. I would like to thank an anonymous reader and the editors of *METh* for their excellent suggestions, all of which I have used to enrich the article.

2. *Early English Drama: An Anthology* edited John C. Coldewey (New York: Garland, 1993) 1.

The Borough of Beccles

Beccles is situated on a rise overlooking the River Waveney in Wangford Hundred in north-east Suffolk, nearly equidistant between the towns of Bungay and Lowestoft. It is one of the oldest towns in Suffolk, and in earlier centuries was 'the most substantial [town] between Ipswich and Norwich'.[3] Along with Ipswich, it was one of two capitals of an Anglo-Saxon division in Suffolk called The Geldable (a place empowered to levy royal geld or taxes). Domesday Book confirms that it already had burgesses at the time of the Conquest. Beccles was one of eleven Suffolk towns that had a market and 'urban status', and one of only six of those towns that had burgesses, though it never became a parliamentary borough. By virtue of its location at the farthest navigable point of the Waveney River, and because it was positioned on what was once 'the main route from London to Yarmouth', it was always commercially significant. Its market dates from the Anglo-Saxon period. As early as the tenth century its thriving port 'provided 60,000 herring a year' for the Abbey of Bury St Edmunds. In 1302 its market had eighty-two stalls, and partly because of its strategic position in the borderland between Suffolk and Norfolk, its market survived the general economic decline of the fifteenth century.[4] During the sixteenth and seventeenth centuries it continued to be important to the Waveney Valley in the marketing of agricultural produce, and in the linen industry, which was 'mainly concentrated in the Valleys of the Waveney and the Little Ouse'.[5]

Though important, Beccles was never large. In 1327 it ranked second among Suffolk towns, having 167 taxpayers. It had between 1,000 and 2,500 residents in the fourteenth century; 1,200 in 1525; 1,100 in 1603; 1,750 in the 1670s; and 2,000 by the end of the seventeenth century.[6]

3. Nesta Evans 'The Holy Ghost Gild and the Beccles Town Land Feoffees in the Sixteenth and Seventeenth Centuries' *Proceedings of the Suffolk Institute of Archaeology and Natural History 37: 1* (1989) 31–43, at 31.
4. Gordon Blackwood *Tudor and Stuart Suffolk* (Lancaster: Carnegie Publishing, 2001) 21, 32; Mark Bailey *Medieval Suffolk: An Economic and Social History, 1200–1500* (Woodbridge: Boydell, 2007) 116, 168–9, 266; Nesta Evans 'The Holy Ghost Gild' 31; Keith Wade and David Dymond 'Smaller Medieval Towns' in *An Historical Atlas of Suffolk* edited David Dymond and Edward Martin (Ipswich: Suffolk County Council, 1988) 162; and Mel Birch *Suffolk's Ancient Sites – Historic Places* (Mendlesham: Castell Publishing, 2004) 35.
5. Blackwood *Tudor and Stuart Suffolk* 21.
6. Bailey *Medieval Suffolk* 128; Blackwood *Tudor and Stuart Suffolk* 5; and Evans 'The Holy Ghost Gild' 41.

The Abbey of Bury St Edmunds, which had acquired Beccles in the mid tenth century, remained its landlord until the Abbey was dissolved in 1539. At the time of the Conquest, the Abbots took most customary rights due from Beccles market, and owned Beccles fair from 1205.[7] As a non-chartered or seignorial borough, Beccles developed a network of seven medieval religious guilds (Holy Ghost, St Michael, Ascension, Holy Trinity, Holy Name of Jesus and St Nicholas, Corpus Christi, and Halfpenny, the first six of which were housed in the Guildhall). Those guilds effectively provided local governance.[8] Burgesses rented the rich grazing lands of the town fen from the Abbot of Bury and before the Reformation assigned administration of those lands (including the game place) to the most important of its guilds, the Holy Ghost Guild, which had been founded in the fifteenth century.[9] The Holy Ghost Guild protected the manorial lands from seizure by the Crown by creating the Lands Feoffment Trust, with the help of merchant William Rede. Although responsibility for the manorial lands had thereby devolved to the Trust after the dissolution, the town had to contend with Rede for ownership of the manorial lands until 1590. In 1584 a limited charter created the Corporation of Beccles, giving it the power to regulate the manorial lands of the fen. While the Corporation had no comparable formal power over the town, it essentially shaped the ways in which the town increasingly governed itself. The often overlapping membership of the Corporation (its portreeves) and the Lands Feoffment Trust (its thirteen feoffees) constituted a local ruling oligarchy.[10]

Medieval and early modern Beccles had a contentious religious history that reflects the presence of competing social, cultural, and economic forces in the area. Beccles' manorial landlords, the abbots of Bury St Edmunds, of course exerted great influence over the town (as described above). The abbey built the parish church in Beccles between 1350 and 1400. In addition to its seven religious guilds, pre-Reformation Beccles had a Hermitage Chapel dedicated to Mary, a leper's hospital dedicated to St Mary Magdalene and St Anthony, and a medieval chapel dedicated to St Peter that was important to the fishermen of Beccles.[11] Pre-Reformation Beccles certainly lived under a strong traditional

7. Birch *Suffolk's Ancient Sites* 35–6.
8. Bailey *Medieval Suffolk* 141.
9. Nesta Evans *Beccles Rediscovered* (Beccles: The Beccles Society, 1984) 57–9, 65.
10. Evans 'The Holy Ghost Gild' 31–2.
11. Birch *Suffolk's Ancient Sites* 35.

religious presence. But at the same time, most of Suffolk's Lollards 'lived in or near the Waveney valley', and Beccles and Bungay 'were considered the chief centres' of Lollard activity in the region. The area expressed vehement and violent opposition to many elements of traditional religion, including the sacraments, devotion to saints, veneration of images, pilgrimages, the papacy, the doctrine of the transubstantiation, and the priesthood. The presence of stone fonts depicting the sacraments in fourteen churches 'near former centres of East Anglian Lollardy' (including Bungay near Beccles) reflects the Orthodox Church reacting to Lollard attacks on the sacraments, and three Lollards were burnt at the stake in Suffolk in the early sixteenth century. During the Marian persecutions in 1556, three Protestants were burned at the stake in Beccles. Such evidence indicates a volatile combination of traditional Catholicism, Lollardy, and eventually Tudor Protestantism in Beccles.[12] The politics of land ownership in Beccles with the aforesaid William Rede were no less contentious. For several decades following the dissolution, the town waged legal battles with Rede for control of the manorial lands (including the game place). The town finally won the contest in 1584 when a charter awarded the lands to the Corporation of Beccles Common. However, lordship of the Manor remained with the Redes and later with Sir Thomas Gresham (1519–79), founder of the Royal Exchange.[13] Thus, drama in Beccles existed within a complex social, religious, and economic environment.

The Playing Tradition in Beccles

The playing tradition in Beccles can be documented over sixty-five years spanning the late medieval and early modern periods. In 1466/7 – the earliest reference to local performers – three players and dancers from Beccles (*Item tribus lusoribus & trepidatoribus de Becclys*) performed for 12d at Mettingham College (a wealthy community of secular canons founded in 1350), four miles west of Beccles.[14] In 1472/3, the College paid four men of Beccles 8d for their play (*Item iiij^or hominibus de Becclis pro ludo suo*); in the same year, the College

12. Blackwood *Tudor and Stuart Suffolk* 69–70, 86.

13. Evans *Beccles Rediscovered* 5–7.

14. London: British Library Additional MS 33987, fol. 82v. Founded in 1350 at Raveningham, Norfolk by Sir John de Norwich, Mettingham College was moved to Norton Subcourse, Norfolk, in 1387, then to Mettingham Castle in 1394, where it remained until the Dissolution. Dedicated to the Blessed Virgin Mary, it had a master and nine chaplains, and supported fourteen boys. Its endowments included Mettingham

paid two men of Beccles 8d for performing with puppets (*Item ij hominibus de Becclis quorum vnus eorum ludebat cum Popyns*).[15] In 1512, accounts from Hickling Priory, in Norfolk include a payment of 2s 3d to the men of Beccles and 'Walss' for their play (*Item hominibus de Beccles & Walss' pro ludo penultimo die decembris*).[16] 'Walss' likely refers to North Walsham, Norfolk (rather than to Walsham-le-Willows, in Suffolk) because of the proximity of the former to Hickling. Like Beccles, North Walsham in Norfolk had local players and a game. While the terms *game* and *play* often alternate without explanation or clarification in documents, I will show that in the particular parish records being discussed here, *game* was specifically used to mean 'play'. In 1584, the

Castle, the manor of Mettingham, Bungay soke, and other income-generating entities (Birch *Suffolk's Ancient Sites* 268–9.

Mettingham college was 'a fairly wealthy institution' (Birch *Suffolk's Ancient Sites* 268), whose account books record payments to innumerable performers between 1395 and 1526 (see London: British Library Additional MSS 33985, 33986, 33987, 33988, 33989, 33990, 40069, and 40070, which include a large number of entries for performance that will be included in the *REED* volume for Suffolk). In addition to performers from Beccles, Mettingham College paid players from the Suffolk towns and villages of Bungay, Dunwich, South Elmham, and Wissett (all within a half-day's ride or less from Beccles); the four large Norfolk towns of Norwich, Walsingham, Wymondham, and Yarmouth; and one place (Belle Monte) that I have not yet been able to identify with certainty. The records variously identify those performers as minstrels, players, dancers (with the players), and taborers. Several of those towns had historical ties – manorial or otherwise – with Mettingham Castle and College.

In addition to players from towns, the many troupes and individuals who performed at Mettingham included apparently local players, players licensed by important patrons, and unsponsored itinerants. The College most commonly paid for performances (usually plays) at Christmas, but also for other performances that occurred at vaguely described 'diverse times'. Payments often referred to no date at all. Of all payments to players representing towns, only one (men of Norwich in 1405/6) occurred at Christmas. The other payments to players from towns (including those from Beccles) specify no date. In addition, performers from towns characteristically received somewhat lower amounts than those given to other troupes, including those paid in the same year as troupes from the towns. One might conclude that players representing towns were visiting during the warmer months, and were perhaps crying the banns of their plays rather than performing the entire play; on the other hand, they might just have been small troupes performing small plays or shows. For a full transcription and discussion of the Mettingham college dramatic records, see *REED: Suffolk* edited James Stokes, 2 vols (forthcoming).

15. London: British Library Additional MS 33987, fol. 139v.
16. Oxford: Bodleian Library MS Tanner 194, fol. [34].

North Walsham churchwardens had 'Receiued of the gamplaiers vjd',[17] and in 1586 and 1589, the Walsham churchwardens received money from collections made by its Christmas Lord (fols 19, 23). The collaboration between Beccles and Walsham in 1512 indicates that the two troupes were performing a Christmastide play together. Their joint effort suggests that the play likely was a production of some size and scope.

Finally, a payment in the churchwardens' accounts of Bungay, in 1565/6, records that people from Beccles attended and contributed to a church-ale and game in Bungay, five miles west of Beccles:

> Item received ye colleccione at the churche ale & game on Trinyte sondaie in all when Master harsar dyd procure his neyburs of Beckylles & other places to come xvij li xiij d.[18]

Bungay most certainly sponsored their own parish play, which they produced at their church-ale during the summer months. So during the sixteenth century, the people of Beccles, who attended that play, were well-acquainted with the notion and particulars of locally produced parish plays.

These few payments to players from Beccles confirm that the town had players; that it had a play; that its players sometimes travelled to perform, sometimes doing so in collaboration with players from other communities; that the times of year when they performed are generally vague in the records, but that they certainly sometimes performed during the Christmas season; that they were capable of mounting a Christmas performance suitable for production in a religious house (that could, therefore, possibly have included music and comedy, given the reference to the Christmas Lord in North Walsham). The entries mentioning players and plays, together with references to game players in North Walsham and Beccles respectively, and to the Game Place in Beccles confirm that Beccles and North Walsham likely shared a common understanding concerning the nature of local performance. These few records also support the well-confirmed impression (arising from Suffolk records in general) that amateur playing circuits in Suffolk included visits to religious houses and private households, where parish players such as those from Beccles could expect a warm welcome and payment either for announcing or for performing their games. The payments for performances that were held in the

17. Norwich: Norfolk Record Office ACC 2004/252, Box 3, fol. 15.

18. Lowestoft: Suffolk Record Office 115/E1/1, 27.

cold winter months certainly would not have occurred in an outdoor playing place. Whether the Beccles players ever staged their play in the Beccles Game Place, and during the summer, the records do not say.

The Beccles Game Place

Local historians have long known about The Game Place in Beccles, and a considerable number of documents contain references to it. The game place was part of a 1,400-acre tract of land between the town and the River Waveney, belonging to the Manor of Beccles (and variously called The Fen, The Commons, the Holy Ghost Lands, or The Town Lands). After 1539 (as discussed above), the tract's ownership passed from the Abbot of Bury St Edmunds to the Beccles Town Lands Feoffment Trust.[19] In 1584 the Corporation of Beccles was given power to 'regulate all matters concerning "Beccles Common or Fenne"'.[20]

As described by David Lindley of the Beccles Museum: 'The Game Place in Beccles was situated in the area between and including [what is now] Station Road and Gaol Lane at the western end where it joins Newgate', at a spot that (game place included) is now 'entirely built up'. David Dymond adds that a plan of Mr William Crisp's farm in Beccles, which is dated 11 October 1821 'clearly shows the jail fronting Newgate and immediately behind it a small rectangle marked as the "Game Place", which in turn abuts a larger area called the "Camping Close"'. The Game Place and the jail (which was latterly built on The Game Place) lay in the corner of a four-acre camping close, directly opposite the Guildhall and its barn, between Smallgate and Newgate, approximately 120 yards from the churchyard.[21] Today it is the site of a Tesco car park.

The earliest surviving mention of the land where The Game Place lay dates from 1544. The document is a demise or lease in which two local priests convey several parcels of land and properties to the Alderman and members of the Holy Ghost Guild of Beccles. Though none of the parcels are identified as The Game Place, Lindley feels that three of the enclosures (nos 5, 6, or 7) in the

19. Evans 'Holy Ghost Gild' 31–2; Evans *Beccles Rediscovered* 65.

20. Evans *Beccles Rediscovered* 57.

21. For this information, and other assistance kindly given, I am deeply grateful to Mr David Lindley of Beccles Museum (e-mail to the author 6 March 2006), and to David Dymond (e-mail to the author 20 April 2006). The plan of the Crisp farm may be found in the Rix Collection at Suffolk Record Office, Lowestoft.

transaction seem likely candidates.[22] The earliest certain mention of the game place itself occurs in 1573 in The Rental of Beccles Manor – a payment of 11d from the 'township of Beccles for the gameplace lying in Newgate'.[23] In 1631, a statement of sale records that John Mason, linen weaver, sold to the Feoffees of the Beccles Lands Trust Charity (for £20) a house that he had built 'vpon [a] p*ar*cell of the towne grownd com*m*onlie called & knowen by the name of the game place lieing in Beccles'.[24] At that time, it was the Feoffees who held the game place upon which the house was built. On 1 December 1635, The Game Place is listed among customary rental payments to the Feoffees of the Beccles Lands Trust, including:

> Item to the Bayliffe for the Mannor of Beccles for rent for certayne land*es* called ffreed*es* & Guspes 1 s. 10 d. and for a peece against those 2 d. And for the holye ghost land 4 d. ob. And for the Game place. j d. in toto 2 s. 11 d. ob. due at Michaellmas 1635. 0 2 11 ob
>
> Item to him more for the like due at Michaelmas 1636 0 2 11 ob …[25]

That same amount is recorded by the Feoffees' Collector in 1693, 1751, 1829, and 1860, preserving the name of The Game Place.

Since the game place sat on ancient manorial grounds, its life as a dedicated recreational site likely much predated that first mention in 1573. When it stopped being used for games is unclear, but many documents show that it retained its name in later centuries long after it was no longer functioning as a place for games.[26] In 1659, a feoffment or deed of gift referred to land called 'the Game Place with the Workhouse'. In 1679, the Corporation of Beccles Fenn built both a House of Correction and a Workhouse 'in a certain place within the town of Beccles, called the Game Place', upon which an earlier workhouse had burned down 'some years since', presumably between 1659 and

22. Lindley, e-mail, 6 March 2006. Concerning the Holy Ghost Guild, see Evans 'Holy Ghost Gild' 31–44.
23. Lindley, e-mail to the author, 6 March 2006.
24. Lowestoft: Suffolk Record Office 994/B1/2.
25. Lowestoft: Suffolk Record Office 994/E1/1, fol. [3v].
26. However, in the mid seventeenth century, players were still performing in the Guildhall. On 7 December 1656, the feoffees recorded a payment of 3s 6d by 'the horse daunc*ers* for the vse of the Guildhall and some damadge' (Lowestoft: Suffolk Record Office 994/E1/1, fol. [97]).

1679. Much later entries in the records of the Court Baron of Beccles Manor – in 1762, 1773, 1800, 1836, 1845, 1850, and 1857 – all refer to the camping close as a four-acre site bounded on the north by the lands of the lord and lady of the manor; on the south by the way of the lord leading towards Hall Meadows; on the east by a 1½ acre meadow called Holstead; and on the west by town-land called the game place. In the Court Baron of 1850, the camping close was referred to as 'Guildhall Close or Camping Close 4 acres'. In 1787, a collector purchased from the feoffees the Workhouse on the site of the game place, in connection with the expansion of the jail. In recent years, the site of the game place had been 'covered by the southern end of Clowes' Printing Works', but since 2005 it has been 'the site of the new Tesco Stores car park bordering Gaol Lane and Newgate ... opposite the back of the Guildhall'. According to Lindley, 'the medieval acting area of the Game Place was close to the late-eighteenth-century theatre building' [a medieval or Tudor building] where travelling companies performed.[27]

The Meaning of 'Game' and 'Play' in Suffolk

The parts of north-east Suffolk and coastal Norfolk surrounding Beccles were rich in parish drama. The terminology that they, and other Suffolk communities, used in referring to local performance – particularly the words *game* and *play* – can help to illuminate the playing tradition in Beccles.

Of the records of local drama that survive in Suffolk, those from nine communities use the word *game* to describe their most lucrative fundraising entertainment, as do several in the nearby parts of Norfolk. In a few of these nine sets of parish records the precise meaning of *game* is uncertain, but in most of them the word *game* described a play. Bungay (situated about five miles from Beccles) provides the most dispositive example. The Bungay game had a script. In 1525/6, the wardens paid 12s for copying out the game book. In 1557/8, they paid for 'the Int*er*lude & game Booke', and for the writing out of parts. The Bungay game had costumes. In 1542/3, the wardens paid for the sewing of *abbes* ('albs') that were worn at the game on Corpus Christi Day. In 1565/6, wardens borrowed apparel for playing from 'my lord of Surrey' in Norwich, and they paid elsewhere for the staining of certain clothing for the interlude. Following the

27. For these many details concerning the history of the game place, I wish to thank Mr David Lindley. He has collected that extraordinary knowledge in a document entitled 'The Game Place & Camping Close', which he most generously made available to me by e-mail on 6 March 2006.

game in 1567/8, they returned apparel to Wymondham, Norfolk (a town that had a game place, and an inventory including 'a list of "apparel" for the game players').[28] In 1576/7, the parish sold 'the game players gownes & coates' from old copes; elsewhere the same account refers to 'the game players apparell'. In 1590/1 the parish sold players' coats, apparently no longer used in community drama. The Bungay game also used props. In 1557/8, a parishioner rode to Yarmouth for game gear. In 1567/8, the wardens purchased nine planks for the cloud, and in 1573, they purchased nails for the stage. And the Bungay game used a scaffold stage. In 1565/6, the wardens paid for a scaffold 'for the Interlude in the churchyarde', and took a collection 'at the churche ale & game on Trinyte sondaie'. In 1566/7, they twice purchased nails for the scaffold, and also paid for making and watching the scaffold. In 1567/8, they paid for disassembling the scaffold. The interchangeable use of *game*, *interlude*, and *play*, as part of a church-ale, confirm that the three terms were one and the same in Bungay; they describe a scaffold play, with written parts, that was staged in the churchyard. A payment 'to Kelsaye the vyce for his pastyme before the plaie and after the playe both daies', and another payment for the dying of *heares* (likely 'wigs') for the interlude players (both payments in 1565/6), strongly suggests that the play or game was a two-day production, and was very likely a morality play. It was always produced within the context of a church-ale, and the parish provided a dinner for the players.[29] In Bungay, it is abundantly clear that *game* meant 'play'.

We know that four of the other eight parishes that used the word *game* had something called a *game* only because they travelled to advertise it. Bramfield received 4d when it 'schewed' its *game* at Walberswick in 1493/4. Thetford Priory paid 'Walsham game et Gyslyngham' 16d in 1505/6. The entry appears to indicate that the two were advertising their co-sponsored *game*. Walsham records, of course, confirm that they used their game place for stage plays (see below), so one might assume that *game* here means 'play'. In the same year (1505/6), Thetford Priory also paid Bardwell and Mildenhall 12d each for their *plays* (probably for their banns), the like amount for *game* and *play* indicating similar activities. In 1504/5, Mildenhall had staged a *play* of St Thomas in the hall yard, at which they collected £7 in contributions for the parish. One might

28. Lowestoft: Suffolk Record Office 116/E1/1, pages 18 and 52; 115/E1/1, pages 8, 34–5, 48; *Records of Plays and Players in Norfolk and Suffolk 1330–1642* edited John Wasson and David Galloway (Malone Society Collections 11; Oxford UP, 1980–1981) 120.

29. Lowestoft: Suffolk Record Office 116/E1/1, 18; 115/E1/1, pages 8, 52, 34–5, 103, 184, 8, 53, 153, 33, 41–3, 48, 35–6.

assume that the Mildenhall *play* being advertised the following year at Thetford was the same parish play of St Thomas. In 1509/10, Mildenhall paid players 13d at the May Ale, and in 1528, many parishioners gave contributions towards a *play* called a 'May Game' (*Item recepimus de diuersis parochianis in mense Maij vltimo preterito pro ludo vocato Maygame lxiiij s*). And in 1540, parishioners contributed 21s for a 'play or church-ale' ('Item of the gatheryng mony ffor the pley or chyrchall xxj s').[30] Based on these records, Mildenhall appears to have used *game*, *play*, and *churchale* interchangeably.

The town of Metfield (approximately 5 miles from Bungay) collected the extremely large amount of 11 marks 4s for its *game* in 1510/11, and an indeterminate amount in 1513/14, the only two references to its *game* that survive. Metfield also contributed to Bungay's *game* in 1510. Long Melford (near Bury) kept a *game* in 1555/6 and again in 1556/7. Long Melford proclaimed its *game* as far away as Braintree, Essex, and Ipswich, an effort that they likely would not have exerted if the *game* were not a play but a mere church-ale or Plow Monday ceremony. Further indicating that the Long Melford *game* at Whitsuntide was likely a play, the parish set up thirteen seats in the churchyard for some who attended. In 1561 at Kenninghall, Norfolk, Sir Thomas Cornwallis, of Brome Hall, Suffolk, paid the violins and the 'game players' (presumably the Kenninghall game players) 40s, in the week leading up to Shrove Tuesday.[31]

In these records, the word *game* never demonstrably refers to something less than a play, and it often coexists synonymously with the words *play*, *interlude*, and *show*; but in other cases it may well have meant some mimetic custom other than a play or interlude. The term also often occurs in connection with a major church-ale. Games appear only intermittently in the records of any place, and when that happens, they appear to be major fundraising events that draw crowds and contributors from places far outside the host community. The term *game* seems to have been used to distinguish 'games' (as pious and worshipful, but imaginative, enactments) from liturgical services or the sacraments. They were 'prayerful play' by the laity, used to teach, delight, raise money, and unify.

30. Ipswich: Suffolk Record Office FC 185/E1/1, fol. 119; Cambridge: Cambridge University Library Add MS 6969, fols 72, 70; Bury: Suffolk Record Office EL 110/5/3, fols 1v, 7v, 20v, 30.

31. Ipswich: Suffolk Record Office FC 91/A7/2 (3), single sheet; FC 91/E5/7/, single sheet; Bury: Suffolk Record Office FL 509/1/15, fols 36v, 39, 39v; Ipswich: Suffolk Record Office HA 411/5/3/3/3/1, fol. [10].

Whatever their uses, in Suffolk, *games* were certainly plays, which further re-enforces the notion that the 'game place' in Beccles is named to indicate a place for the staging of plays.

The Meaning of 'Game Place' in Suffolk

Suffolk had many more identifiable outdoor recreation sites than did any other part of the country. In Suffolk, those sites are most often called 'camping closes' (after an ancient sport resembling modern-day football), although they may sometimes bear other names as well. Some of those sites (especially the ones demonstrably manorial in origin) included a designated corner called 'The Game Place'. Not every camping close had a game place, but every identifiable game place lay within, or adjacent to, a camping close. So, a study of game places in Suffolk necessarily starts with camping closes; and since at least one Suffolk game place (the one at Walsham-le-Willows) within a camping close was indisputably used to stage plays, the study of local drama in Suffolk must include consideration of both game places and camping closes as outdoor theatres.

The definitive work on camping closes and game places has been done by the great Suffolk historian, David Dymond. As he says: 'All sorts of communities had them [camping closes]', from villages to 'major towns and market centres', especially in 'wood-pasture areas such as High Suffolk … heavy land which carried dispersed settlement and supported a mixed farming economy in which dairying used to be of special importance'. It is likely, he concludes, 'that the majority of parishes in East Anglia had a facility of this kind, whatever its name'.[32] Camping closes are a signature feature of Suffolk and, to a lesser extent, of other East Anglian counties. As Dymond shows, Medieval East Anglia (especially Suffolk) was addicted to 'camping' or 'camp-ball' (from the Anglo-Saxon *campen*, 'to contend'), a particularly violent field sport.

Many parishes designated parcels of land of various sizes as 'special sites for communal recreation', that is for 'camping' and other activities. Although the sites were most commonly called 'camping closes', they could be called by other names, from 'wrestling close' to 'Maypole pightle'. While a few closes included within them a parcel of land separately identified as 'The Game Place' (as discussed above), in other instances, the terms *camping close* and *game place* might

32. David Dymond 'The Camping Close: A Lost Social Institution' *Rural History 1* (1990) 165–92.

be used interchangeably. Activities on the closes could range from sports to plays. The closes were often manorial lands that became part of the glebe (lands that were part of the benefice of a parish incumbent), and many camping closes and game places were 'adjacent, or very close, to the parish church', commonly on the north side, or within 'a village nucleus'.[33] The evidence for these closes, including those with game places, most often appears in tithe apportionments, wills, glebe terriers, manorial surveys, and early maps, evidences dating from the second half of the fifteenth century through the nineteenth century. Using such sources, Dymond and others have identified approximately seventy camping closes in Suffolk, 36 in Norfolk, 29 in Cambridgeshire, and 14 in Essex.

Using printed sources and original records, I have been able to verify sixty of the total of seventy parishes with camping closes that Dymond mentions (TABLE 1).[34] For thirty-five of the seventy, no performance records survive (in most cases because no local records survive); for twenty-five of the seventy, at least one performance record of some kind does survive. Because so many of the closes were originally part of manorial lands, I have listed their parishes by the hundred in which they lay. The greatest number of parishes with both a camping

33. David Dymond 'Camping Closes' in *An Historical Atlas of Suffolk* edited by David Dymond and Edward Martin (Ipswich: Suffolk County Council, second edition 1989) 154; 'The Camping Close' 166.

34. According to Dymond, a total of 14 camping closes and related sites have been identified in Essex, 29 in Cambridgeshire, 36 in Norfolk, and 70 (by far the greatest number) in Suffolk (Dymond 'Camping Closes' 214 note 16). See also Charles Candler 'On the Significance of Some East Anglian Field-Names' *Norfolk Archaeology 11* (1892) 148–9; R.W. Ketton-Cremer 'Camping, a Forgotten Norfolk Game' *Norfolk Archaeology 24* (1932) 88–92; and Robert Forby *The Vocabulary of East Anglia* 2 vols (London: J.B. Nicholls and Son, 1830; reprint Newton Abbot, 1970) *1* 50–54.

Some of the communities in other East Anglian counties identified by Dymond and others in the publications cited above as having camping or related closes are:

Cambridgeshire: Barton, Bassingborn, Cambridge, Chesterton, Cottonham, Harston, Littleport, Oakington, and Orwell, among others.

Essex: Billericay, Braintree, Canewdon, Chigwell, Colchester, Copford, Dedham, East Hanningfield, Gosfield, Great Tey, Halstead, Navestock, Norton Woodseats, and Thaxted.

Norfolk: Calthorpe, Carbrooke, Cawston, Colkirk, Crostwick, Denver, Ditchingham, East Bilney, Elsing, Felbrigg, Garboldisham, Harleston, Hevingham, Kirby Cane, Lyng, Mattishall, Necton, Norwich, Ranworth, Shouldham Priory, Stiffkey, Swaffham, Tunstead, Weston Longville, Wymondham (games – a three-day night-and-day play), and Yarmouth.

TABLE 1: SUFFOLK PLACES WITH CAMPING CLOSES (BY HUNDREDS)

Hundred	Parish	Has dramatic records
Babergh	Bures	no
	Cockfield	no
	Groton	no
	Lawshall	no
	Shimpling	no
	Stoke-by-Nayland	yes
Blackbourn	Ashfield, Great	yes
	Bardwell	yes
	Coney Weston	no
	Elmswell	no
	Hopton	no
	Ixworth	yes
	Knettishall	no
	Market Weston	no
	Norton	no
	Stanton	yes
	Walsham-le-Willows	yes
	Wattisfield	yes
Blything	Bramfield	no
	Cratfield	yes
	Leiston	no
	Rumburgh	yes
	Heveningham	no
Bosmere/Claydon	Akenham	yes
	Bramford	yes
	Claydon	no
	Needham Market	no
Bury (Liberty of)	Bury	yes
Colneis	Felixstowe	yes
Cosford	Hadleigh	yes
	Semer	yes
	Layham	no
	Whatfield	no

Hundred	Parish	Has dramatic records
Hartismere	Wetheringsett	no
	Eye	yes
Hoxne	Fressingfield	yes
	Saxstead	no
	Weybread	yes
Lackford	Icklingham	yes
	Lakenheath	no
Loes	Eyke	no
Risbridge	Clare	yes
	Little Thurlow	no
	Stradishall	no
Risbridge/Hinckford (Essex)	Haverhill	no
Samford	Capel St Mary	no
	Hintlesham	no
Stow	Stowmarket	yes
Thedwastre	Debenham	no
	Drinkstone	no
	Fornham St Genevieve	no
	Framsden	yes
	Great Barton	yes
	Pakenham	yes
	Stanningfield	no
Thingoe	Hawstead	no
Thredling	Winston	no
Wangford	Beccles	yes
	Mettingham	yes
Wilford	Ufford	no

close and a performance record of one kind or another lay in Blackbourne Hundred (six instances), the next highest were in Blything and Thedwestry Hundreds (three each). Over the decades and centuries, as the closes passed from manorial ownership into the possession of post-Reformation parishes, towns, and individuals, most of the camping closes gradually lost their original identity and evolved away from their original uses. It is striking that in an island kingdom where land was, and is, at such a premium, a county like Suffolk could have so many dedicated open-air playing places in communities of every size.

In the course of his studies, Dymond has become convinced that camping closes 'are indistinguishable from other kinds of recreational site, and indeed are the missing game-places or playing places long sought by literary historians'.[35] Game places and camping closes do seem the logical place to begin in seeking likely venues for the signature open-air plays of Suffolk and other parts of East Anglia. Fortunately, descriptions of the size and shape of many camping closes and game places survive in tithe apportionments, tithe maps, field books, and occasionally other kinds of documents.

Game places, lying as they did within camping closes, were obviously more compact than a typical camping close. Beccles' game place was 'a small rectangle' abutting a four-acre camping close in that town. In Walsham-le-Willows, the size of the game place is variously described (during the course of the sixteenth century) as being a half-acre; or a half-acre, ten perches; or a half-acre, sixteen perches, one foot. The Walsham game place lay within an open space at least three times larger than the game place that may have been the camping close there.[36] In Great Ashfield, 'Le Playing Place' was one and one-fourth acres in size. In Great Barton, the 'pleisto' or church green was one acre. And in Hintlesham, 'The Playing Place' was one-fourth acre.[37] The playing places about which we can know something tended to be of a similar one-acre size.

35. David Dymond 'Place-Names as Evidence for Recreation' *Journal of the English Place-Name Society 25* (1992/93) 16.

36. Personal letter concerning the Beccles Game Place from David Dymond to the author, 20 April 2006; Chicago: University of Chicago Library MS Bacon 969, fol. 59v. Kenneth M. Dodd 'Another English Theater in the Round' *Shakespeare Quarterly 21: 2* (Spring 1970) 129, 135.

37. Cambridge: Cambridge University Library Additional MS 3390, fol. 215 (Great Ashfield); Bury: Suffolk Record Office TE 14/4/1, single sheet (Great Barton); Ipswich: Suffolk Record Office FAA 2701/19/89, single sheet (Hintlesham).

Camping closes, though occasionally compact, were most often much larger than game places, ranging in size from one to twelve acres. The camping close at Clare, for example, occupied more than five acres. Bramfield had two camping fields, called Little and Great, respectively seven acres and four acres in size. The camping close at Little Thurlow was three acres; at Lakenheath six acres; at Market Weston seven acres; at Needham Market three acres; at Capel St Mary one and three-fourth acres; at Ixworth one acre; and at Whatfield one and three-fourth acres. Framsden had two sites, 'The Great Playing Close' and 'The little Playing Close', respectively twelve acres and five acres. Exceptionally, the camping close at Saxstead was a mere three-fourth acre. Camping closes generally had a parallel shape typical of back-and-forth field sports, although they could vary widely (in one case becoming triangular) based on the availability of space in the community.[38]

In their names, Suffolk recreational sites confusingly blend wording associated with both game and playing places and camping closes. Precision, consistency, and clarity are not qualities that can be associated with the naming of outdoor recreational sites in Suffolk (at least not in ways that we as yet understand. In practical terms, 'game places' could easily have accommodated many of the surviving plays associated with East Anglia, other than the huge *Mary Magdalene* or *Castle of Perseverance*. And in one case – at Walsham-le-Willows – they certainly did). Camping closes, on the other hand, were so large that they could easily have accommodated the building of a temporary theatre-in-the-round and scaffold staging within their confines. Although the principal function of camping closes was to be sporting venues (as their name indicates), there is no reason to think that they could not also have been used to stage plays. Precedents for the multiple use of such sites exist elsewhere in the kingdom. In Cornwall, some of the open-air amphitheatres (*plain-an-guary*)

38. Bury: Suffolk Record Office T 146/1, fol. 6 (Clare); Ipswich: Suffolk Record Office FD 35/A1/a, 6 (Bramfield); Bury: Suffolk Record Office T 103/1, 8, T/103/2, single sheet (Little Thurlow); Dymond 'The Camping Close' 175 (Lakenheath); Bury: Suffolk Record Office T 30/1, 2 (Market Weston); Dymond 'The Camping Close' 180 (Needham Market); Ipswich: Suffolk Record Office FDA 57/A1/1a, 1b, and Dymond 'The Camping Close' 186 (Capel St Mary); Dymond 'The Camping Close' 167, 188 note 8 (Ixworth); Bury: Suffolk Record Office T 226/1, 3 (Whatfield); Ipswich: Suffolk Record Office FDA 105/A1/1a, 9 (Framsden); Bury: Suffolk Record Office FDA 211/A1/1a, 9 (Saxstead). For photographs (or maps) of camping closes at Swaffham (Norfolk), Ash Street, Little Thurlow, Lakenheath, Market Weston, Needham Market, Saxstead, and Capel St Mary, see Dymond 'The Camping Close' 166–7, 178, 175, 177, 180, 174, and 186.

were demonstrably used both for drama and for sports at St Just in Penwith and elsewhere.[39] In Edinburgh, Scotland, the playfield on Greenside was used to stage the *Satyre of the Thrie Estatis* on or about Sunday, 18 August 1554. On 7 October 1552, the town council had proposed a new playfield near there which would accommodate both 'interludis', and 'lesure pastymes' including shooting and bowling.[40]

Game Places, Camping Closes, and Drama in Suffolk

Theatre historians have long laboured to clarify the relationship between game places and parish drama in East Anglia, especially as it relates to those late medieval plays that required large, outdoor, circular playing places, and which are now associated with the region. In 1977, David Galloway discussed the game place in Great Yarmouth, dismissing out of hand the view held by J.T. Murray (and followed by E.K. Chambers and Glynne Wickham) that the Yarmouth 'game place' had something called a *game house* – in effect a purpose-built theatre much predating those in London. A year later, Richard Beadle, citing the comment by fifteenth-century friar John Capgrave of King's Lynn, Norfolk, that the Roman amphitheatre 'was a circular playing-place *swech as we haue her in þis lond*', wondered 'whether the mode of staging "in the round" was not once common in later medieval East Anglia'. A year after that, Galloway reported on a third game place, this one at Wymondham, Norfolk, that certainly functioned as a venue for performance (Wymondham loaned properties to Bungay for its play), though he also dismissed Beadle's notion that 'tentys' mentioned in Yarmouth documents related to the game place meant enclosures that were used in staging, saying instead that the word likely meant 'tenements'.[41] However, precedents for the theatrical use of the term certainly exist elsewhere in the kingdom. In Cornish drama, staged in dedicated outdoor

39. *REED: Cornwall* edited Sally L. Joyce and Evelyn S. Newlyn (University of Toronto Press, 1999) 401; and Richard Carew *The Survey of Cornwall* (London: John Iaggard, 1602; reprinted Amsterdam and New York: Da Capo Press, 1969) T3v–V4r.

40. Anna J. Mill *Mediaeval Plays in Scotland* (1924; reprinted New York and London: Benjamin Blom, 1969) 181–2 note 3, 351–2.

41. David Galloway 'The "Game Place" and "House" at Great Yarmouth, 1493–1595' *Theatre Notebook 31* (1977) 6–9; Richard Beadle 'The East Anglian "game-place": a possibility for further research' *REED Newsletter 1* (1978) 3; and Galloway 'Comment: The East Anglian "Game-place": Some Facts and Fictions' *REED Newsletter 1* (1979) 24–6.

playing places, the word *tentys* referred to scaffold structures that were used as on-stage 'homes' of major characters. For example, among the several references to stage structures in Cornish drama are these: in the *Ordinale De Origine Mundi*: *hic ascendit episcopus in tentum suum* ('here the bishop goes up to his seat': *sd* between 2660–61); and in the *Passio Domini Nostri Ihesu Christi*: *hic descendit pilatus et iet in tentum cayphas* ('here Pilate goes down, and Caiaphus shall go into his tent': *sd* between 1616–17).[42] In a major contribution, Robert Wright demonstrated that medieval and early modern East Anglia, including Suffolk, had an incredibly rich tradition of parish drama that was financially supported by hub-like networks of neighbouring communities, though he did not focus on the game places themselves.[43]

In seeking to clarify the relationship (if any) between the outdoor sites and the dramatic records in Suffolk, four categories of communities suggest themselves: communities that had game places which they certainly used to perform plays; communities that had both playing places and plays, but left no record connecting the two; communities that had plays, but left no record confirming that they had a playing place; and communities that had a playing place, but left no record confirming that they had a play. The only game place in Suffolk that was unquestionably used to stage plays is the famous game place at Walsham-le-Willows. More than a dozen documents situate Walsham's game place as being at a corner of the community's camping close. A Walsham field book made in 1577 confirms that the game place was a dedicated open-air theatre for the staging of plays:

> The sayd game place in the tenure of diuers men to the vse and behofe of the towne of walsham ^\aforesayd/ is customary ground holden of the sayd manor of walsham and a place compassed rownd *with* a fayer banke ^\cast vp on a good height & havinge/ ~~sett v~~ many great trees called populers growynge about the same banke, in the myddest a fayre round

42. *The Ancient Cornish Drama* translated Edwin Norris, 2 vols (1859; reprinted New York and London: Benjamin Blom, 1968) *1* 202–3, 350–1. See also examples of stage tents in *1* 356–7, 374–5, 386–7, and 456–7. For discussions of the analogous use of tent and stage house in the *Ordinalia*, see *The Cornish Ordinalia: A Medieval Dramatic Trilogy* translated Markham Harris (Washington DC: Catholic University of America Press, 1969) xxi; and Jane A. Bakere *The Cornish Ordinalia: A Critical Study* (Cardiff: University of Wales Press, 1980) 155–8.

43. Robert Wright 'Community Theatre in Late Medieval East Anglia' *Theatre Notebook 28: 1* (1974) 24–39.

place of earth wythe a stone wall about the same to the height of the earth made of purpose for the vse of Stage playes.[44]

Walsham-le-Willows, Finningham, Gislingham, Rickinghall Inferior, and Rickinghall Superior all bordered Allwood Green, the largest green in Suffolk. Some evidence suggests the likelihood that the five collaborated in the production of plays. In 1505/6, Walsham co-produced a play with the parish of Gislingham, Suffolk, which the two communities advertised at Thetford ('*Item solutis* in regard to Walsham game et Gyslyngham xvj d').[45] The much-earlier manorial records of Rickinghall contain the famous Rickinghall Fragment (1369/70), seemingly part of a play dramatising a tyrant king who places himself above all authority, including that of God.[46] Of the five bordering parishes only Walsham is known to have had a game place. The nearby village of Wattisfield also had a possible site (imprecisely called 'the play ground'). Of possible venues, it seems most likely that the jointly produced play in 1505/6 was staged at either Walsham or Wattisfield. The play represented by the Rickenhall Fragment may have been as well, if either of those two game places existed at that early date. The evidence from this cluster of villages also strengthens the possibility that since game places are far more scattered than are camping closes in the records, villages might have joined together to stage plays in those game places. The fact that communities from various neighbouring hundreds worked together on drama suggests that hundredal affiliations were not necessarily a determinative factor in the co-operative production of parish plays. In any event, in the equivocal world of the documents, Walsham offers rare absolute certainty concerning the relationship between game place and plays in this part of Suffolk.

44. Chicago: University of Chicago Library MS Bacon 969, fol. 59v. For a thorough study of the documents and the playing place, see Kenneth M. Dodd 'Another English Theater in the Round' *Shakespeare Quarterly 21: 2* (Spring 1970) 125–56.

45. Cambridge: Cambridge University Library Additional MS 6969, fol. 72. As early as 1392, Walsham-le-Willows had a plough ale 'at the time of sowing wheat'; *The Court Rolls of Walsham Le Willows 1351–1399* edited Ray Locke (Suffolk Records Society 45; Woodbridge: Suffolk Records Society/Boydell, 2002) 179. Though this ale far predates the first record of the game place, the record shows the presence of customary entertainments in Walsham from a very early time.

46. London: British Library Additional Roll 63481B, single sheet: edition in *Non-Cycle Plays and Fragments* edited Norman Davis *EETS SS 1* (1970) cxiv–cxv and 116–17.

For twenty-one communities, we have records that they had both entertainment traditions of one kind or another and camping closes. But those records contain no evidence confirming that the closes served as performance venues. Beccles falls into this second category. The difficulty in confirming that communities such as Beccles staged their 'game' in the game place (though it may seem obvious that they would have) lies in the fragmentary nature of the records. Some are very sketchy indeed. Further, references to the games most often appear as payments or receipts in financial accounts, while references to game places most often appear in tithe apportionments, rentals, or similar legalistic, non-accounting records. While civic or parochial records often specify that a professional troupe being paid had performed on a certain day, in a church or hall or dwelling, before a particular audience (often the local oligarchy and its families), scribes almost never felt it necessary to confirm the obvious fact that the parish game had been held in the game place or in the churchyard (as untypically occurs in the Boxford churchwardens' accounts). In these twenty-one instances, it is only possible to identify two unlinkable facts: the community had a game, and the community had a game place.

For example, the village of Bardwell advertised its 'game' (its play) at Thetford Priory in 1505/6, and it also had a camping close, but Bardwell parish records mention only church-ales, minstrels and banner-cloths used in processions. Ixworth also paid for what the record calls its 'play' (not called its *game*), which they advertised at Thetford Priory in 1508/9. Ixworth also had a camping close. But Ixworth lacks the parish records that might be able to confirm a connection between the camping close and Ixworth's play. The village of Cratfield had something called 'The Great Church Ale' (and many other ales as well), but the records offer no clue as to whether the ale included a *game*, although Cratfield had a camping close. The town of Eye had players who performed on Corpus Christi Day, and Eye had a camping close, but its few churchwardens' accounts reveal no connection between the two. In the village of Fressingfield, in 1509, the feoffees of the local Guild of St Margaret of Antioch transferred two parcels of land and premises thereon to the churchwardens and parishioners of the village for ninety-eight years, specifically for the keeping of church-ales and other activities 'nesessary to the profyte of the said church or parishe', clearly making it a dedicated recreation site. The transaction confirms that Fressingfield had annual fundraising festive diversions, and that those diversions required a sizeable space. The village of Felixstowe had, by 1498, a site called 'le campyngclos', and in 1497/8, its King and Queen of the May (a mimetic event by definition) received 2d from Felixstowe Priory, but other records capable of documenting a relationship between the close and the May games do not exist.[47]

Sixty-six Suffolk communities, great and small, have left one or more performance records of one kind or another, but no record confirming that any of the sixty-six also had a dedicated outdoor playing place. Performance in these sixty-six places ranges from masques (as at Hengrave, Little Saxham, and Newmarket) to plays (as at Boxford) to traditional mimetic customs (as at Blythburgh, Long Melford, and numerous other places) to music almost everywhere. The venues that can be identified include churches, churchyards, halls in private dwellings, halls in religious foundations, guild halls, mayor's houses, streets, greens, and commons. Given the profusion of camping closes in Suffolk, it might be expected that dedicated outdoor sites for some of the 66 communities that have only performance records may yet turn up; but to date they have not.

Thirty-six additional Suffolk communities certainly had variously named dedicated recreational sites, but they left no evidence of a local performance tradition. The principal reason, in most cases, is that many of those communities lack records of the kind where evidences of performance might typically be found.

Conclusions

What, then, can we know about early drama in Beccles, and what does Beccles tell us about early drama in Suffolk? The town certainly had something that it called 'The Game Place', situated at one corner of the Beccles camping close on what were originally manorial lands. Beccles maps and other records clearly distinguish between the four-acre camping close (as a whole) and the much

47. For Bardwell, see Cambridge: Cambridge University Library Additional MS 6969, fol. 72, and Bury: Suffolk Record Office FL 522/11/20, fols 4, 6, 13, 18, 36, 67, 119, 120; for Ixworth, see Cambridge: Cambridge University Library Additional MS 6969, fol. 90v; for Cratfield, see Ipswich: Suffolk Record Office FC 62/E1/1, fol. [4v]; for Eye, see Ipswich: Suffolk Record Office EE 2/L1/4, sheets O and R; for Fressingfield, see Ipswich: Suffolk Record Office FC 90/L3/8, single sheet; and for Felixstowe, see David Dymond 'The Camping Close: A Lost Social Institution' *Rural History 1* (1990) 178; and London: The National Archives, Public Record Office SC 6/HENVII/691, mb 1. Concerning camping closes for these six communities, see Dymond 'The Camping Close' 169, 172–3, 178, and 184; and Arthur Hadrian Allcroft *Earthwork of England: Prehistoric, Roman, Saxon, Danish, Norman, and Mediaeval* (London: Macmillan, 1908) 601.

smaller Game Place within it. Since Suffolk records characteristically use the words *game* and *play* synonymously, Beccles likely used its game place to stage plays, while using the much larger camping close for the football-like sport of camping, and other diversions. We can know that Beccles had parish players who performed locally, but who also travelled to perform in other places, sometimes together with troupes from those other communities. We can know that players from Beccles certainly performed during the Christmas season (therefore most probably indoors), but we lack a verifiable link between the players and the outdoor Game Place in Beccles.

What does Beccles contribute, contextually, to the picture of early drama in Suffolk? Beccles lies at the centre of a densely populated area including north-east Suffolk and south-east Norfolk (the River Waveney making a border between the two) in the northern part of what is known as High Suffolk. The area was characterised by a gentle landscape, compact towns, non-nucleated parishes, pasture lands, cattle, sheep, and marketable agriculture, including peas and other crops. During the medieval and early modern periods, the Waveney and its tributaries provided access to the ports at Lowestoft and Yarmouth, and thereby to North Sea trade. Camping closes existed in every part of Suffolk, as do records of parish and civic drama. But the records of local drama in the Waveney River Valley are notably copious. Extending from west to east, Walsham-le-Willows, Thetford (Norfolk), Mettingham, Bungay, Beccles, and Yarmouth (Norfolk), together with other communities, including Wymondham, Norfolk, all left records of a significant tradition in parish-sponsored drama that is complex in its staging, widely advertised, and sometimes multi-parish in its production. So, we can know that, in having its own players, camping close, and Game Place, Beccles was unexceptional; it mirrored the pattern not only in north-east Suffolk but in the county as a whole.

In having a Game Place, however, Beccles is notable. The records make reference to only two Game Places in Suffolk (at Walsham-le-Willows and Beccles), and two in Norfolk (at Yarmouth[48] and Wymondham). All four game

48. Other communities throughout Suffolk had sites whose names may or may not indicate a Game Place. Wattisfield (near north of Walsham) had something called a 'Play Ground'. Great Ashfield (between Walsham and Bury) had a camping close that 'was once apparently known as "le Playing Place"' (Dymond 'Lost Social Institution' 169). Akenham (north of Ipswich) had a 'Maypole Pightle' near the churchyard. Hintlesham had a piece of glebe land west of the churchyard called 'The Playing Place'. However, Hintlesham, though close to Boxford, was not one of the 28 parishes contributing to the play at Boxford in 1535 – some of them much farther away from Boxford than was

places are in north-east Suffolk or the part of Norfolk relatively near Suffolk. All four towns were important in different ways. Walsham was an agricultural hub; Beccles was the most important port town on the River Waveney; Yarmouth was the major North Sea port in the area; and Wymondham was an important market and abbey town. However, it is not clear that their collective status as towns had anything to do with the fact that they had game places. And the fact that the four towns had game places seemingly did not at all determine whether or not they also had a play; the records show that towns everywhere in and near the Waveney had plays. Although Bungay had but half the population of Beccles and no recorded game place, it had a large, two-day, play, known as far away as Norwich. Thetford (Norfolk) welcomed local players from numerous other Suffolk communities who were announcing their own plays. A small triangle of proximate communities (Wattisfield, Stanton, and Walsham-le-Willows) illustrates the density of the local playing tradition. Wattisfield had something called a 'Play Ground', and the Wattisfield churchwardens paid the expenses of a Father Wilby (apparently representing Wattisfield) 'when he went to the playe at Stanton'. Walsham, of course, staged plays on its Game Place, and it co-produced a play with Gillingham in 1505/6, one of five communities, including Walsham, that bounded the huge Allwood Green. Manorial records from Rickenhall (one of the five) include 'The Rickenhall Fragment' (see above).

The Suffolk records provide considerable other evidence of networking concerning their plays among parishes throughout Suffolk, south Norfolk, and north Essex. Those circuits certainly did not stop at county boundaries. Records from twelve Suffolk communities contain evidences of inter-parish playing circuits among eighty-two communities (including the twelve) from the three counties. Because the records that survive are inevitably fragmentary, many other likely instances of inter-parish co-operation in matters of custom, ceremony, and performance may well have been lost to us. Apparently, no place was too small to have its own players. To cite one example, in 1481 Sir John Howard paid the players of the hamlet of Thorington Street for their performance at Stoke-by-Nayland. The evidences of local networking among villages and towns about which we can know something (however fragmentary) include:

Hintlesham. Framsden (between Debenham and Wickham Market) had a 'Playing Close' immediately south-east of the church (in earlier times, the word 'close' indicated a more compact space than a field). Great Barton (near Bury) had a 'Playstow'.

Boxford: Assington, Brent Eleigh, Bures St Mary, Chelsworth, Chilton, Dedham, Edwardstone, Groton, Great Waldingfield, Hadleigh, Kersey, Lavenham, Layham, Lindsey, Little Cornard, Little Waldingfield, Long Melford, Milden, Monk's Eleigh, Nayland, Newton, Preston, Polstead, Shelley, Stoke-by-Nayland, Stowmarket, Stratford St Mary, Sudbury.

Bungay: Beccles, Mettingham, Norwich, Yarmouth (Norfolk).

Dennington: Saxstead, Wilby.

Hengrave Hall: Brome, Bury St Edmunds, Cambridge – all musicians.

Long Melford: Braintree (Essex), Ipswich.

Metfield: Bungay, Mendham.

Mettingham College: Beccles, Beaumont (Essex), Bungay, Gillingham (Norfolk), Norwich, South Elmham, Walsingham (Norfolk), Wymondham (Norfolk), Yarmouth (Norfolk).

Mildenhall: the hamlets of Beck Row, Halywell, and West Row; Thetford (Norfolk).

Stoke-by-Nayland: Billericay (Essex), Boxford, Chelmsford (Essex), Coggeshall (Essex), Colchester (Essex), Esterford Kelvedon (Essex), Hadleigh, Lavenham, Sudbury, Thorington Street.

Thetford (Norfolk): Suffolk parishes: Bardwell, Gislingham, Ixworth, Mildenhall, Walsham-le-Willows.

Walsham-le-Willows: Gislingham, possibly Rickenhall.

Wattisfield: Stanton.

Walberswick: Blythburgh, Bramfield, Halsworth, Southwold, Wenhaston, Yoxford.

The density and ubiquity of the venues are extraordinary. No one place (for example, Ipswich or Bury) was the single centre of dramatic activity in the county. The county might more usefully be described as a series of microcultures, each with distinctive playing traditions within a common culture. Ipswich, for example, had an extraordinary tradition involving Corpus Christi celebration and drama. In the areas north and south of the River Waveney, towns and villages had their own plays, and sometimes their own game place. Though Beccles and other communities had a very powerful manorial landlord in the Abbey at Bury, the management and farming of manorial lands devolved to towns during the late Middle Ages, and the Waveney Valley was also the primary area of Lollardy in the county. Records show that the complexity of that local culture was mirrored in its drama.

As far as I have been able to determine, the possible relevance of the Beccles Game Place to the staging of plays in East Anglia has not been discussed in studies of early theatre in East Anglia. More generally, the relationship between recreational sites in Suffolk (and elsewhere in East Anglia) and the plays themselves has not been materially advanced in recent years. The records of performance and the records of playing places have not, as it were, been talking to each other, and neither of them has been talking very usefully to the play texts. In the absence of identifiable venues, this great provincial playing tradition remains curiously disconnected from the culture within which it flourished.

In the drama-rich environment of Suffolk, some payments and other entries in the records identify the venues where performances occurred – predictably in churches, halls, inns, or private dwellings. But the greater number of records list no venue. The many camping closes, game places, and playing places offer themselves as a likely first choice in seeking possible venues, especially for the great number of plays demonstrably staged during the warmer months of the year. Particularly rewarding could be a close study of the relationship of game spaces and camping closes to the built environment which they most often adjoined. With its parish churches, streets, other glebe properties, and private or public buildings, the surrounding environment had immediate relationships with the recreational sites. The search for lost theatres in isolation could usefully give way to the study of more complex venues. For example, the Bungay parish records combine theatrical and mercantile concerns – staging for players, and stalls for tradesmen and tradeswomen in a setting at once festive, pious, fiscal, and performative. Stage directions in *The Conversion of St Paul* describe movement between places and stations – with the appearances and exitings of horses, together with processional elements – that invites one to consider how the players might have blended scaffold staging, built structures, and more than one kind of open space. These dedicated recreational sites, and their immediate surroundings, may yet prove to be our most eloquent and instructive witnesses to the early drama in Suffolk.

University of Wisconsin – Stevens Point

PENDENS SUPER FERETRUM: Fergus, Aelred, and the York 'Funeral of the Virgin'

Jamie Beckett

In studies of the York Corpus Christi Play, the pageant sometimes known as 'Fergus' has proved somewhat enigmatic. Various records attesting to the pageant survive, though no script was ever entered into the York Register, and moreover both the popularity of the piece and the number of times it was actually staged have been brought into question.[1] Perhaps the most intriguing account given of the pageant comes from 1432/3, when a complaint is recorded in the A/Y Memorandum Book concerning the apparently controversial nature of the production:

> *vero quia Cementarij huius ciuitatis murmurabant inter se de pagina sua in ludo corporis christi vbi ffergus fflagellatus erat pro eo quod materia pagine illius in sacra non continetur scriptura & magis risum & clamorem causabat quam deuocionem Et quandoque lites contenciones & pugne inde proueniebant in populo ipsamque paginam suam raro vel nunquam potuerunt producere & ludere clara die sicut faciunt pagine precedentes*.

> indeed, because the Masons of this city have become accustomed to murmur about their pageant in the Corpus Christi Play in which Fergus was beaten because the pageant's subject is not contained in sacred scripture and used to produce more laughter and noise than devotion. And whenever quarrels, disagreements, and fights used to arise among the people from this they have rarely or never been able to produce their pageant in daylight as the preceding pageants do.[2]

1. For a good overview see *The York Plays: A Critical Edition of the York Corpus Christi Play as recorded in British Library Additional* MS *35290* edited Richard Beadle, 2 vols *EETS SS 23* and *24* (2019 and 2013) *2* 424–9.
2. York City Archives MS E20 (A/Y Memorandum Book 1431–1432) fols 257r–257v, in *Records of Early English Drama: York* edited Alexandra F. Johnston and Margaret Rogerson (University of Toronto Press, 1979) *1* 47–8; translation based on *REED: York 2* 732; Beadle notes that the dating should read '1432–1433': Beadle *York Plays 2* 425 note 778.

This complaint offers a rare example of audience response to the York Cycle, and to the passions and conflict which these performances had the capacity to stir: we are told that this pageant led to 'more noise and laughter than devotion', as well as 'quarrels, disagreements and fights'. The idea that such a boisterous response to biblical or pseudo-biblical drama occurred in this period should perhaps come as little surprise.[3] But it is through this record of the response that we have been able to characterise the apparently unique content of this 'lost' play, offering tantalising details of the performance and its oddities: namely that the piece could be characterised as the pageant 'in which Fergus was beaten'; that this beating was perhaps framed (at least in part) as the cause of this controversy; and that the subject of the pageant was not considered to be contained in 'sacred scripture'.

The record is framed within the A/Y Memorandum Book as part of a complaint by the Goldsmiths over the expense of producing both Herod's court and the Magi – costs which they sought to share. Accentuation of this 'murmur' of dissent among the Masons might be read as a convenient means on the part of the Goldsmiths to motivate change, an endeavour which was ultimately successful. The text later stipulates that the Masons should be given responsibility for staging *Herod*, and discard their former production for the foreseeable future. The complaint of 1432/3 provokes a variety of questions, not least concerning the content of the pageant, and the reason why it gave rise to such a fractious and unruly response among spectators. So, we might ask, what was the pageant 'in which Fergus was beaten' ostensibly about?

Looking back to the *Ordo paginarum*, we can see that the beating of Fergus was 1415 a component part of the pageant also known as *Portacio corporis marie*, or 'The Funeral of the Virgin', assigned to the Masons. This area of the *Ordo* is damaged, but using the earlier readings by Toulmin Smith, the description of the pageant reads: *Quatuor Apostoli [portantes feretrum] Marie & fergus pendens super feretrum [suum ij ali]is Iudeis cum vno Angelo.*[4] This text corresponds with what

3. See for example Sarah Carpenter 'New Evidence: Vives and Audience-Response to Biblical Drama' *METh 31* (2009) 3–12.

4. A/Y Memorandum Book fol. 254r, in *REED: York 1* 23, 26; *2* 709; Twycross has suggested that the *Ordo* may denote a procession of tableaux at this point in the history of the Cycle, distinct from the scripted pageants which survive in the *York Register*. Nevertheless, the use of the name 'Fergus' in this early record remains pertinent. If the *Ordo* titles do represent tableaux, the visual details listed were likely at least to have informed the later scripted performances; Meg Twycross 'The *Ordo paginarum* Revisited, with a Digital Camera' in *'Bring Furth the Pagants': Essays in Early English Drama Presented to Alexandra*

we know of the Funeral of the Virgin narrative from other sources, including the popular *Legenda Aurea* and the N. Town Plays.[5] In the story three Jewish figures attempt to unsettle the funeral bier of the Virgin Mary, as it is being carried by several apostles. On touching the holy coffin, the ringleader becomes stuck to it and his friends are blinded. Only by converting to Christianity, and through the intercession of the Virgin, are the aggressors restored to their senses.

The 'Funeral' narrative seems to have been a fairly popular tale associated with Marian devotion in the late medieval period, and is depicted in at least two windows at York Minster, as elsewhere.[6] Philip Butterworth has suggested that the performance of the narrative had a comic element, likely mediated through the slapstick of a removable arm stuck to the funeral bier.[7] Although the story is apocryphal, it is difficult to see how the complaint that the subject of the pageant was not contained within scripture (*materia pagine illius in sacra non continetur scriptura*) could be taken as cause for trouble, especially when regarded alongside other non-canonical aspects of the York Cycle, from the role of Uxor Noe to Joseph's troubles about Mary.

The contentious subject of the pageant, however, may have been distinct from the simple narrative of the Virgin's funeral. I propose that the 'non-scriptural' subject of the pageant which is criticised may refer not to the apocryphal nature of the Virgin's funeral, but to the use of characters, themes, or content considered to be derived from another source entirely. The fact the pageant should be characterised in the complaint as *vbi ffergus fflagellatus* may offer us an insight into what proved controversial about the production, and where it appeared to deviate from the 'sacra scriptura' – centrally, through the beating of the figure named 'Fergus'.

F Johnston edited D.N. Klausner and K.S. Marsalek (Toronto University Press, 2007) 105–31, especially 111.

5. See Beadle *York Plays 2* 424–5; Mark R. Sullivan 'The Missing York Funeral of the Virgin' in *The Dramatic Tradition of the Middle Ages* edited Clifford Davidson (New York: AMS Press, 2005) 150–4.

6. See Clifford Davidson and David E. O'Connor *York Art: A Subject List of Extant and Lost Art* (Early Drama, Art and Music 4; Kalamazoo: Medieval Institute, 2003) 68. Hardwick suggests that a window depicting several monkeys carrying a coffin at York may even parody the scene; see Paul Hardwick 'Making Light of Devotion: The Pilgrimage Window in York Minster' in *Medieval English Comedy* edited Paul Hardwick and Sandra Hordis (Turnhout: Brepols, 2007) 65.

7. Philip Butterworth 'Substitution: Theatrical Sleight of Hand in Medieval Plays' *European Medieval Drama* 9 (2005) 209–29.

That the name 'Fergus' denotes the Jewish ringleader in the York 'Funeral' has been generally accepted, though the origins and use of the name in this context have remained a source of interest. In versions of the narrative as written or performed in England and on the continent, the name given to this ringleader would be considered recognisably Jewish by late medieval audiences – as Anna Mill notes, he is referred to variously as 'Japhia, Isachar, Reuben, the High Priest Adonijah, Bezerlay', as well as simply 'Judea aldorman' in the *Blickling Homilies*, or *primus princeps* in the N. Town *Assumption of Mary*.[8] This list demonstrates the variety of guises and labels which the lead antagonist of the Funeral of the Virgin narrative could be given to inhabit, whether a prince, priest, or even alderman, but the chief characteristic shared by all of these names is their unambiguous Jewishness.

By contrast, the appellation 'Fergus' notably carries Caledonian rather than Jewish associations. Mark Sullivan, among others, has reasoned that the use of this name marks out the antipathy of the people of York to the Scots, who led military excursions into Yorkshire sporadically throughout the late thirteenth and early fourteenth centuries, and remained a threatening presence throughout the fifteenth.[9] The character Fergus therefore represents an amalgamated Scoto-Jewish figure of hatred, bringing together the localised enemy of the Scot with the much-maligned Jew. The Scottish adversary was a tangible threat, and may have provided a stand-in for the Jew whose communities had been expelled from England in 1290, and represented an otherwise absent foe.

Although the assumption that 'Fergus' references Scottish enmity seems fairly likely, in the following pages I wish to argue that the use of the name was inspired by far more specific associations than a simple anti-Scots polemic. I contend that 'Fergus', used as shorthand for the 'Funeral' pageant, actually referenced a specific enemy of the people of York who was not merely a representative of Scotland, but also a distinct 'Other' with a complicated past, posing an ancient threat to the region of the north-east. But to locate this Fergus we must look backwards into the history of twelfth-century Yorkshire, and consider how this history was transmuted into a controversial performance of the early fifteenth century.

8. Anna J. Mill 'The York Plays of the Dying, Assumption, and Coronation of Our Lady' *PMLA* 65: 5 (1950) 868.

9. Sullivan 'Missing York Funeral' 150–4.

Fergus of Galloway and Aelred of Rievaulx

From around 1130 until his deposition in 1160, a figure named Fergus of Galloway ruled over a vast swathe of land in the south-west of modern-day Scotland, extending from the west coast on the Irish Sea as far as the region of Annandale in the east, and up to the lands of Carrick and the river Doon in the north.[10] Fergus was a leader of some renown, lord and self-styled 'king' of a Galloway which was entirely autonomous of Scottish rule. He was a major player in Anglo-Scottish politics of the twelfth century, a politician who shrewdly maintained a policy of alternating allegiance between Scottish and English rulers to maintain political freedom.[11] His region represented a bastion of Gaelic culture looking westward to Ireland and the Isle of Man, against the pervasive and colonising powers of Anglo/Scoto-Norman influence to the east and the south.[12] And, I argue, it is to him that we must look to find the antecedent of the 'Fergus' mentioned in York's 'Funeral' pageant.

A record of the ousting of Fergus of Galloway from power comes to us through the *Vita Aelredi*, a hagiographical account of the life of Aelred of Rievaulx written shortly after his death in 1167 by the abbot's fellow Cistercian and friend Walter Daniel:

> the father went down to Galloway to visit and comfort a daughter-house of Rievaulx. There he found the petty king of that land incensed against his sons, and the sons raging against their father and each other. It is a wild country where the inhabitants are like beasts, and is altogether barbarous ... There chastity founders as often as lust wills, and the pure is only so far removed from the harlot that the more chaste will change their husbands every month, and a man will sell his wife for a heifer ...
>
> As I have said, our father on a visit to the place found the princes of the province quarrelling amongst themselves. The King of Scotland could not subdue, nor the bishop pacify, their mutual hatreds, rancour, and tyranny. Sons were against father, father against sons, brother against

10. Daphne Brooke *Wild Men and Holy Places: St Ninian, Whithorn and the Medieval Realm of Galloway* (Edinburgh: Canongate Press, 1994) 79.
11. Richard D. Oram 'Fergus, Galloway and the Scots' in *Galloway: Land and Lordship* edited Richard D. Oram and Geoffrey Stell (Edinburgh: Scottish Society for Northern Studies, 1991) 121.
12. See Hector L. MacQueen 'The Laws of Galloway: A Preliminary Survey' in *Galloway: Land and Lordship* 131–43.

> brother, daily polluting the unhappy little land with bloodshed. Aelred the peacemaker met with them all … He eagerly urged their veteran sire to put on a monastic habit and by his marvellous admonishment bent him to that course, and taught him – who had taken the life of thousands – to become a partaker of the life eternal, to such effect that he ended his days in a monastery of religious brethren … His sons, holding their father in great veneration, live together to this day in peace and tranquillity …[13]

Daniel's inclusion of this trip to Galloway in Aelred's *Vita* is fairly easy to understand. Galloway is presented as a land ripe for religious and political reform, showcasing the prospective saint's skills both as a temporal diplomat and an evangelising peacemaker. In this 'wild country where the inhabitants are like beasts' barbarity reigned, bereft of civilisation and godliness. The people of the region are defined by their brutishness as well as their carnality – something highlighted by references to their sexual deviance, and their habitation of a landscape polluted by blood. Aelred restores the land to God, with both the 'petty king' and his sons transformed by the abbot's 'marvellous admonishment'. Aelred reforms the land and turns the barbarous Fergus into a pious monk, seeking Christ's redemption.[14]

There are suggestions that Aelred had a particular interest in Galloway. Among his writings, he is thought to have authored the twelfth-century *Vita Niniani*, written in celebration of the early saint who had reformed the vicious Picts of Galloway, and established the ancient bishopric of Candida Casa, or Whithorn, there. Aelred held a particular devotion to the early northern saints, Ninian among them. He likely wrote the hagiographical text especially for Christian, Bishop of Whithorn, and included miracle stories in the text which were intended to press Fergus of Galloway into further spiritual and political reform of his land.[15] In this account of Aelred's visit to Galloway, written some years later, Walter Daniel is clearly trying to align his former abbot with the

13. Walter Daniel *The Life of Ailred of Rievaulx* translated F.M. Powicke (London: Nelson, 1950) 45–6; the 'daughter-house' of Rievaulx mentioned is Dundrennan.
14. For comments on the Cistercian and Augustinian forays into Galloway, see William Aird '"Sweet Civility and Barbarous Rudeness": A View from the Frontier. Abbot Ailred of Rievaulx and the Scots' in *Imagining Frontiers, Contesting Identities* edited Steven G. Ellis and Lud'a Klusáková (Pisa UP, 2007) 59–75.
15. Jean Truax *Aelred the Peacemaker: The Public Life of a Cistercian Abbot* (Collegeville, Minnesota: Liturgical Press, 2017) 159–60.

saintly Ninian. Indeed, his story is certainly at least partly fictionalised, as it does not mention the influence of Scottish military forces on Fergus' choice to retire to the cloister, clearly outlined in the *Chronicle of Holyrood* – a text which, further, makes no reference to Aelred's involvement or even his presence at the conflict.[16]

But the form of Aelred's activities in Galloway makes an interesting analogue to the Funeral of the Virgin narrative. Fergus, a barbarous king matched by two barbarous princes, raises discord typified by ungodly savagery in a once-sacred land, just as the three Jews rail against the reverent scene of the Virgin's burial. Fergus and Galloway suffer from the familial rift raised by civil war: the body politic is dismembered and beaten just as the Jewish prince is bluntly disjointed, his hand adhering to the funeral bier and his associates blinded. Only when the 'petty king' turns to Christ is proper order restored in the country of Galloway: unity reinstated through the force of the divine.

In his comments on the 'Funeral', Richard Beadle points out that the beating of Fergus while he dangles from the funeral bier is an innovation of the York pageant on the 'Funeral' narrative.[17] Alongside the specific name given to the Jewish prince, the beating of Fergus – an aggression which I suggest was committed by the blinded princes, rather than the solemn apostles – establishes a possible analogue with the strife of the Galwegian civil war, where 'Sons were against father, father against sons'. To read Aelred as an apostle of Christ with particular care for the Virgin is easy, considering the special dedication of the Cistercian Order to Marian devotion.[18]

Walter Daniel's narrative of Aelred's trip to Galloway presents us with a hazy analogue for the content of the York 'Funeral'. But to provide evidence for the real connection of this account from the *Vita Aelredi* to a performance of the fifteenth century, we must look to the chronicles and written sources via which this story and its characters were mediated through the high to the late medieval period.

16. Anon 'The Chronicle of Holyrood' in *Church Historians of England* translated and edited Joseph Stevenson (London: Seeleys, 1856) *4: 1* 747.

17. Beadle *York Plays 2* 424–5.

18. Emilia Jamroziak *The Cistercian Order in Medieval Europe: 1090–1500* (Abingdon: Routledge, 2013) 174–5.

The Battle of the Standard and the Galwegian Peril

The account of Aelred's trip to Galloway, written by Daniel around 1167, was informed by other contemporary discourses surrounding the Galwegians during this period, not least the writings of the abbot himself. Extended references to the savage and barbarous men of Galloway begin shortly after events of the late 1130s, when the Galwegians played a prominent role in the Scottish military incursions of David I into northern England during the tumultuous reign of Stephen. The Galwegians are often defined as a group distinct from the body of the Scots, who supposedly cause trouble and threaten the martial endeavour of their fair-weather allies.[19] From 1137 David's forces ravaged the north-east of England, slaughtering thousands and wreaking general destruction in Northumberland, County Durham, and Yorkshire. The turning point of the campaign was the famed English victory near the town of Northallerton in 1138, located between York and Durham and referred to as the Battle of the Standard.

Various accounts of the Battle of the Standard circulated in the high medieval period, mutually inspiring and informing each other.[20] But two of the most influential (and possibly earliest) appear to have been the writings of the Augustinian prior Richard of Hexham, whose institution was positioned just below the Scottish border, and Aelred of Rievaulx, whose Cistercian house lay only twenty miles from the battlefield.[21] Links between the Augustinians and the Cistercians were well-established by the middle of the twelfth century, and continued into the succeeding centuries. Importantly, both orders took a keen interest in the writing, copying, and transmission of local histories between their institutions, offering us a tangible link between these monastic authors and the producers of the 'Funeral' pageant.[22]

19. The Galwegians are blamed for attacking the church of St Michael at Hexham against David's orders, and for almost derailing the Scottish army because of an argument over a woman in Durham; Richard of Hexham *De Gestis Regis Stephani et de Bello Standardii* in *Chronicles of the Reigns of Stephen, Henry II, and Richard I* edited Richard Howlett, 4 vols (Rolls Series 82; London: Longman, 1884–89) 3 (1886) 154.

20. On their mutuality, see Matthew Strickland *War and Chivalry: The Conduct and Perception of War in England and Normandy, 1066–1217* (Cambridge UP, 1996) 295.

21. Oram also includes Roger of Howden as an influential, if slightly later, source on the Battle of the Standard: see Richard Oram 'The Mythical Pict and the Monastic Pedant: The Origin of the Legend of the Galloway Picts' *Pictish Arts Society Journal* 4 (1993) 14–27.

22. Jamroziak *The Cistercian Order* 223–4.

Richard of Hexham's *De Gestis Regis Stephani et de Bello Standardii*, written shortly after 1140, seems to have influenced Aelred's own *Relatio de Standardo*, which is dated around 1156.[23] They differ in their form, Richard adopting a matter-of-fact documentary style, and Aelred offering what we must regard as a semi-fictionalised record, putting speeches into the mouths of prominent participants in the battle, many of whom were patrons of Rievaulx. But both accounts share a focus on the men of Galloway, distinguished from the rest of the Scottish troops for their savagery. Both men were allies of David, and sought to minimise the responsibility attached to him for the atrocities committed by the Scots-led army, blaming the Galwegian forces instead.[24] To do this, they represent the men of Galloway as barbarous, irreligious, and faintly comic figures – characteristics which align well with what we know of the nature of the York 'Funeral' pageant's own Galwegian, Fergus.

Recounting the savagery of the 1130s campaign, Richard's account speaks of Galwegian forces tearing through Northumberland and County Durham on a bloody rampage, 'sparing no rank, no age, no sex, no condition' from their massacre, and taking matrons and virgins into slavery.[25] He notes the oath of protection sworn by David I to the church of Hexham and its properties, broken by two blundering Galwegians who pillage the altar of St Michael near Hexham, shattering crucifixes and slaughtering clergy and children, only to meet with divine retribution for their deeds.[26] Notable here is not only the purported barbarism of the men of Galloway, but their apparent godlessness; more than savage enemies, in his text and Aelred's the Galwegians – with their long history of Christian worship, under Ninian – become heathens.

This characterisation is informed by the attempt of English forces to frame their repelling of the Scots, both subsequently and at the time, as a form of crusade. Aelred repeatedly asserts that the military action was 'in the defence

23. See Antonia Gransden *Historical Writing in England c.500 to c.1307* (London: Routledge, 1996) 181–5; Truax *Aelred the Peacemaker* 142–3, and Elizabeth Freeman 'Aelred as a Historian among Historians' in *A Companion to Aelred of Rievaulx (1110–1167)* edited Marsha L. Dutton (Leiden: Brill, 2017) 114.

24. Oram 'The Mythical Pict' 22–4. Also Brooke *Wild Men and Holy Places* 99, and Strickland *War and Chivalry* 293–6.

25. Richard of Hexham *De Gestis Regis Stephani* in *Chronicles* edited Howlett 3 152–3.

26. Richard of Hexham *De Gestis Regis Stephani* in *Chronicles* edited Howlett 3 154.

of the Church of Christ against the barbarians'.[27] Archbishop Thurstan of York instigated the Battle of the Standard, and choreographed its iconography: Radulph, Bishop of the Orkneys, carried the 'Standard' into the fray, mounted with a Holy Pyx, alongside the banners of the patron saints of York, Beverley, and Ripon.[28] The forces serving under David are ostensibly the focus of this holy war, but it is chiefly the Galwegians who were presented in these texts as ungodly 'Others'. To this end, both Richard and Aelred also use the label 'Picts' to describe the men of Galloway, a race previously used by Bede to identify the unruly residents of western Scotland, converted to Christianity by Ninian. In describing them as 'Picts', both chroniclers stress the ancient estrangement of Galloway from the rest of Christian civilisation, and the nature of Galwegians as savage outsiders.[29]

The relevance of this discussion of the Galwegians to the York 'Funeral' comes in the small leap which is made to align these outsiders from Galloway with contemporary figures of 'Otherness', the Jews. Anti-Semitic narratives of 'blood libel' became increasingly popular throughout twelfth and thirteenth century England, with stories of supposed child-martyrs such as William of Norwich or Little Hugh of Lincoln.[30] Richard and Aelred direct these same accusations towards the soldiers of Galloway, a heathen army distinct both from the pious English and the Scots, whose leader they had apparently led astray. Both men talk of the Galwegian soldiers slaughtering a 'multitude of children' before drinking their blood, Aelred describing men who 'satisfied their thirst with the cruel cup', 'calling themselves happy … [that] they could drink the blood of the Gauls'.[31]

27. See Aird '"Sweet Civility"' in *Imagining Frontiers* 63–6; quotation taken from *Aelred of Rievaulx: The Historical Works*, translated Jane Patricia Freeland, edited Marsha L. Dutton (Kalamazoo: Cistercian Publications, 2005) 248.

28. For uses of Aelred's narrative, see Marianne Garrity '"Hidden Honey": The Many Meanings of Aelred of Rievaulx's *De bello standardi*' *Cistercian Studies Quarterly* 44: 1 (2009) 57–64.

29. See Gransden *Historical Writing in England* 175; also Oram 'The Mythical Pict' 14–20.

30. See Anthony Bale 'Fictions of Judaism in England before 1290' in *The Jews in Medieval England: Historical, Literary and Archeological Sources* edited Patricia Skinner (Woodbridge: Boydell, 2003) 130–1; also Alan Dundes 'The Ritual Murder or Blood Libel Legend: A Study of Anti-Semitic Victimization through Projective Inversion', in *The Blood Libel Legend: A Casebook in Anti-Semitic Folklore* (Madison: University of Wisconsin Press, 1991) 336–78.

31. Richard of Hexham 'Chronicles' in *Church Historians of England* 43; Speech of Walter Espec in *Ailred of Rievaulx: Historical Works* 255. 'Gauls' here likely refers to the contemporary Galwegian understanding of the English as Anglo-Normans.

Attacks particularly on children, pregnant women, and unborn babes in these accounts accentuate the idea of innocence desecrated by barbarity, and it is easy to find parallels within the contemporary child-martyr narratives featuring villainous Jewish figures. Like the Jews, Galwegians were reputed to hold law, customs, and rituals mysterious and threatening to Christian society. Indeed, the people of Galloway did hold unique laws and customs alien to the English, reflecting their estrangement from Anglo-Norman culture.[32] But as in contemporary representations of the Jews, the 'Otherness' of the men of Galloway was also ridiculed, and made comic.

Aelred's text mocks the Galwegians for their convention of entering into battle naked, their savagery transmuted into comic carnality, exhorting the reader to 'laugh rather than fear' the soldier who runs into the fray with 'nearly bare buttocks'.[33] The bodies of the Galwegians become comic objects of mockery, the painful acts committed on them treated with humorous rhetoric. Aelred compares the bodies of Galwegian soldiers shot with arrows to hedgehogs, while Richard relishes the statement that some were 'slain immediately' and the rest 'disgracefully fled'.[34] In the York 'Funeral', we see Fergus suffer bodily pain, turned to slapstick in both his beating and the adhesion of his arm to the Virgin's bier, a treatment as applicable to Galwegians, in these histories, as to the Jews.

The Battle of the Standard, mediated through the writings of Richard and Aelred, was passed down through the following centuries, and as Richard Oram notes, spread the idea of Galloway as a barbaric and inhospitable region widely through Cistercian and Augustinian houses as far as continental Europe.[35] But the battle held particular importance in the history of the north-east of England, both due to its significance as a local military victory framed as a holy war, and

32. MacQueen 'Laws of Galloway' 131–43. This legal code was often regarded as alien by contemporary Scots and English, including the flexible marital customs mocked by Walter Daniel in the passage above: it persisted until the end of the sixteenth century in Galloway.

33. *Aelred of Rievaulx: Historical Works* 253. Also see Ronan Toolis '"Naked and Unarmored": A Reassessment of the Role of the Glaswegians at the Battle of the Standard' *Transactions of the Dumfriesshire and Galloway Natural History and Antiquarian Society* 78 (2004) 79–92.

34. *Aelred of Rievaulx: Historical Works* 266; Richard of Hexham 'Chronicles' in *Church Historians of England* 50.

35. Oram 'The Mythical Pict' 24.

because of the influence of Richard and Aelred's work in shaping northern history writing more broadly.[36] In the north Aelred's *Relatio* continued to be copied widely, especially among the Cistercian institutions in Yorkshire. These religious houses held a vested interest in preserving and circulating accounts of local history pertinent to their interests, especially those involving their illustrious and influential leaders.[37] Through the copying of these accounts, stories of the savagery of the men of Galloway continued to circulate.

An early-fifteenth-century catalogue of the library at Meaux, in the East Riding of Yorkshire, records ownership of a copy of the *Relatio*, alongside many other works by Aelred. This copy was used by the abbot Thomas Burton when he wrote the chronicle of the abbey in the late fourteenth or early fifteenth century, looking back to the early history of his institution. Burton combines passages from Aelred's *Relatio* with Henry of Huntingdon's *Historia Anglorum* in his account of the Battle of the Standard, and importantly makes reference not just to the Scottish enemy, but also the Galwegians.[38]

Resonances of the Galwegians as a savage and ungodly force inspired by Aelred's writing on the Battle of the Standard influenced works on other themes. The metrical chronicle of Peter Langtoft of Bridlington, an Augustinian canon writing between 1297 and 1307, speaks of the wretched people of Scotland and Galloway (*D'Escoz e de Galewaye le popel maluré*) fighting the English at Falkirk

36. See Helen M. Jewell 'The North–South Divide: The Origins of Northern Consciousness in England' (Manchester UP, 1994) 40–2; for the continued growth of the Cistercians in the North see Michael Carter '"It would have pitied any heart to see": Destruction and Survival at Cistercian Monasteries in Northern England at the Dissolution' *Journal of the British Archaeological Association 168: 1* (2015) 77–110, at 79.

37. Jamroziak *Cistercian Order* 223–4; copies of Aelred's *Relatio* circulated through the monastic institutions of Rievaulx, Sawley, Meaux, and Kirkham in Yorkshire, as well as copies in York and Durham, into the sixteenth century: Elizabeth Freeman 'Aelred of Rievaulx's *De Bello Standardii*: Cistercian Historiography and the Creation of Community Memories' *Cîteaux 49: 1* (1998) 22–7.

38. Freeman 'Aelred as a Historian' 142; see Thomas Burton *Chronica Monasterii de Melsa* edited Edward A. Bond, 3 vols (Rolls Series 43; London: Longmans, Green, Reader, and Dyer, 1866–68) *1* 122: *Dum autem acies Scottorum Loevensium, qui gloriam primi ictus postpositis Galwensibus a rege Scottorum invito proripuerunt* ... The catalogue of the library lists the presence of various works by Aelred including *Alredus de Standardo, [Vita] Edwardi Regis, Laus David regis Scotiae* and *Alredus in institutione reclusae*; *Chronica Monasterii de Melsa* (1868) *3* xcix, xcvi, xciv.

in 1298, clearing marking a distinction between nations.[39] Langtoft's awareness of the men of Galloway and their textual reputation was likely drawn from the *Relatio* or other works influenced by Aelred and Richard, even though his brief account of the Battle of the Standard does not necessarily reference them.[40] The way both Burton and Langtoft make specific reference to Galwegians as a separate people from the Scots is indicative of their reliance on these older texts, as by the late thirteenth century the region of Galloway had been fully absorbed into the body of Scotland.

Having established the continued representation of Galwegians as savages distinct from the Scots, specifically in Yorkshire in the fourteenth and fifteenth centuries, it is also pertinent to demonstrate the continued association of Galloway with the name 'Fergus'. In the *Vita Aelredi* Walter Daniel does not mention the ruler of Galloway by name, and neither do any of the accounts of the Battle of the Standard – though Richard of Hexham does mention that a son of Fergus was taken as security by the English in the terms surrender.[41] But the name 'Fergus' lived on past his death in the chronicles, chiefly through accounts of the associated savagery of his sons, Gilbert and Uchtred. Writing around 1192, Roger of Howden records a visit to Galloway he had made in 1174, an attempt to establish diplomatic ties between the region and the English Crown which was unsettled by continued civil war in the region – the same conflict which Aelred had supposedly quashed.

Importantly, even though Fergus is no longer physically present, he is repeatedly made reference to as dynastic head of the Galwegians. Referring to the dispute taking place between *Hutredus et Gillebertus filii Ferregus* the rulers of *Galwalenses* or Galloway, Roger also tells of the savagery of *Malculumb, filius Gilleberti filii Fergus*, who had his uncle butchered, his eyes, tongue, and testicles

39. *The Chronicle of Pierre de Langtoft, in French verse, from the earliest period to the death of King Edward I* edited Thomas Wright, 2 vols (Rolls Series 47; London: Longmans, Green, Reader, and Dyer, 1866 and 1868) 2 312–13.

40. *Chronicle of Pierre de Langtoft 1* 479. His description of the battle seems to rely heavily on Aelred's, marked out by the special attention he gives to Walter Espec (as in the *Relatio*) and the speech of Robert de Brus. Whether or not Peter Langtoft refers to the participation of the Galwegians is somewhat ambiguous, as in the published version of his text Bishop Radulph cries out '*Tuez les Escoz, defolez les Walays!*'. As the Welsh had no part in this battle, it is likely that he was referring to the Galwegians.

41. He is referred to as *filium Fergusi comitis* by Richard of Hexham *De Gestis Regis Stephani* in *Chronicles* edited Howlett 3 178.

removed.[42] In a later work, the same writer talks of the renewed submission of Galloway to Scotland in 1186, this time in reference to a different dispute between *Rollandum, filium Uchtredi filii Fergus* and *Dunecano filio Gilberti filii Fergus*.[43] Clearly the name 'Fergus' was still predominantly associated with Galloway at this time, and in subsequent annals we see the mid-twelfth-century ruler continually marked out as the patriarchal head of the apparently dysfunctional and savage Galwegian nation.

Writing at a similar time, William of Newburgh, an Augustinian canon of Bridlington with known links to Rievaulx, also records this episode, but in language more similar to that used in Daniel's *Vita Aelredi*.[44] Like Roger, in his *Historia Rerum Anglicarum* William talks of Uchtred as being 'tormented by tortures' (*excruciatum suppliciis*), and of the savagery of the people, but also of the impact of this on the land, and the divine retribution which this bloodshed represented. He refers to Uchtred and Gilbert as *Hi nimirum Fergusi* ('those [people], without doubt, of Fergus'), consciously associating this episode with Aelred's trip to Galloway.[45] Evidence that this account of barbarity, and of Fergus' role as paterfamilias, was in circulation in Yorkshire into the fifteenth century can be found in the *Chronicle of Jervaulx*, which copies much of William's material, repeating references to Fergus as well as association with the blood and barbarism of civil war in Galloway. The inclusion of this text for publication by the early antiquarian Roger Twysden in 1652 may further denote its broader circulation.[46]

In a tangible historical sense, Fergus was well remembered in Scotland as a dynastic progenitor – of Alan of Galloway, and ultimately John Balliol – and as a religious benefactor.[47] But his name also passed into literary usage as

42. *Chronica Magistri Rogeri de Houedene* edited William Stubbs, 4 vols (Rolls Series 51; London: Longmans, Green, 1868–71) *2* (1869) 79–80.
43. *Chronica Rogeri de Houedene* edited Stubbs *2* 309.
44. Freeman 'Aelred as a Historian' 142.
45. William of Newburgh in *Chronicles of the Reigns of Stephen, Henry II, and Richard I* 186–7.
46. John of Brompton in *Historiae Anglicanae Scriptores X* edited Roger Twysden (London: Cornelius Bee, 1652) cols 720–1284, at cols 1105, 1116, and especially 1092–3. No modern edition of this manuscript has been made. The text is displayed in two numbered columns per page.
47. Andrew McDonald 'Scoto-Norse Kings and the Reformed Religious Orders: Patterns of Monastic Patronage in Twelfth-Century Galloway and Argyll' *Albion: A Quarterly Journal Concerned with British Studies 27: 2* (1995) 187–219, at 192 and 195.

a representative of Galloway, fictionalised as a knightly protagonist in the Old French *Roman de Fergus*, as well as the Middle Dutch *Ferguut*, which survives in multiple manuscripts from the mid-to-late thirteenth century.[48] It is likely that in northern England the name Fergus became a byword for the region of Galloway, but also for the Galwegians, and the savagery by which they were known in the area, mediated through local histories of the Battle of the Standard.

Coming back to the account of Aelred's visit to Galloway at the beginning of this argument, we might find in this episode – and certainly the way it was recounted after the twelfth century – a central legend which tied together both the savagery of the Galwegians, and their defeat (analogous to reform) through divine mediation. While Fergus represented the savagery of Galloway, as a local saint Aelred perhaps signified the spiritual potency of the region. It appears that Aelred continued to be a popular northern saint until at least the Reformation, and that his 'taming' of Fergus, or Galloway, was a well-known story. Although few manuscripts of the *Vita Aelredi* survive, passages of the hagiography were certainly in circulation through the twelfth and thirteenth centuries, and clearly influenced a popular mid-fourteenth-century work called the *Sanctilogium Angliae Walliae Scotiae et Hiberniae* attributed to John of Tynemouth (sometimes named John of York).[49]

The *Sanctilogium*, for a long time associated with John Capgrave, went on to be printed by Wynkyn de Worde in 1515 and achieved wide circulation under the title *De Nova Legenda Anglie*.[50] Importantly, the abridgement of Daniel's *Vita* retains the story of Aelred's trip to Galloway, recounting the abbot's special efforts and saintly prowess in dealing with the barbarous Galwegians.[51] Cutting

48. See Thomas Clancy 'Scottish Literatures Before Scottish Literature' in *The Cambridge Companion to Scottish Literature* edited Gerald Carruthers and Liam McIlvanney (Cambridge UP, 2012) 13–26; Guillaume le Clerc *Fergus of Galloway* translated D.D.R. Owen (London: Dent, 1991); *Dutch Romances: 2: Ferguut* edited and translated David F. Johnson and Geert H.M. Claassens (Cambridge: D.S. Brewer, 2000). The knightly Fergus is sometimes regarded as a parodic rendering of Perceval.

49. Various manuscript versions of this work survive in the north of England, and copies are known to have been made at both Durham Cathedral and York Minster. See John Block Friedman *Northern English Books, Owners and Makers in the Late Middle Ages* (Syracuse, NY: Syracuse UP, 1995) 91–2.

50. Mary Beth Long 'Corpora and Manuscripts, Authors and Audiences' in *A Companion to Middle English Hagiography* edited Sarah Salih (Cambridge: D.S. Brewer, 2006) 62.

51. *Descendens in Galwediam Alredus, inuenit regulum terre illius contra filios suos iratum, filios in patrem seuientes, et in se inuicem fratres*; *Nova Legenda Anglie: As collected by John of*

out large chunks of the *Vita Aelredi*, the printed text is perhaps most interesting in this context for the editorial decisions it represents. The work likely stripped Daniel's narrative down to hagiographical incidents perceived to be most essential to the abbot's story, and Aelred's actions in Galloway were clearly deemed important (or popular) enough to remain.

Similarly the story is also included in the *Kalendre of the New Legende of Englande*, produced by Robert Pynson in 1516. This is the only printed translation of the collected saints' lives from Latin into the vernacular, and an even further abridgement of the *Sanctilogium*: it is known as the last English hagiographical collection to be printed before the Reformation.[52] The *Kalendre* offers extremely brief summations of saints' lives, and here Aelred's trip to Galloway takes up only half a line of text, but the inclusion of the episode goes some way to demonstrate the importance of the narrative – especially as it is placed alongside a reference to the abbot's wildly popular work on the life of King Edward the Confessor, of which numerous copies survive:

> And he refourmyd the hole cou<u>n</u>trey of gallway/ and wrote the lyfe of Seynt Edwarde kynge and consellore and dyd many other thynges ...[53]

Although both Wynkyn de Worde and Pynson printed in London, we might assume that the story of the Cistercian abbot and the Galwegians still held wider fame in the north, where texts associated with Aelred remained popular.[54] Ultimately, the story of Aelred's intervention in Galloway was wide-reaching, and became a key feature of the saint's life. The suggestion that the story of Aelred's reform of Galloway, characterised by the 'taming' of Fergus in particular, was a fairly popular narrative by this point in the early sixteenth century gives further credence to my central hypothesis; that the details of this narrative were well known at this point in the fifteenth century makes it possible for them to be aligned with content of the 'Funeral' pageant in York.

Tynemouth, John Capgrave, and others, and first printed, with New Lives, by Wynkyn de Worde, AD. MDXVI edited Carl Horstman, 2 vols (Oxford: Clarendon Press, 1901) *1* 43; see also *Nova Legenda Anglie* (London: Wynkyn de Worde, 1516) at *Early English Books Online* (accessed 1 August 2017).

52. *Nova Legenda Anglie 1* 43.

53. *Kalendre of the newe legende of Englande* (London: Robert Pynson, 1516) at *Early English Books Online* (accessed 1 August 2017) image 13 of 162.

54. See Friedman *Northern English Books* 91–2.

Layering narratives, amalgamating characters

Interestingly, the only other reference to 'Fergus' being used as shorthand for the Jewish ringleader of the 'Funeral' narrative comes from the *Northern Homily Cycle*, where the name appears not in the text itself, but rather as a label above it.[55] To be precise, it seems that the phrase *Fergus conuersus & baptizatus est* appears only in the expanded versions of the text, and more specifically the two manuscript versions written in a northern dialect, BL Harley 4196, and BL Cotton Tiberius E.VII, both of which are dated to the early fifteenth century, and further, their origins are placed with the Augustinian canons of York or Yorkshire.[56] Thus use of the name 'Fergus' in these manuscripts to denote the Jewish antagonist of the 'Funeral' was likely made both at roughly the same time as the reference in the *Ordo paginarum*, and in at least a proximate locale.

As has been demonstrated, records of the Galwegians as savage aggressors in the north-east, tied particularly to Aelred, were largely passed into the later medieval period through the works (and in the libraries) of the Yorkshire Cistercians and Augustinians. While the Cistercian Order remained at least ostensibly aloof from communications with the laity, the Augustinians (or Austins), whether canons or friars, had the capacity to spread these narratives of Galwegian savagery into the wider urban communities of the north.

Alexandra Johnston has argued persuasively that the Austin Friary at York played an influential role in the content of the city's Corpus Christi Cycle, through their library and through their interactions with the laity.[57] Given that it was likely the York Austins who included the name *Fergus* in the *Northern Homily Cycle*, this institution might provide further evidence for the bringing

55. Beadle *York Plays 2* 424–5.

56. See James H. Morey *Book and Verse: A Guide to Middle English Biblical Literature* (Chicago: University of Illinois Press, 2000) 323–30. The most accessible version of the *Northern Homily Cycle* is the edited edition made by Horstman, who fortunately uses BL MS Harley 4196 and BL MS Cotton Tiberius E VII as his base-texts. See *Altenglische Legenden: Neue Folge. Mit Einleitung und Anmerkungen* edited Carl Horstmann (Heilbronn: Henniger, 1881) 117 line 418.

57. Alexandra Johnston 'The World Made Flesh: Augustinian Elements in the York Cycle' in *The Centre and Its Compass: Studies in Medieval Literature in Honour of Professor John Leyerle* edited Robert A. Taylor (Kalamazoo: Medieval Institute Publications, 1993) 225–46; also Johnston 'The York Cycle and the Libraries of York' in *The Church and Learning in Later Medieval Society: Essays in Honour of R.B. Dobson* edited Caroline Barron and Jenny Stratford (Harlaxton Medieval Studies 11; Donington: Shaun Tyas, 2002) 355–70.

together of the story of Aelred's reform of Fergus with the 'Funeral' narrative in the city – though, as Beadle remarks, whether the performance influenced the written narrative, or vice versa, is difficult to assess.[58]

From the point at which the antagonist of the York 'Funeral' is referred to as 'Fergus', we might also assume that a layering of narratives was occurring through which the story of Aelred and the Galwegians was attached to the performance of the Virgin's burial. On one side, Fergus, representing the Galwegians, for so long styled in northern chronicles as akin to Jews, played the part of the heathen prince unsettling the bier. On the other stood Aelred, representing both localised spiritual authority and Cistercian devotion to the Virgin Mary, played the apostle pall-bearer who defeats and reforms Fergus' sinful ways.

Beyond other dramatic renderings of the same narrative – notably in N. Town and the Bourges Cycle – Marian miracle stories with Jewish antagonists were popular throughout the later Middle Ages, well into the fifteenth and sixteenth centuries.[59] Butterworth has already grouped these narratives together, alongside other works such as the *Croxton Play of the Sacrament*, collectively characterised by the portrayal of Jews as particularly carnal villains, often comically suffering disembodiment, mutilation, or blindness as a result of their spiritual transgressions.[60] But to go further, Denise L. Despres and Jeffrey J. Cohen have both argued that the popularity of these accounts was often vested in their historicity: the stories offer the ability to recall specific historical moments, drawing on the tangible past of a community, and so strengthening its identity.[61]

In these stories Jews did not only represent forces of 'alterity' or 'Otherness' in English society, but rather a 'necessary element in the devotional world of the late medieval laity', which utilised the memory of these figures to establish corporate identities.[62] In York, the use of 'Fergus' in the 'Funeral' pageant demonstrates an attempt to give the pseudo-biblical story a certain tangibility

58. Beadle *York Plays 2* 425 note 775.

59. See Sylvia Tomasch 'Postcolonial Chaucer and the Virtual Jew' in *The Postcolonial Middle Ages* edited J.J. Cohen (Basingstoke: Palgrave Macmillan, 2000) 243–60.

60. Butterworth 'Substitution: Theatrical Sleight of Hand' 209–30.

61. Denise L. Despres 'The Immaculate Flesh and the Social Body: Mary and the Jews' *Jewish History 12: 1* (1998) 47–69; Jeffrey Jerome Cohen 'The Flow of Blood in Medieval Norwich' *Speculum 79: 1* (2004) 26–65.

62. Despres 'Immaculate Flesh', especially 56–62; Cohen 'Flow of Blood' 29–30, 65.

and local relevance. We might read the York 'Funeral' and its use of the character 'Fergus' as featuring the transposition of a local historical narrative onto the universal history of the world which the Cycle ultimately represented. Yoking a temporal enemy to a more abstract and universalised 'Other' likely offered a means to create and propagate a story of specifically local Jewish antagonism: a Marian miracle of anti-Semitic conquest which the people of York could claim for their own.

A very similar and contemporaneous example of the appropriation of the 'Funeral' narrative as a means to frame a localised secular enemy exists within the stained glass of St Peter Mancroft church in Norwich. Here two panels survive from the mid fifteenth century depicting the Funeral of the Virgin Mary, donated by the wealthy local mercer Robert Toppes. In this scene the Jewish antagonist is portrayed as a knightly figure, and intriguingly the arms are identifiable as those of William de la Pole, Duke of Suffolk, a local magnate and agent of the Crown.[63] Suffolk was the object of local animosity for various reasons, not least for his interference in civic affairs, and the reputed lawlessness of his retainers in Norwich, and East Anglia more broadly.[64]

Toppes himself was exiled as a result of Suffolk's arbitrations in Norwich, but later, after a reform of the civic government, returned to become mayor around the time the window was created. Suffolk on the other hand, having previously been criticised for his regime of disorder and injustice in the locality, as well as his role in the loss of English territory in France, was imprisoned as a traitor by 1450, and soon after executed by enemies while fleeing to the continent.

A surprising number of parallels can be drawn between the attributes afforded to Fergus of Galloway and William de la Pole in these accounts. Both men had been powerful magnates; they were known for the savagery of their associates, and for the lawlessness spread by them; they were 'reformed' and vanquished, only to die soon after their fall from power, to be reconciled with God. It is difficult not to see Toppes' window as a means to inscribe the

63. See David King *The Medieval Stained Glass of St Peter Mancroft, Norwich* (Corpus Vitrearum Medii Ævi 5; Oxford UP for the British Academy, 2006), clxxxvi–clxxxvii and 74.

64. Lorraine Attreed 'The Politics of Welcome: Ceremonies and Constitutional Development in Later Medieval English Towns' in *City and Spectacle in Medieval Europe* edited Barbara A. Hanawalt and Kathryn L. Reyerson (Minneapolis: University of Minnesota Press, 1994) 215; John Marshall '"Fortune in Worldys Worschyppe": The Satirizing of the Suffolks in *Wisdom*' *METh 14* (1992) 37–66; King *St Peter Mancroft* liii–liv.

narrative of Suffolk's local wrongdoing and defeat into the memorialising space of his parish church, through the story of the Virgin's funeral. As with Fergus in the 'Funeral' pageant, the memory of local enemy Suffolk is amalgamated with the narrative of the Jewish aggressor, in an attempt to influence the audience's reading of both figures. The universalised antagonist is melded together with a figure of enmity pertinent to the interests of a certain locality, inscribing a specific version of a shared past onto the pseudo-biblical narrative as a means to strengthen a sense of community, by forming a collective memory.

But where Suffolk was an enemy of the recent past, whose association with the 'Funeral' was inscribed in glass, at York memories of Fergus had been mediated through almost three centuries for spectators, and attached to the Jewish prince through the far less rigid medium of performance. At the time of the window's creation William de la Pole, Duke of Suffolk, was still a clearly defined figure of antagonism in Norwich, within living memory of many of those who experienced the glass. Fergus of Galloway, on the other hand, was a figure from the distant past at the time of the York Cycle's staging, making him a more slippery and indistinct 'Other'. The sense of shared identity and community which the use of 'Fergus' was intended to rouse clearly failed to some degree, if we are to believe the Mason's complaint. And this was likely because certain spectators were less clear in exactly who he was, or what he represented, than others.

Quarrels, disagreements, and fights

Essentially I have argued that the use of the name 'Fergus' in the York 'Funeral' represents not only the synthesis of figures spiritually conceived as fulfilling the role of the 'Other' – one of the Jewish people, and the other of the so-called 'Celtic Fringe' – but also an attempt to relay local narratives of earthly, historical conquest over a pseudo-biblical pageant, creating a homegrown miracle of Marian holiness. But how well this synthesis was actually received by audiences throughout the history of the pageant's performance remains unclear – though the supposed infrequency of staging may offer some answer to this. If this melding of narratives did represent an attempt to create a localised Marian miracle legend, why should it cause the friction and tension mentioned in the Mason's complaint, rather than a renewed sense of community cohesion against a foreign 'Other'?

As I have argued, the reason why the character 'Fergus' was used in the York 'Funeral' pageant was because the name represented a figure of Galwegian godlessness and savagery, tied to the past of the region. But while certain producers and spectators of the play likely have understood this association, others may have held different ideas of what 'Fergus' represented. And it is the multiplicity of associations held by the name in this period which may have made the position of the character as a reformed 'Other' deeply contentious. The idea that different spectators disagreed, argued, or fought for the precedence of their own interpretation of 'Fergus' offers an useful lens through which to read the response recorded in the Masons' complaint.

To some spectators 'Fergus' may have indeed represented a Scottish aggressor – suitable, perhaps, for portrayal as a fearsome 'Other'. Even if they appreciated the former distinction made between Galloway and Scotland, ultimately 'Fergus' could have represented a more generalised Caledonian aggressor. But even this view is complicated by the content of the pageant: if 'Fergus' was regarded as a Scot, would spectators in York have welcomed his reform and embraced his entry into the devotional community of the city at the end of the performance?

Considering the ongoing military action carried out over Scottish and English territory throughout the fourteenth and fifteenth centuries, perhaps a reformed Caledonian aggressor was not the best character to welcome onto the streets of York.[65] To complicate ideas of reception further, York, and more broadly Yorkshire, had a high Scottish immigrant population throughout the fifteenth century, who may have bristled at the portrayal of a savage Scottish caricature beaten on the streets.[66] The potential for tensions arising over this generalised Scoto-Galwegian Fergus, on both sides, would have surely been great.

But added to this, Fergus and Galloway had further long-held and complex associations with the north-east region, and with York in particular. Ironically through Ninian, the saint who Aelred had wished to emulate, the bishopric of Galloway was historically tied to the see of York, an ancient connection

65. Beadle points to points of 'marked hostility' towards Scots in the city during this period, and 'severe legislation' enacted against aliens in 1419 by the Corporation; Beadle *York Plays 2* 425.

66. The surnames of at least 14 Freemen recorded are associated with Scotland: see *Register of the Freemen of the City of York: Vol. 1, 1272–1558* edited Francis Collins *Surtees Society* 96 (1897); 927 resident Scots were assessed for Alien Subsidies in York and the three Ridings 1440–89, and of these 288 were householders; 55 were assessed in York alone: for data see the 'England's Medieval Immigrants Project', managed by the University of York at <https://www.englandsimmigrants.com> [accessed 10 March 2016].

which (again, ironically) was renewed during Fergus' reign in the mid twelfth century.[67] Although the English Church made various claims to supremacy over Scottish bishops well into the fifteenth century, various bishops of Galloway (or Whithorn) actually served as suffragans to York until the early fifteenth century, after which the association was cut.[68]

Bishop Oswald of Whithorn, a native of Galloway, was the last to serve as a suffragen of York and inhabited the north-east exclusively from the late 1390s to at least 1418, with records demonstrating that he carried out many duties in the parish churches of York itself.[69] So to complicate things even further, while some spectators may have interpreted the reform of 'Fergus' in the 'Funeral' as representing the ancient reform of Galloway by the Church of York, others may have felt aggrieved at seeing Galwegian figures – like poor Bishop Oswald, likely familiar to at least some audience members – depicted as Jewish antagonists. The performance may even have roused anger in some spectators due to York's very recent loss of influence over the Galwegian bishopric, the death of Oswald likely occurring little over a decade before the Masons' complaint was registered.

67. See Richard Oram 'The Medieval Bishops of Whithorn, their Cathedral and their Tombs' in *'Clothing for the Soul Divine': Burials at the Tomb of S. Ninian: Excavations at Whithorn Priory, 1957–1967* edited Christopher Lowe (Edinburgh: Historic Scotland, 2009) 131–44; Alan MacQuarrie *Medieval Scotland: Kingship and Nation* (Stroud: Alan Sutton, 2004) 110.

68. This ancient association is cited by John de Allhallowgate in references to both Ninian's founding of Whithorn, or *Candida Casa*, and the status of Galwegian bishops as suffragans of York: see 'Chronicon Metricum Ecclesiae Eboracensis' in *The Historians of the Church of York* edited James Raine, 3 vols (Rolls Series 71; London: Longman and HMSO [vol. 3], 1879–94) *2* (1886) 460–2; also Robert Brentano 'Whithorn and York' *Scottish Historical Review 32* (1953) 144–6.

69. Unfortunately for Oswald he was elected to Galloway just as the Great Schism occurred, and a rival pope supported by the Scottish Crown appointed a alternate prelate in his place. See Oram 'The Medieval Bishops of Whithorn' 141–2. Oswald ordained priests in various parish churches in York, and the last reference to his life comes when he was serving as master of Friarside Hospital, County Durham, in 1418. See *A Catalogue of the Register of Robert Waldby, Archbishop of York 1397* edited David Michael Smith (Borthwick Texts and Calendars 2; York: Borthwick Institute of Historical Research, 1974) 10–12, 37–43; R.N. Swanson *A Calendar of the Register of Richard Scrope, Archbishop of York 1398–1405* (York: Borthwick Institute of Historical Research, 1981) v–vi; *A History of the County of Durham* edited William Page, 3 vols (Victoria County History; London: Constable, 1905–28) *2* (1907) 123; Walter Skirlaw, Bishop of Durham, left Oswald a mitre and a prayer book in a testamentary bequest; *Testamenta Eboracensia Part 1* edited James Raine *Surtees Society* 4 (1836) 310.

This complex range of associations which Fergus and Galloway held for spectators in late medieval York is of course largely conjectural. But the multiplicity of possible responses to 'Fergus' in the 'Funeral' pageant – many of them overlapping or contradicting each other – seems to align well with the conflict and contention noted in the 1432 complaint. Whereas the abstract figure of the Jewish prince or priest, unsettling the Virgin Mary's bier, is an easily established 'Other', the attempted amalgamation of this character with a contentious figure of local history, Fergus, aroused more complicated and conflicting responses – especially in the context of the early fifteenth century. The failed attempt made in the 1470s to bring back the 'Funeral' pageant may attest to the popular potential that producers saw in the pageant, but also its problematic associations.[70] It is especially interesting that the pageant continued to be referred to as 'Fergus', suggesting that the melding of a localised historical enemy of York with the Marian miracle story had, at least, stuck.

The Masons' complaint still continues to raise more questions than answers. But as a rare record of audience response to a 'lost' performance, it allows us to consider the extremely broad range of popular associations and local narratives which likely shaped the York Cycle, beyond what we may now consider to be biblical or apocryphal texts. It demonstrates the way in which these pageants were not simply evocations of biblical stories to be passively consumed by audiences, but rather dynamic performances shaped and constructed through the mediation of producer and spectator alike. In these pageants, perhaps distinct from any alternate literary or visual narratives of the period, the 'Other' is a demonstrably malleable entity, formed by communal assent. The case of 'Fergus' demonstrates the tensions and potential for conflict inherent in the multiplicity of minds and voices which made up a medieval audience. And, of course, the capacity for such voices to raised more in noise and laughter than in devotion.

University of Durham

70. Beadle *York Plays 2* 426–8.

GEORGE GASCOIGNE AT OXFORD

James McBain

Anyone who has read the diary of Richard Madox, Elizabethan Fellow of All Souls College, Oxford, will know that he should probably not be valued as England's greatest theatre critic. On 22 February 1582, for example, he writes 'We went to the theatre to see a scurvie play set owt by one virgin which ther proved a fyemarten with owt voice so we stayd not the matter'.[1] *Fyemartin* here refers to a 'freemartin', which is a bovine term, used to describe a hermaphroditic calf.[2] Had Madox been more interested, we might have been able to identify the 'scurvie' performance that he had left, but it has sadly not proved possible so far.

We should be grateful that he was slightly more careful with his record of 8 January 1582, therefore. Madox, his brother, and their friends, Richard Lateware of St John's College and George Abbot of Balliol College, go out 'clubbing', a use of a term which incidentally predates the *OED*'s earliest identification of it by over fifty years.[3] Clubbing in early modern Oxford seemed to consist of wandering between colleges and greeting friends with improvised orations. Madox's party ultimately reach their destination for the evening, Trinity College, and he records the following, 'We supt at the presidents lodging and after had the Supposes handeled in the haul indifferently'.[4] We might speculate about the production's failings, but there is scholarly consensus that the play referred to here is George Gascoigne's *Supposes*, a translation of Ariosto's erudite comedy, *I Suppositi* (1509). We know from the text, first published in 1573, that the play premiered at Gray's Inn in 1566 and, with the subsequent edition of 1575, we also have a hint at its initial reception; Gascoigne modestly added a brief Latin note to confirm that the audience had applauded, *Et plauserunt*.[5]

1. Richard Madox *An Elizabethan in 1582: The Diary of Richard Madox* edited Elizabeth Story Donno (London: Hakluyt Society, 1976) 88.
2. *Oxford English Dictionary* sv *freemartin* n. 1.
3. *Oxford English Dictionary* sv *club* v. 4.
4. Madox *Diary of Richard Madox* 74.
5. George Gascoigne *Supposes* in *A Hundreth Sundrie Flowres* edited G.W. Pigman III (Oxford: Clarendon Press, 2000) 58.

Recent interest in the Inns of Court as a cultural context has helped to focus attention on both Gascoigne and the festive entertainments, such as the Revels at Gray's Inn, at which *Supposes* was first performed.[6] We know rather less about drama at Trinity College, Oxford, however, although what we do know is relevant to an erudite performance. In December 1555, for example, a number of members of the Privy Council wrote to the Master of the Revels with a request to borrow costumes for a 'learnyd Tragedye':

> Wheras the fellos and scholars of the newe College yn Oxford entende thys Chrystmas to sett foorth a learnyd Tragedye to the glorie of god and increase of learning & for the moore decent settynge foorth of the same have made sute hyther to boroe out of the Revells certayne sutes of apparel.[7]

Since Trinity had been founded in the same year, it seems quite likely that it was the college referred to here, rather than New College itself, which would suggest an ambition to establish a dramatic tradition immediately. In an audit-book of 1559, there is a record of payment for costumes and scenery for a performance of Terence's *Andria*, which is noted along with the expense of hosting the Heads of other colleges as part of the Christmas festivities for that year.[8] There was some sort of show produced on Trinity Sunday, 1564;[9] and then there were plays over the festive period of 1578/9, although we sadly lack details of what they were. As is often the case, we usually just have occasional records of exceptional expenses rather than direct references to particular performances; the 1578/9 record is not for any theatrical costs but rather for a payment to the stonemason 'working about the window in the hall at the time of the plays'.[10] It is entirely possible that plays were regularly performed at Trinity and that the play Madox attended was just one of those, although it should be noted that the play has

6. Study of Inns drama has been transformed by the publication of the relevant *REED* volumes: *REED: Inns of Court* edited Alan H. Nelson and John R. Elliott Jr, 3 vols (Cambridge: D.S. Brewer, 2010). See also *The Intellectual and Cultural World of the Early Modern Inns of Court* edited Jayne Elisabeth Archer, Elizabeth Goldring, and Sarah Knight (Manchester UP, 2011).
7. *REED: Oxford* edited John R. Elliott and others, 2 vols (University of Toronto Press, 2004) *1* 98.
8. *REED: Oxford 1* 101.
9. *REED: Oxford 1* 111.
10. *REED: Oxford 1* 168.

previously been included among a group produced within an apparent drama 'festival' of 1582.[11]

Assuming that the identification of the Trinity play is correct, it means that *Supposes* is very unusual for having been performed at two different academic institutions within the early modern period. We also (again unusually) have reported reactions to both performances and, with this essay, I wish to consider possible responses to the play in a little more detail by speculating more broadly on the productions' respective audiences. *Supposes* would furthermore be remarkable within Oxford academic drama more locally as the 'odd one out', the sole example of a play performed within the University that was written by a contemporaneous English author without an apparent connection to it. The *REED* volumes for Oxford detail just four examples of plays at the University (and I am consciously separating gown plays from town plays here) that came from 'extramural' sources: Bale's *Three Laws* and Foxe's *Christus Triumphans* are plays that have possible associations but no firm evidence of actual performance at Oxford (I'm putting Foxe as extramural in the sense that he'd lost his Fellowship by this stage, but obviously we can see him as an Oxford man too); Richard Edwards' *Damon and Pithias* was played in the warden's lodgings at Merton College in January 1568, which was a revival of a play that was performed at Court at Christmas 1564/5. Edwards studied at Oxford, becoming a Student or Fellow at Christ Church, and he was brought back to use his experience as Master of the Children of the Chapel Royal to produce his two-part *Palamon and Arcite* as part of the Queen's visit of 1566, shortly before his death. So it is reasonable, I think, to consider him as something of an Oxford insider.[12] Gascoigne, by contrast, was probably at Cambridge prior to study at Gray's Inn.[13] The unusual nature of an extramural contemporaneous play therefore begs the question of why it might have been chosen. Gascoigne had died in 1577 and while the text of his play had been printed twice by 1582, there would not be another edition until the *Whole Works* of 1587. Trinity was therefore not responding to a newly available text, although the fact of an academic comedy being readily available in print might well be seen

11. John Finnis and Patrick H. Martin 'An Oxford Play Festival in 1582' *Notes & Queries* 50: 4 (2003) 391–4.
12. *REED: Oxford 2* Appendix 9 853–5.
13. G.W. Pigman III 'Gascoigne, George (1534/5?–1577) *Oxford Dictionary of National Biography* (Oxford UP, 2004); online edition May 2010 <http://www.oxforddnb.com> [accessed 23 July 2017].

as relevant, especially if the play could be seen as particularly pertinent to an academic environment.

Supposes is relatively well known, but a brief narrative summary might be useful to give a sense of the familiar patterns and unlikely coincidences upon which it relies. Essentially the set-up is that a wealthy Sicilian law student, Erostrato, and his servant, Dulippo, have been in Ferrara for two years and have switched places so that the former can work within the household of Damon and thereby access his daughter, Polynesta. Meanwhile Damon is in negotiation with a rich, old lawyer called Cleander for Polynesta's hand and so Erostrato (or rather Dulippo as he actually is) tells Damon that he would like to marry her, that he is even wealthier than Cleander, and that his father, Philogano, will be along in a fortnight to secure everything and prove his wealth. The problem, of course, is that they cannot really send for Philogano or they will have to come clean about the right Erostrato neglecting his studies in favour of sex. And so Dulippo dupes a visiting Sienese merchant into believing that recent political turmoil means that Ferrara is now pitched against his people and that, for safety, he should stay with him – and to fool anybody who asks, he should pretend to be his father – and so it goes on. It just so happens that Damon finds out about the loss of his daughter's virginity and Erostrato is locked up. Then the real Philogano appears and, not being able to find his son, naturally assumes that he has been murdered and subsequently impersonated. And he therefore employs Cleander to prosecute Dulippo. But it then turns out that Dulippo is, of course, Cleander's long lost son and everyone ultimately gets what they want towards a happy resolution.

Even from this brief description, and perhaps even in the absence of prior knowledge of the play, it is hopefully obvious that it imitates many of the characters, plots, and methods familiar from Roman comedy. I did not mention all of the characters from *Supposes*, but alongside the typical clever servant, the 'doubled' father, the acquisitive old lawyer (who simultaneously represents the old man in love), and the sexually wayward son that I mentioned, we have also got typical figures such as a gossipy Nurse, and a parasite. Indeed, the editors of the scholarly edition of Ariosto detect references to nineteen of Plautus' twenty complete surviving plays within *Supposes* and to all six extant plays by Terence.[14] The play is almost an anthology of New Comedy, in other words, which is precisely the way, I would argue, that it is supposed to be understood.

14. Ludovico Ariosto *Tutte le Opera di Ludovico Ariosto* edited Cesare Segre, 5 vols (Milan: Mondadori, 1984) 4 xxi–xxiii.

The full extent of the play's imitation is possible to miss, however. In his encyclopaedic series of volumes, *British Drama*, Martin Wiggins lists only Ariosto's prose and verse texts as narrative sources for *Supposes*, along with Plautus' play, *The Captives*.[15] Thinking about sources for a translation is clearly a complicated business because a decision has to be made about whether to list the sources for the source text itself – hence *The Captives* here. And yet it is a slightly odd inclusion because, as Ariosto's original prologue makes clear, in a typically Terentian manner, *Supposes/I Suppositi* is explicitly announced as being based upon a combination of more than one source text:

> In this play, among other things, you are to suppose that the servant is a free man, and vice versa. The author admits that he has followed Plautus and Terence in this. Plautus interchanges Philocrates and Tyndarus in *The Captives* and Terence does the same thing … in *The Eunuch*. The author has done this because, as far as is within his power, he wants to imitate the celebrated poets not only in their customs but also in the very plots of their stories.[16]

If we are including sources for Ariosto, as mediated through Gascoigne, we might suggest that either both the Terence and Plautus sources should therefore be included, if they are useful to the reception of Gascoigne's play, or perhaps neither, if the idea is that the reader should go back to the major source(s) and trace imitation from there. It is more complicated than that, of course, anyway, since we could potentially list twenty-five rather than two Roman comedies that are available within the text. In any event, Gascoigne's prologue is entirely different and so a judgement has been made upon more than an explicit announcement of source material; rather than simply draw attention to particular source texts, Gascoigne instead also foregrounds the method of supposition which the play performs. Ariosto's introduction is thus replaced with a brief and far more general 'Prologue or Argument', which, within a little over twenty lines, attempts to use the word 'suppose' as many times as possible. So, for example, he introduces the idea of servants and masters being substituted and then continues:

15. *British Drama 1533–1642: A Catalogue* edited Martin Wiggins with Catherine Richardson, 8 vols (Oxford UP, 2012) *1* 441.
16. Ludovico Ariosto *Supposes* in *Three Italian Renaissance Comedies* edited Christopher Cairns (Lewiston: Mellen Press, 1996) 59.

> I suppose that even already you suppose me very fonde, that have so simply disclosed unto you the subtilties of these our Supposes: where otherwise in deede I suppose you shoulde have hearde almoste the laste of our Supposes, before you could have supposed anye of them arighte.
> 'The Prologue or Argument'

Clearly the joke works here by the suggestion that revealing how characters will be switched somehow diminishes, rather than enhances, the experience of the play. And in case we missed it, the point is then confirmed for us in the opening scene when Polynesta reveals to her Nurse that the two men have switched identities so that Erostrato can gain sexual access to her. Equally, of course, we do not need to wait until the end to imagine the arc of the plot's trajectory. The invocation of supposition in other words relies upon an awareness of Roman comedy and its familiar methodologies. From the moment that we hear Cleander mention the loss of his son, our prior experience of how antefacts work in New Comedy suggests to us that he will turn up in the shape of (or rather be revealed as) Dulippo, just as we know that the real Philogano will appear at dramatically the most opportune time.

At the smaller scale of how the characters interact with each other, we can similarly see precisely how the play functions in the same way as New Comedic precedent. Dulippo, who has been described as an 'author-surrogate',[17] motivates the plot by telling lies, to Damon and the dim-witted Sienese visitor, to name but two. But he does so convincingly because he formulates narrative in the way in which rhetoricians explained that ancient comic writers had done. This is what Lorna Hutson describes as mimetic illusion and she has demonstrated, I think persuasively, that this was also the method for finding and formulating arguments taught by the synthesis of rhetoric and dialectic within University Arts courses in the sixteenth century.[18] Improbable stories thus become probable because they contain all of the topics or elements that were deemed critical for plausible narration (motive, time, place, opportunity, means, method, and the like), to quote the list provided by Quintilian. I will return to this idea shortly.

There are numerous ways of thinking about how and why Gascoigne alters Ariosto's prologue; his removal of specific reference to Terence and Plautus and the explicit emphasis on an imitation of ancient comic method. On the one

17. Lorna Hutson *The Invention of Suspicion: Law and Mimesis in Shakespeare and Renaissance Drama* (Oxford UP, 2007) 192.
18. Hutson *The Invention of Suspicion* 128–37.

hand, to an educated audience, there is really no need to provide the explicit direction; if you know your Roman comedy, the obvious clues are there – and indeed, the delivery of those clues becomes the very substance of the play. But what if you do not know your comedy quite so well? If you did not recognise the various types and motifs, and indeed motives, then you might well need to wait until the end of the play to find out what happens, as Gascoigne ironically suggests. It would still be a good play, but it would be a very different experience.

I would suggest that it is not a great leap to think that many members of an Oxford audience in 1582 would be primed to appreciate the delivery of those intertextual clues. The centrality of Roman comedy to humanist curricula is very well known, with Terence particularly being routinely anatomised as a ready-made example of recyclable and rhetorically aware Latin. Grammar school students learned how to compose through Terence – and, as ever, Colin Burrow is brilliant in describing how, at a more fundamental level, schoolboys learnt how to speak through him:

> Terence was valuable: his 'hey you's, 'I just died's, his 'ohmygod's provided excellent models for a genuinely useful day-to-day Latin speech ... The Pelian groves, Hyrcanian tigers, and rhetorical ornaments of tragic drama and epic poetry might be useful for orators composing funerary laments or florid addresses to monarchs on public occasions. But for buying a drink or negotiating in the playground under your master's eye, Terence was your man.[19]

We know that classical comedies figure regularly among booklists of students and academics at the Universities and also that they were regularly performed at academic institutions too; I mentioned above that Trinity staged *The Andria* in 1559; two of the eight plays that were apparently performed as part of the Oxford play festival of 1582 were by Plautus. I have always been slightly troubled by precisely how this works, however. We know that some schools, such as Westminster, performed plays in Latin (including Roman New Comedy) and so there is surely a possible sense in which playing Terence particularly is both literally and metaphorically child's play, albeit that I fully accept that performing a whole play, with the added value to skills of memory and delivery, is very different from the intensive focus on parts that would form the imitative experience at the majority of schools. But *Supposes* works well with this in mind. While borrowing

19. Colin Burrow *Shakespeare and Classical Antiquity* (Oxford UP, 2013) 140.

from, or imitating, many of the elements of Roman comedy (the stock characters considered above, for example, the knowing use of settings and the game of forcing the audience to imagine what's going on behind closed doors, the Terentian tactic of one character inviting another to narrate and consider their situation, etc.) Ariosto, and then Gascoigne, also adapt and develop that material. Lorna Hutson has drawn attention, for example, to the psychological depth involved at the point at which Philogano realises that his erstwhile servant has been imitating his son, and therefore assumes (wrongly) that he must also have murdered him:

> Philogano: Out and alas, he whom I sent hither with my sonne to be his servaunt, and to give attendance on him, hath eyther cut his throate, or by some evill meanes made hym away, and hath not onely taken his garments, his books, his money, and that which he broughte oute of *Sicilia* wyth him, but usurpeth his name also …
>
> Oh miserable *Philogano*, oh unhappie olde man: oh eternall god, is there no judge? no officer? no higher powers whom I maye complaine unto for redresse of these wrongs?
>
> 4. 8. 25–9, 31–4

As Hutson states:

> No *senex* figure of Roman comedy sounds quite so distraught on discovering how he's been made a dupe in his absence. The difference from Roman comedy lies in Ariosto's brilliant exploitation of the horror of surmise. Filogono's imagined scenario of his son's murder is indeed more likely than the play's 'real' explanation, and its pathos plumbs unexpected emotional depths in the comic convention of paralogism, or mistaken conjecture.[20]

I would not disagree, but I think we can go slightly further and suggest that it is a more complicated example. Just as Ariosto imitates his sources and produces something that is recognisably like (but not the same), so Gascoigne, in turn, adapts and develops Ariosto. We know that, for all of its success and popularity, the use of Roman comedy within grammar school education drew opposition for the apparent mediation of immorality – it is not difficult to see the issue with disobedient young men getting away with premarital sex purely because it just so happens that, unbeknownst to all (except an experienced audience),

20. Lorna Hutson 'The evidential plot: Shakespeare and Gascoigne at Gray's Inn' in *The Intellectual and Cultural Worlds of the Early Modern Inns of Court* 245–63, at 253.

the young woman is well-born after all. It is a story well known and so I will not follow it here; it is why we have Christian Terence and the many attempts to use the parable of the Prodigal Son throughout the century as a replacement narrative spine. Gascoigne's later play, *The Glass of Government*, takes this opposition to New Comedy head-on; it can be read as a straightforward mediation of the attitudes of people like Ascham, or it can be read as an ironic satire of *The Schoolmaster* and texts that have a similar agenda. It is striking within this context to note that many of the additions that Gascoigne makes to his source text within *Supposes* involve morality and can be seen to work in a similarly knowing way. Gascoigne's Erostrato speaks of self-reproach and shame, for example, which Ariosto's equivalent never feels (2. 1. 57–9); and Damon, the father, reproaches himself for his lack of care with a speech (very different in Gascoigne to Ariosto) that focuses upon parental duties to instil morality:

> For of all the dueties that are requisite in humane lyfe, onely obedience is by the parents to be required of the childe, where on the other side the parents are bound, first to beget them, then to bring them foorth, after to nourish them, to preserve them from boldily perils in the cradle, from daunger of soule by godly education, to matche them in perfect consort enclined to virtue, to banish them all ydle and wanton companie.
>
> 3. 3. 50–6

If this feels like a set piece that is not quite integrated, that might well be how we are supposed to take it. Here we have a rather dry moral intrusion into a play that elsewhere delights in the disobedience of young men and women who act safe in the knowledge that the narrative will look after them. Indeed, some of Gascoigne's other alterations serve to make the play more salacious by manipulating the audience's imaginations; there is a point at which it is falsely reported that the lovers were 'taken a bed' (5. 2. 36–7), which causes the audience to imagine them *in flagrante*, while Ariosto's equivalent merely reports that the affair had been discovered.

So suppose we see the way that Philogano reacts (above) as having a moral as well as psychological dimension. The audience might empathise and consider what it must be to imagine the murder of one's child; the young men present might see the stark effects of bad behaviour and decide to mend their ways. But while Philogano is certainly a development of the source figure of a comedic *senex*, everything that contextualises this point emphasises that we are watching a play that is imitating New Comedy and we know very well that all will be well. It is a bit like a magician's trick; once we understand how it is performed, we might admire the skill involved, but we will not be fooled again. So, aware of what is happening here, we might well admire Ariosto's (and Gascoigne's) skill in enabling the manipulation of the character within the scene, but that is not to say that we are taken in by it ourselves. If we take that line, we are tangentially acknowledging the application of a method of dialectical invention taught at the universities in the sixteenth century, the method by which a student would learn to find an argument, or compose a narrative, and make it seem credible – a method that relies on the manipulation of both information and an audience.[21] The method both supports the success of the play and also undermines the potential realism of this scene. We can trace the circumstances that cause the final misapplication of logic and we find it incredibly satisfying. On the contrary, an inability to recognise source material, both the imitative framework of New Comedy and the signposted circumstances of manipulated plot, might mean that the play is more *affective* than it would otherwise be. That is not at all to suggest that there could not be a nuanced spectrum of response, of course there could be, but even a decision to suspend an accreted awareness of architextual imitation and to focus on the emotive literariness is something different from unknowing subjection. And if we subsequently recognise that there is something slightly different here, our thoughts are simultaneously brought back to the source from which it differs.

This possible gap in audience awareness, something that relies upon learning, provides the dramatised joke at the heart of the slightly earlier Cambridge play, *Gammer Gurton's Needle*, that the rural villagers are easily fooled by the slightly higher intellect of Diccon. Thus he knows how to formulate his lies to make them seem rhetorically and dialectically probable by providing all of the circumstances which an unwitting audience would use to build their delusion:

> Yea, that I do doubtless, as ye shall hear anon:
> A' see a thing this matter toucheth within these twenty hours, (*time*)
> Even at this gate before my face, by a neighbour of yours. (*place and person*)
> She stooped me down and up she took
> the needle or a pin – (*manner and deed*)
> I durst be sworn it was even yours, by all my mother's kin!
>
> 2. 4. 15–19

21. Lorna Hutson 'Rhetoric and Early Modern Law' in *The Oxford Handbook of Rhetorical Studies* edited Michael MacDonald (Oxford UP, 2017).

At the heart of *Supposes*, we have a similar set piece demonstration of how an emphatically false argument is conceived and delivered. Dulippo fools the Sienese visitor by producing evidence that seems credible because of the way that it seems to make sense. He is careful to include topics and circumstances of time, place, person, manner and deed that serve as evidence to support his lie. He craftily takes information from the visitor and uses it against him: for example, he hears that the visitor has been travelling for a month and therefore describes the political turmoil as happening within the last week; he provides details that seem possible, if not probable, such as that 'the duke had charged upon great penalties that the Inholders and vitlers should bring word daily of as many Sieneses as come to their houses' (*2*. 1. 121–2); he explains that he wishes to help the now desperate visitor in recompense for courtesy that he had previously received in Siena and so on. Like Diccon, Dulippo is also aware of his stagecraft and describes the delivery of his manipulation too; Dulippo says, 'I would you had heard me, and seene the gestures that I enforced to make him believe this', and Erostrato replies, 'I believe you, for I know you can counterfeit well' (*2*. 1. 119). It is a use of learning, even if it is not quite the end to which Oxford learning was intended to be directed.

In thinking about the migration of *Supposes* from Gray's Inn to Trinity College, Oxford, and the relative fields of learning which might be at play, we should also question how we might evaluate the performance at the Inns of Court too. The answer to that might seem obvious from the most recent critical attention that the play has received. Lorna Hutson, most notably, has argued for how the evaluation of evidence within the play is almost current with some of the ways that lawyers (and local justices) would soon be trained to think about circumstances and plausibility.[22] I do not totally disagree, but I do think that the most convincing elements of her reading are those which she develops more generally from the use of circumstance and plausibility as vital elements of rhetorical and dramatic narrative, rather than specific legal reference. Ariosto had studied Law, before he was allowed to move to Classics, and the saturation of legal material within the play, which Gascoigne merely translates (and his is a generally close translation), is very similar to that found throughout Roman New Comedy. There are certainly brief satirical barbs at lawyers for being greedy and self-serving, but they are familiar and taken from the original. And while the play provides, for Ariosto, a new synthesis of material that enables him to consider modern city-states, I would maintain that the play is primarily about

22. See Hutson 'The evidential plot' and *The Invention of Suspicion*, especially 185–202.

Roman New Comedy itself, the way that it worked and the way that students/readers/audience members were taught to approach, understand, and learn from it. We know that in Ferrara, from 1486 onwards, and the performance of Plautus' *Menaechmi*, classical comedies, both in Latin and Italian translation, were performed regularly, alongside vernacular plays based on classical narratives. And so we might assume that many among Ariosto's original audience would appreciate and respond to the many sources at play.

We might equally assume that many among the audience at Gray's Inn would be similarly equipped to respond. In his study of *Shakespeare and Classical Antiquity*, Colin Burrow makes a persuasive case for how Shakespeare shaped comedies written for Inns performances to first demonstrate awareness of, and secondly to develop, the shared anticipation of classical comedy among the audiences for *The Comedy of Errors* (Gray's Inn 1594) and *Twelfth Night* (Middle Temple in 1602). Acutely aware of the limits of his education among 'an audience of smartly Latinate young men',[23] Shakespeare explicitly demonstrates his knowledge of conventions in *Errors*, but was able to play more confidently with them by the time of *Twelfth Night*. Ironically, however, I would argue that it would not be quite the same case at Gray's Inn in the 1560s. Lorna Hutson envisages a similar audience to that which we might imagine watching *The Comedy of Errors*:

> We need to recover the combination of knowingness and novelty and the sense of fun that would have greeted Gascoigne's play when it was first performed to an audience as well-versed in Latin comedy as the lawyers of the Inns.[24]

I have written elsewhere, however, about the way that many of the literary figures that we associate with the Inns, men such as Gascoigne, were exceptional among their peers through their level of education, particularly the earlier we go backwards through the sixteenth century.[25] It is entirely likely that 'smartly Latinate young men' would actually have been in the minority, even at festive celebrations when the Inns would be visited by former members and connections. And while we have known, at least since Lisa Jardine's work on University

23. Burrow *Shakespeare and Classical Antiquity* 143.
24. Hutson 'The evidential plot' 247.
25. James McBain '"Attentive Mindes and Serious Wits": Legal Training and Early Drama' in *The Oxford Handbook of English Law and Literature, 1500–1700* edited Lorna Hutson (Oxford UP, 2017) 80–96.

curricula, that a decent level of Latin was a prerequisite for entry, there were no such requirements at the Inns.[26] It has previously been argued that the *REED* editors had, perfectly reasonably, made different assumptions about language dependent on location: that a lost 'roman comedy' at the Inns of Court is assumed to have been in English while the example of Peter Heylyn's 'English tragedy' at Oxford is assumed to have been in Latin.[27] The possibility was raised that Heylyn's work, and others, might well have been in English instead. But it is important to state that the argument does not work the other way around because there is simply no evidence of a tradition of Latin plays at the Inns.[28] Indeed, while there are interludes, plays, masques, revels, and disguisings, Gascoigne's play is the earliest example of a formal comedy that we know of at one of the Inns, which obviously contrasts markedly with the Universities, with a tradition of regular comedies from the late 1520s onwards at Oxford and from 1510 at Cambridge.

I am not claiming that comedy would have been entirely new to the assembled audience at Gray's Inn in 1566, of course, but I think that it would be fair to make the slightly more modest claim that the average law student would have far less experience of both Latin and vernacular learned comedy than the average student at one of the Universities. And, in case we are thinking that there would be too much of an overlap, it is worth recalling figures provided by Rosemary O'Day that in 1561, only 13% of men gaining admittance to one of the Inns had previously spent time at one of the Universities (the figure rises to 46% for 1581) and that a minority within the group had stayed long enough to have completed degrees.[29] We think of the Inns as being a particularly

26. See, for example, Lisa Jardine 'Humanism and the Sixteenth Century Cambridge Arts Course' *History of Education 4: 1* (1975) 16–31.
27. Stephanie Allen, Elisabeth Dutton, and James McBain 'Rehabilitating Academic Drama' in *The Routledge Research Companion to Early Drama and Performance* edited Pamela King (Abingdon: Routledge, 2017) 221–36.
28. In summarising plays known to have been performed at the Early Modern Inns, in the introduction to *REED: Inns of Court*, Alan Nelson states that 'Inns of Court comedy is [now] represented uniquely by *Supposes*', *1* xxi. Nelson then refers to the extant cast-list for the lost 'roman comedy', which suggests a hybrid performance in its combination of recognisable types (old man, parasite, courtesan), political figures (Clodius and Cato, for example), and the figure of 'Melancholy'. The play, if it was ever produced, presumably did not rely on familiarity with authentic Latin models and was therefore very different from *Supposes*.
29. Rosemary O'Day *The Professions in Early Modern England, 1450–1800* (Harlow: Longman, 2000) 129.

conducive environment for literature and they obviously were productive places for writers, such as Gascoigne. But I think that there is an essential difference between an institution and its training as providing a context for performance, such as the Inns, and the situation, such as at Oxford, where some of the material considered might well become pre-text too.[30]

Much of what we know about legal training at the Inns comes from reports written to inspire reform to bring education there more into line with humanist studies elsewhere, both in terms of language and literature. The complaint that law students often started so young as to neglect the possibility of other study recurs too, but, as the percentage of students with prior experience at university increases towards the turn of the century, that complaint looked after itself. Recently Lorna Hutson has also argued very persuasively that university dialectic came to influence legal reasoning from the early seventeenth century, which, along with supporting a sense of change with an increasingly educated intake at the Inns, simultaneously testifies to there being established habits of argumentation based upon circumstances at the universities earlier on.[31]

I am suggesting that *Supposes*, which might initially seem to be an outsider at Oxford, albeit one that makes perfect sense, is in many ways an outsider at Gray's Inn too. Indeed, it could be argued that it would ironically have been much more of an outsider at the Inns than at Oxford, if we think quite narrowly in terms of how likely an audience might have been to appreciate the depth of its engagement with the many hypotexts that can be found within it. But then, to think so narrowly would be to reduce the potential that this example of dramatic migration has for inviting us to think about how an audience and play might relate. There is no reason not to suppose that Madox is referring to Gascoigne's work; it is very likely to be the same play, in terms of a text, but then it is also not the same play, both between different audiences and between members of the same one in terms of how it might have been understood. A good way of explaining what I mean is to borrow from a relatively recent essay, in which Emma Smith uses film genre criticism as a way of thinking about the life cycle of early modern revenge plays. Ultimately drawing upon the work of the art historian, Henri Focillon, film genre criticism, in basic terms, identifies a generic life cycle of a particular form and splits it into distinct phases, so we have a rough pattern of 'classic – parody – contestation – critique', in the

30. *Oxford English Dictionary* sv *pre-text* n.3: 'The literary, historical, or biographical material which informs or contextualises a literary work'.

31. Hutson 'Rhetoric and Early Modern Law'.

terms of Christian Metz.[32] In the slightly more complicated version of Thomas Schatz, these phases are developed in more detail, so we have: first, a phase of experimentation to establish conventions; a classic period when conventions are understood by artists and audience; a period of refinement, in which the form is embellished with stylistic details; and then finally a baroque (or self-reflexive) stage when 'the form and its embellishments are accented to the point at which they themselves become the substance or content of the work'.[33]

The important thing to appreciate from this model, I think, is that it is a two-way engagement between artist and audience. Smith quotes Leo Braudy (early modernist and film historian) and his articulation, that 'Genre films essentially ask the audience, "do you still want to believe this?" Popularity is the audience answering 'Yes'. Change in genre occurs when the audience says, "That's too infantile a form for what we believe. Show us something more complicated"'.[34] I think this model is very helpful, but there is an obvious objection which is that the relatively stable categories rely upon a relatively stable idea of an audience. It is clearly too bland to think about an audience *en masse* as sharing the same perspective, even if your job is involved in decisions about whether a Hollywood studio should finance a proposed film. There is some value in tentatively drawing some distinction between likely audiences at different places, nevertheless. We might speculate that the play might have seemed the equivalent of 'baroque' to many in the audience at Trinity, but it might have seemed more akin to 'classic' for many at Gray's Inn. Gillian Austen has described *Supposes* as 'avant-garde' for the original audience, which we might locate somewhere closer to the initial 'period of experimentation', if the generic identity of the play is explicitly seen to be available at all.[35]

Academic drama, like household drama, invites us to speculate about audiences and to populate performances, even if only to a limited extent. There are inherent risks to that speculation, but it nevertheless seems necessary if we are to be able to consider the audience beyond the fragmentary remains that 'they applauded' or that the play was 'handled indifferently'.

Université de Fribourg

32. Emma Smith 'Genres: Cinematic and Early Modern' *Shakespeare Bulletin 32: 1* (2014) 27–43, at 30.
33. Smith 'Genres: Cinematic and Early Modern' 30.
34. Smith 'Genres: Cinematic and Early Modern' 30.
35. Gillian Austen *George Gascoigne* (Cambridge: D.S. Brewer, 2008) 49.

ELIZABETH NEVILE'S WEDDING ENTERTAINMENTS:
A Yorkshire Family Celebration in 1526 and its Contexts

Diana Wyatt

Among the papers of the Strickland-Constable family of Wassand Hall in the East Riding of Yorkshire, now lodged at the East Riding Archives and Local Studies in Beverley, is a modest little booklet measuring only 20 cm x 15 cm, of paper bound in a piece of recycled parchment, which is listed in the ERA catalogue as 'Sir John Nevile's memoranda book. 1595'.

The booklet, containing only twenty-eight (unnumbered) folios, in fact appears to be a compilation of memoranda and accounts made mainly for the weddings of Sir John Nevile's children in the 1520s and 1530s, prefaced by a pedigree of the family (Nevile of Chevet, West Riding) up to 1595, which occupies the first half of the booklet; the cover is marked 'H.N.' for Henry Nevile, the great-grandson of Sir John.[1] It is not immediately clear how this manuscript ended up in the records of the East Riding family of Strickland-Constable, but it is likely that it passed from family to family when Rosamond Estoft, the granddaughter of this Henry Nevile's grandson Sandford Nevile, married Yarburgh Constable of Wassand (1676–1731).[2]

The Nevile family settled in the West Riding on the marriage of Sir John Nevile in the early sixteenth century to a West Riding heiress, the widowed Lady Tempest, née Elizabeth Bosvile, and Sir John seems to have largely rebuilt the family house at Chevet, which his wife had inherited from her own family. They are known also to have owned property at Mile End in Stepney, Middlesex, but Chevet was evidently the family seat, where it is most likely that family celebrations, including the weddings detailed in the Memoranda Book, took place.[3]

1. The manuscript among the Strickland-Constable papers (East Riding Archives and Local Studies DDWS/8/1/1/1) is evidently the original, but excerpts from it were printed in John Croft *Excerpta Antiqua: or, A Collection of Original Manuscripts* (York: William Blanchard, 1797) 78–81. Croft, however, gives no indication of the provenance.
2. See *Dugdale's Visitation of Yorkshire* edited with additions by J.W. Clay, 3 vols in 4 (Exeter: William Pollard, 1907) 3 50.
3. For details of Sir John Nevile's life and career see *The History of Parliament*, <http://www.historyofparliamentonline.org/volume/1509-1558/member/neville-sir-john-ii-1488-1541> [accessed 3 August 2017].

The manuscript contains expense accounts for food and clothes for four Nevile weddings between 1526 and 1533: those of Sir John's daughters Elizabeth (to Roger Rockley, 14 January 1526), Anne (to Thomas Drax) and Mary (to Gervase Clifton), and of his son Henry to Dorothy Dawney, as well as notes on his considerable expenses on a number of other special occasions from 1520 to 1529. All these notes are of interest for what they tell us about Sir John and his sense of the lavish output appropriate to his status, and will be discussed later. However, it is an extra note in the account of Elizabeth's wedding that is the most interesting in the context of entertainment. After listing, at some length, clothes and food, the account suddenly pauses to describe entertainment given as part of Elizabeth's prolonged wedding celebrations (PLATE 1):

ffor night

> ffirst a play, and, streight after the play, a maske, and when the maske was done, then the banquett, which was 110 dishes and all of meat, and then all the gentlemen and Ladys danced and this continued from Sunday to the Saturday after

This detail offers an intriguing insight into the activities, and particularly the entertainments, performed during the wedding – evidently an extremely lavish celebration, given that it 'continued from Sunday to the Saturday after'. Having noticed it during my initial examination, I turned to the accounts of the other weddings in the manuscript in the hope of finding similar details, but there are none. It is impossible to say whether Elizabeth's was the most lavish (perhaps because the first?) of all the four weddings of Sir John's children accounted for in the Memoranda Book, or whether her father was simply more concerned in general with expenses than activity – which, on reflection, makes it unclear why these teasing details of entertainments have been included at all. The manuscript does raise a few questions of its own, which may suggest an answer to that little puzzle. Despite the catalogue identification of the book as 'Sir John Nevile's memoranda book', in fact the family pedigree to the 1590s occupies the first half of the book – fourteen out of a total of twenty-eight folios – and only the second half contains Sir John Nevile's various notes of expenses for his children's weddings and other special occasions: his visit to Guînes in the north of France to participate in Henry VIII's famous meeting with Francis I of France at the Field of the Cloth of Gold in 1520; hospitality given to judges during Sir John's tenure as High Sheriff of Yorkshire in 1527/8; and the extensive building works at Chevet which were completed in 1529.

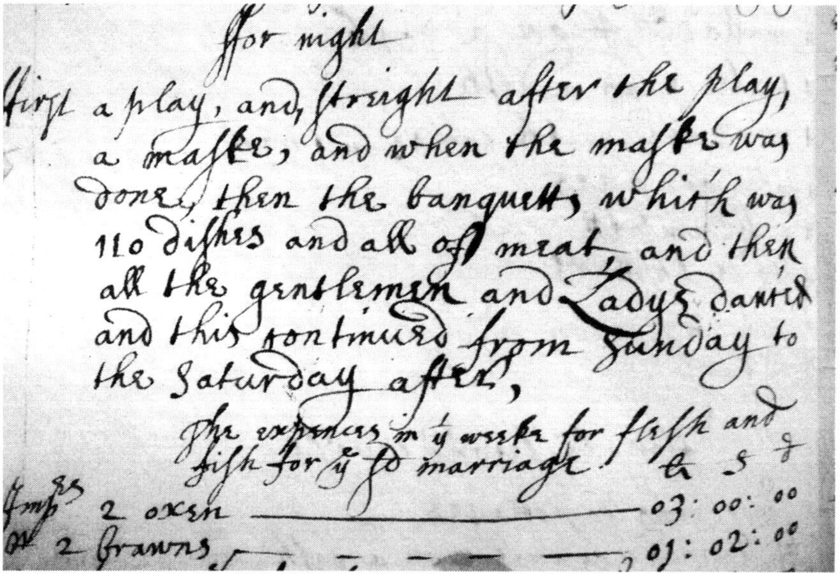

ffor night
first a play, and straight after the play,
a maske, and when the maske was
done, then the banquett, which was
110 dishes and all of meat, and then
all the gentlemen and Ladys danced
and this continued from Sunday to
the Saturday after,
The expences in ye weeke for flesh and
fish for ye sd marriage. li s d
Imprs 2 oxen ———— 03: 00: 00
It 2 brawns ———— 01: 02: 00

PLATE 1: Beverley: East Riding Archives and Local Studies, MS ERALS DDWS/8/1/1/1 fol. 15v, reproduced by kind permission of the depositor

Comparison between the hand of the pedigree, which was evidently compiled by Henry Nevile, Sir John's great-grandson, the 'HN' of the title page, and that of the wedding entries strongly suggests to me that they are identical: in other words all Sir John's notes that appear in the Memoranda Book were copied by Henry, as being of interest to him in the context of the family's pedigree and its acquired status. Since as far as I know there is no surviving original version of Sir John's accounts, we have only this copy, made almost seventy years later, to go on. There may originally have been more information about entertainments at the other weddings, which Henry omitted because they added nothing to his own picture of his family's importance and social connections. However, even if some sections were omitted by Henry Nevile, for the most part it does read like an accurate copy, using the first person in places and reproducing the exact dates on which Sir John made certain notes. In fact a strong sense of Sir John Nevile's personality, at least his pride in being able to extend his mansion and to entertain so grandly, emerges from these notes, which adds to the sense that they have been copied carefully and accurately.

Beyond the question of how closely the existing manuscript follows Sir John's original notes, the record of Elizabeth's wedding raises questions about the exact status of these particular Neviles, how lavish their festivities might have been, how closely Sir John might have followed the fashion of the royal court and the greatest households in the country, and the form and appearance of the entertainments mentioned, the play and 'maske'.[4]

The family's status is not hard to discover. Sir John Nevile's branch of the Neville family was a rather junior one from Liversedge in Lincolnshire, and he himself was his father's third son; in that he did not inherit his father's property, he may well have considered himself a self-made man, which would help to explain the emphasis in the Memoranda Book on how much he spent on his house and hospitality. Born before 1488 (according to his biography in *The History of Parliament*), he raised his status early in the sixteenth century by marrying Elizabeth, the heiress of the West Riding Bosvile family who brought him the property of Chevet near Wakefield.[5] He initiated a twenty-year programme of building there, which suggests radical modernisation if not, indeed, complete rebuilding; luckily, a set of accounts for this building survives, as well as the notes in the Memoranda Book, which together give us a good idea of the extensiveness and layout of the house.[6] The survival of the building records is especially fortunate, because the house itself has not survived: having passed by marriage from the Neviles to the Pilkington family in the eighteenth century, it remained in the Pilkingtons' possession until it was sold to Wakefield Council in 1954, briefly opened to the public, and then demolished, evidently because of mining subsidence, in the 1960s. Photographs of the house in its final years indicate much alteration since Sir John Nevile's time, although one staircase, said to be from the early sixteenth century building, had been retained.[7]

4. I adopt the manuscript spelling *maske* throughout this article, rather than the later *masque*, which may suggest a slightly different kind of entertainment.
5. For Sir John Nevile's biography, see reference to *The History of Parliament Online* at note 2 above.
6. For manuscript see Leeds University Brotherton Library, Bradfer-Lawrence Collection MD335/3/2. See also Wm.E. Preston 'A Sixteenth-Century Account Roll of the building of a house at Chevet' *Yorkshire Archaeological Journal* 35 (1936) 326–30.
7. A brief account of the Chevet site, now part of Newmillerdam Country Park, can be seen at <http://www.pennineheritage.org.uk/exhibits/show/historic-homes-of-yorkshire/chevet-park> [accessed 3 August 2017]. It includes photographs of the house taken in the early twentieth century.

William E. Preston's article in the *Yorkshire Archaeological Journal* includes a useful transcript of the building accounts, which give a very good idea of the extent of the house and outbuildings.[8] The accounts are headed 'Thys be the chargeus of the beyldyng of my howse at Cheyet sens the viij yere of our soveraine lord Kyng Henry the viijth [April 1517–April 1518] as doye apere by the (Indenre of accounntts).' Joseph Hunter, in *South Yorkshire* (quoted by Preston) mentions a beam incorporated into the structure of the house with the inscription 'Thys hows was mad by John Nevyll knyght and Dame Elizabeth hys wyf in the yere of our God MCCCCCXXIX', which suggests a period of continuous rebuilding, additions and improvements covering twenty-two years – a thorough and presumably expensive project designed to ensure that the house would befit the status of an MP and courtier such as Sir John became. The rooms mentioned in the accounts include the hall, the 'old greet chambur', the (new?) 'grett chambur in the neythur end of the hall', the gilt chamber, the great and little galleries, the chapel, the gate house and various outbuildings including brew house, stables, granary and ox house.

The accounts also detail numerous windows and chimneys, and it is in a list of new windows that we find the intriguing mention of 'the qwens chambur' and 'the kyngs grett chambur'. Preston suggests that either there had already been royal visitors or the Neviles were preparing for the possibility. There appears to be no surviving evidence for a royal visit to Chevet either in the Bosviles' time or in Sir John Nevile's, but the impression given by the Memoranda Book is that Sir John would certainly have welcomed a visit from King Henry VIII: he was evidently proud both of his royal connections and of his own ability to spend freely on appropriate occasions. More interestingly, a note calendared in the *Letters and Papers of Henry VIII, Volume 16* (1540–41) of several actual or projected 'gests' made or planned by the king includes the itinerary of 'The King's summer gests from Windsor to York': the planned Yorkshire leg is from Sheffield to 'Burton Abbey, Mr Nevill's, and Wakefield, hassellwoode, and York'.[9] It is known that Henry VIII visited Yorkshire only once, during the admonitory Northern Progress of June–October 1541, when quite a different route was followed, so these 'summer gests' including a stay at Chevet evidently never took place. However, on this evidence it seems not to

8. For details see note 6.

9. Calendared in *Letters and Papers of Henry VIII, Volume 16 (1540–41)* 323 #677: viii. Accessed online at <http://www.british-history.ac.uk/letters-papers-hen8/vol16/pp315-331> on 16 August 2017.

have been unrealistic for Sir John, during the years when he was building both his house and his career as a courtier, to prepare for such a visit.[10]

The notes in the Memoranda Book on the 'home improvements' at Chevet interestingly imply that Sir John completely rebuilt the house and added all the outbuildings, despite the 'old' chambers listed in the building accounts, which would seem to be parts of the Bosvile house. At any rate the sheer pride in his own capacity to spend grandly, as well as to keep out of debt in so doing, shines out of this note dated 28 November 1540:

> Alsoe the s*aid* Sr Iohn Nevile hath builded the manor house of Chevet clearly out of the ground with Barnes, Bake houses & Brewhouses, Stables, Garners, oxe houses, & all other out houses and alsoe hath bought with his penye all manour of Implements belonging to the said house as well moueable as vnmoueable that is within the said house or houses thervnto belonging
>
> Alsoe the said Sr Iohn Nevile hath made all the paile about his parke and translated 3 or 4 times and alsoe made all the ponds wh*ich* I will put in Iudgement of euery wise man that seeth the house within and without what it stands me in and all this haue I done within this 24 yeares Lord I thanke him of his goodnes and at this pr*esent* day wh*ich* is the 28 day of Nov: in the 32 yeare of the Reigne of our Souereign lord King Henry the eight owes neuer a peny to any man liueing for the said houses or house or any parcell belonging therunto.[11]

Sir John's career seems to have kept pace with his establishment as a property-owner: he was knighted after the successful siege of Tournai by Henry VIII in 1513, and in 1520 he accompanied Henry to Guînes for the famously extravagant meeting with Francis I of France at the Field of the Cloth of Gold, where he was chosen to take part in the jousts. The extraordinary

10. Events strangely overtook him, however: see concluding paragraphs below.

11. This note on the building of Chevet is prefaced by a note on the building of his other house at Mile End (now in east London, then Middlesex), which he says cost £900 and 25 marks (a total of £916 13s 4d, or what would now be expressed as £916 66p), towards which the King gave £100. Corroborative evidence for that gift is calendared in the *Letters and Papers of Henry VIII, Volume 3 (1523)* 1316 #3146:17: 'Sir John Nevyll, of Chevet, York, and Elizabeth his wife. Grant, in survivorship, of a messuage with land, three cottages and three gardens in Mylesende, in the parish of Stepney … 12 May 15 Hen. VIII. Del. Westm., 17 June'. Accessed online at <http://www.british-history.ac.uk/letters-papers-hen8/vol3/pp1303-1316> on 11 August 2017.

ostentation and obvious expense of Henry's preparations for the meetings with Francis I are shown in a contemporary picture of the event, not only in the huge numbers in Henry's train but in the specially erected buildings and the entertainments laid on. The lists in which Sir John Nevile and others jousted can be seen at top right of the painting. Of course, Sir John himself can hardly have stretched to any such extravagant spectacle at Elizabeth's wedding or any other family celebration, but the picture (and many of the surviving documents of that occasion as well as others at court) reminds us that this is the kind of lavish royal spectacle that Sir John Nevile regularly saw and even participated in. The *Letters and Papers of Henry VIII* usefully tell us that even by that point in his career, Sir John Nevile had frequently taken part in royal jousts listed among the Revels accounts of Richard Gibson between 1515 and 1518. One entry gives a representative flavour of the richness of costume and sheer spectacle of such events: in July 1517, the King held a joust at Greenwich, with a team of fourteen jousting on his side. The King's costume was parti-coloured: cloth of silver with white velvet cut-work and gold damask fringing on the right side, and black satin, with black velvet cut-work, blue tinsel and damask gold embroidery on the left. He rode a horse with trappings in the same style and his spare horse had white velvet trappings embroidered with gold.[12]

Sir John Nevile was one of fourteen knights and gentlemen jousting on the King's side, who were dressed in white velvet and satin. The King's own costume, naturally, was the most spectacular of all, and its parti-coloured silver/black design reminds us how much such jousts, like the maskes Henry also delighted to take part in, were staged performances.

Sir John continued to rise in the 1520s and 1530s: having already been Sheriff of Yorkshire by 1520, he held the office again twice, as well as a number of royal appointments over the years; he was an MP in 1529, had been appointed a Knight of the Body to Henry VIII by 1533, and was one of fifty 'gentlemen pensioners' lined up to greet the newly arrived Anne of Cleves when she crossed the Channel and proceeded from Dover to Rochester for her first meeting with Henry in January 1540.[13] So although not in the highest

12. Calendared in *Letters and Papers of Henry VIII, Volume 2 (1517)* 1510; Revels Accounts #9 vi. Accessed online at <http://www.british-history.ac.uk/letters-papers-hen8/vol2/pp1490-1518> on 3 August 2017.

13. Calendared in *Letters and Papers of Henry VIII, Volume 15 (1540)* 5 #14. Accessed online at <http://www.british-history.ac.uk/letters-papers-hen8/vol15/pp1-19> on 16 August 2017.

rank of Nevilles, Sir John had a certain status both at home and at court; he knew the king personally, mixed with the great and the good, or at any rate the wealthy and powerful, and by virtue of his wife's inheritance as well as his own efforts, was in a position to spend sufficiently freely on big events to feel a degree of satisfaction in his position and achievements – at least the tone of the notes on his expenses in the Memoranda Book (assuming accurate copying by his great-grandson Henry) suggests as much.

For example, on his participation at the Field of the Cloth of Gold, recorded several years later in a curious mixture of third and first person, we find this note:

> Alsoe the said S*ir* Iohn Nevile spent at ye great Triumph that the Kings Maiestie had at the Campe besides Guynes of my selfe wife and s*er*vants for the Kings Honnor 300ld 25 Marke w*hi*ch I will take of my Consience I spent noe lesse.

Having established that Sir John Nevile evidently had the wealth, the social status, the familiarity with court customs and fashions, and the evident desire to establish himself as a landowner and courtier, which might well prompt him to spend extravagantly on the food, clothes and entertainments for a family wedding, we must examine the evidence that helps to illuminate that bald reference to the play and the maske at Elizabeth's.

In the absence of detail in the Memoranda Book itself, we must rely on analogies, and fortunately there are enough in existence to help us to fill in the picture of these celebrations, particularly the maske. Meg Twycross and Sarah Carpenter quote a significant reference by Edward Hall to what appears to be a new departure from the established form of the disguising, performed at Henry VIII's court for Epiphany 1512:

> the kyng with a .xi. other were disguised, after the maner of Italie, called a maske, a thyng not seen afore in England, thei were appareled in garmentes long and brode, wrought all with gold, with visers and cappes of gold & after the banket doen, these Maskers came in, with sixe gentlemen in silke bearing staffe torches and desired the ladies to daunce, some were content, and some … refused, because it was not a thing commonly seen …[14]

14. Meg Twycross and Sarah Carpenter *Masks and Masking in Medieval and Early Tudor England* (Aldershot: Ashgate, 2002) 169. The Hall quotation is from Edward Hall

Twycross and Carpenter comment on that last detail of Hall's, that apart from the wearing of particular 'long and brode' costumes, 'the apparent novelty Hall notes seems to be restricted to … the maskers not dancing just among themselves but taking partners [unmasked ladies] from the audience. Hall identifies this as Italian, new, and slightly risqué'.

By the 1520s, however, this new foreign fashion seems to have become established. Royal Revels accounts, mentioned above in the context of jousting, also include a wealth of information on masking and similar entertainments. The closest in date – by a curious coincidence dated 14 January 1526, the exact date of Elizabeth's wedding – lists costumes for a masking at court over the Christmas season of 1525/6, calendared in the *Letters and Papers*:

> A meskeler of 6 gentlemen in gowns of cloth of gold and silver, the othersideblack tinsel satin, with great hoods of tinsel satin and tippets of cloth of gold, with buskins of black velvet, and visors bearded with silver. 8 maskelers: 8 long taffeta gowns and hoods; 8 coats of cloth of gold and tinsel satin; 8 dark purple velvet bonnets; 8 pair of black velvet buskins; 8 visors bearded with gold; 9 bonnets over and above the number.[15]

'Meskeler' or 'maskeler' (a term frequently used in Richard Gibson's Revels accounts as well as by Edward Hall), clearly connotes masking activity: in the first item it seems to denote a mask or a set of maskers; in the second it seems to mean sets of costumes for maskers, or even the individual maskers. W.R. Streitberger points out the fluidity of this term even in Gibson's own usage, as of most terms used in the period for performance activity:

> He uses 'mask', meskelyn', and 'meskellyer' to describe a type of entertainment given as part of the revels, to refer to a visor, and to refer to the costumes worn by one of these entertainments.[16]

The Union of the Two Noble and Illustrious Houses of Lancaster and York edited H. Ellis (London: J. Johnson, 1809) 526.

15. Calendared in *Letters and Papers of Henry VIII, Volume 4 (1526)* 838 #1888. Accessed online at <http://www.british-history.ac.uk/letters-papers-hen8/vol4/pp831-849> on 3 August 2017.

16. W.R. Streitberger *Court Revels, 1485–1559* (Toronto, Buffalo, London: University of Toronto Press, 1994) 4. Streitberger's comprehensive research illustrates vividly the difficulty of knowing exactly what any given term denotes, and he underlines the need for caution in interpretation. For full Hall reference, see note 14. Interestingly these are

This record, being concerned simply to record expenses, says nothing about the precise activities of these 'meskelers'. The beards indicate at least that they were dressed as men, and interestingly the immediately preceding entry in these accounts lists eight costumes for ladies: velvet bonnets, 'hers' (i.e. hairs, wigs?), cloth of gold for gowns and foresleeves. They are not, admittedly, stated to be masking costumes, but as the Revels Office was paying for them, the strong implication is that they too were costumes for an entertainment, possibly for ladies to pair the eight 'maskelers' in the second of the two entries quoted above, or a group of 'lordes' for whom costumes were also provided, though for what exact purpose is not stated.

The grandeur of court revels – between Christmas and Twelfth Night or indeed during the continuing celebrations of the 'long' Christmas season lasting until Candlemas, the Purification of the Virgin on 2 February – must have been beyond Sir John Nevile's reach, but the coincidence of dating of the Revels entry and Elizabeth Nevile's wedding day serves as a useful reminder not only that the 'long' Christmas season was not unusually chosen for weddings, but also that masking, as a fashionable adaptation of disguising, was by then becoming a usual form of celebration of various important events in any household of sufficient wealth and status.

Suzanne Westfall has kindly allowed me to draw on an unpublished paper in which she discusses the ordinances for the wedding of a nobleman's daughter contained in the Second Northumberland Household Book.[17] Both the first and second Household Books were compiled for Henry Algernon Percy the 'Magnificent' Fifth Earl, in the early sixteenth century; Henry the Magnificent died in 1527, so the period of both Northumberland books is appropriately close to that of Elizabeth Nevile's wedding in January 1526. The Percies' Yorkshire bases at Wressle and Leconfield were both in the East rather than the West Riding – but certainly close enough geographically to the Neviles' more modest seat of Chevet to provide an instructive comparison. Sir John Nevile's court connections and evident desire to emulate royal and noble customs make it

the only two citations for *maskeler* in the *Oxford English Dictionary* (*maskeler* n.); Hall's phrase 'in maskeler' evidently means 'in disguise'.

17. Suzanne Westfall '"We must be married, or we must live in bawdry": Wedding Revels at the Earl of Northumberland's Household' (paper given at the International Medieval Congress, Kalamazoo, 2015). The Second Northumberland Household Book is Bodleian MS Eng. hist. b. 208. The orders for the marriage of an earl's daughter are at fols 23–30.

likely that his family celebrations would follow the fashion of his most powerful and influential neighbours the Percies.

Westfall quotes extensively from the ordinances governing every moment of the elaborate ceremonial to be observed, underlining the extraordinary care for precedence and propriety throughout (even to the extent of detailing the fashion of headdress to be worn by the bride at the wedding service depending on whether she is a maiden or has been married before). After dining separately from her new husband, the bride, according to the twenty-sixth article, should (after resting a while in her chamber) be approached by a gentleman usher who will 'schew hir that the mynstrallis be redy' and she will enter the hall to dance. Westfall points out that the music was 'probably provided by Percy's retained household minstrels, a taboret, a luter, and a rebec-player, perhaps augmented by local minstrels, itinerant patronised troupes, or minstrels that noble guests had brought along'. We have no information about the provision of music at Elizabeth Nevile's wedding, but there must have been music provided for the dancing, and presumably for the play and the maske too. The Northumberland ordinances provide both for this early-evening music and dancing, and for further food and entertainment in the evening: Westfall outlines the twenty-eighth article, which 'describes the service of private suppers, again segregated by gender, followed by everyone's procession into the great hall to – and we finally get to it – enjoy a "bankett" … And, most importantly to us, to "se suche passe tymes as is their ordirid for theim As Disguisinges enterludes or playes"'.

The Northumberland ordinances evidently reflect a growing fashion in the households of the nobility and gentry: Suzanne Westfall notes that 'The combination of banquet and disguising appears to be a typical structure for wedding revels'. The play(s) and dancing provided for in the Northumberland Household Book are also specifically mentioned in the Nevile Memoranda Book as part of the structure of celebratory activity. What is especially interesting about this evidence from the Memoranda Book is that although examples of plays, maskes and banquets at weddings are readily available from the Elizabethan period, it is harder to find any from as early as the 1520s. Despite its lack of detail, this little manuscript offers the earliest evidence I have found of a specific instance of the pattern in practice.

The play and the maske performed at Elizabeth Nevile's wedding are neither described nor named in the Memoranda Book; nor does the manuscript give us any information about the identities of the performers in either case. So far no *REED* evidence has emerged for Sir John Nevile as a patron of players, so it is impossible to know whether he retained any in-house players, or musicians or choristers who might have performed plays as well as music. However, it is not improbable that a household capable of providing the kind of celebrations Sir John Nevile evidently hosted would retain staff who could provide music and plays as needed. The Earl of Northumberland's Household Books again offer suggestive analogies: the First Book provides, in a check-roll of household staff, for 'My Lordes Chapleyns in Householde vj Viz. The Almoner and if he be a maker of Interludys than he to have a Servaunt to the intent for Writynge of the Parts'.[18] Elsewhere in the First Household Book is a note that four persons are to be appointed as players, to perform plays and interludes at Christmas and other occasions as required. The fifth Earl of Northumberland, of course, was remarkable even in an outstandingly wealthy and powerful family for the extent to which he seems to have favoured richly ceremonious entertainments; moreover he had been brought up at court. Clearly the Neviles of Chevet and Mile End cannot have rivalled the scale and expense of the Northumberland celebrations, both of weddings and of other family occasions. All the same, from what is known of Sir John, he is likely to have emulated the style and lavishness of entertainments of the Earl's households at Wressle and Leconfield, or even those at court, albeit on a smaller scale. So Chevet household musicians may have provided the performance of the play, which a household chaplain may have written; alternatively musicians attached to the households of wedding guests – at Elizabeth's wedding, perhaps the groom's family the Rockleys – may have supplied either text or performers. Otherwise, players may have been hired, though the maskers were presumably either wedding guests or family members, or a mixture of both.

Ian Lancashire, writing about the Twelfth Night celebrations described in the Second Northumberland Household Book, illuminatingly discusses the household hierarchy and concern with precedence which is likely to have dictated the order of performance itself. The precise wording of the record in the Nevile Memoranda Book – 'ffirst a play, and, streight after the play, a maske, and … then the banquett' – may suggest something about the identity of the performers of play and maske respectively. According to Lancashire:

> The centerpiece of the dramatic spectacle was the dramatic pageant containing the morris dancers; these must have been the earl's

18. *The Regulations and Establishment of the Household of Henry Algernon Percy the fifth Earl of Northumberland at his castles of Wressil and Leckinfield* edited Thomas Percy (London: A. Brown, 1905) 44.

> henchmen, those young nobles with whose court education he was entrusted and who were the ornament of his retinue. The henchmen's apparel, with some such end in mind, was the main household expense for Christmas 1514–1516 [*sic*]. In turn the morris was embedded in a disguising and dance of gentlemen and gentlewomen; and these gentry were introduced by performers who were the earl's paid servants, actors of 'aithir play as an entirlude A comody or trigidy' and minstrels. As the henchmen outrank the disguisers, and they the hired performers, so the semi-dramatic dance of the henchmen, I suggest, combines and exceeds the simple play before and the dance after.[19]

With the caveat as before that the Nevile household was not of such high status as Northumberland's, and so is unlikely to have contained similar noble henchmen, it is worth observing that the play at Elizabeth's wedding may have been performed first as much for reasons of household precedence as anything else: if the players were of lower rank (being either household servants or a local hired troupe) than the maskers, the movement would be from hired performance to private entertainment shared among the family and their guests. The *appearance* of the maskers, however, may not have been so obviously set apart from that of the lower-status players: it is likely that, once the play finished and the players had exited, the maskers – family or guests – entered the hall apparently from outside, dressed exotically, perhaps in the Venetian fashion which had been new at court as recently as 1512. The maskers and other family members and guests presumably then shared in both the banquet and the dancing which followed ('and then all the gentlemen and Ladys danced'). In such a situation, as Twycross and Carpenter note, 'there is rarely a distinct body of "spectators" watching a distinct body of "performers"'.[20]

Suzanne Westfall, discussing wedding revels in the Henrician period, notes that, in general:

> The nobility followed the royal example of celebrating marriages with disguisings and banquets. In 1536, the Earl of Rutland celebrated a triple wedding that united the houses of Oxford, Westmorland, and Rutland.

19. Ian Lancashire 'Orders for Twelfth Day and Night circa 1515 in the Second Northumberland Household Book' *English Literary Renaissance 10: 1* (Winter 1980) 6–45, at 18.

20. Twycross and Carpenter *Masks* 102.

> King Henry himself appeared in a mask of Turks and presented the guests with a banquet of forty dishes before returning to York Place.[21]

A performance by the King himself was certainly more than the Neviles of Chevet could hope for (even if their hopes of a royal visit seem to have been not unrealistic: see pages 145–6 above). But the detail in that record cited by Westfall, of the maske featuring Turks, reminds us that there is no particular reason why Elizabeth's wedding maske might not feature Turks, or other exotic figures such as evidently became, and remained, the fashion for weding maskes as the sixteenth century progressed. Forty-six years after Elizabeth Nevile's wedding, George Gascoigne's 'Deuise of a maske for the right honorable Viscount Mountacute [Montagu]' of 1572, published in 1573, features Venetian maskers and a narrative – one of very few sixteenth-century maske texts to survive – referring to Venetian wars against the Turks, from which the speaker has fled. Italian costumes, incidentally, do seem to have become established by then as the norm: the headnote to Gascoigne's published text amusingly explains that eight prospective wedding guests, having decided to present a maske at the wedding, had already had their costumes 'cut of the Venetian fashion', as if that had become the obvious fashion for masking, before it occurred to them that their appearance as Venetians might require some explanation, whereupon they asked Gascoigne to write an introductory speech establishing a fictional Venetian context.[22]

Not all surviving examples of wedding revels mention meals as well as performances, which makes it more interesting that the Memoranda Book does record a sumptuous banquet to follow the entertainment:

> and when the maske was done, then the banquett, which was 110 dishes and all of meat, and then all the gentlemen and Ladys danced …

Suzanne Westfall pertinently reminds us that a 'banquet' in the usage of the period does not mean an entire feast, but a lavish sweet course which forms part of a much greater feast, lasting for hours, with the dancing, masking and plays in between courses.[23] The banquet at Elizabeth's wedding was certainly

21. Westfall 'We must be married' (unpublished conference paper 2015). See note 17 for full details.
22. 'Gascoignes deuise of a maske for the right honorable Viscount Mountacute' in George Gascoigne *A Hundred Sundry Flowers* (1573) (Menston, Yorks: Scolar Press, 1970).
23. Westfall 'We must be married' (unpublished conference paper 2015). See note 17 for full details.

generous (apparently more so even than the king's gift to the Earl of Rutland's celebration): '110 dishes', as the Memoranda Book rather proudly puts it, 'and all of meat'. That 'meat', incidentally, may seem a flat contradiction of the definition of 'banquet' as a sweet course, but the word is clearly used here in the wider sense of 'food' or 'nourishment' (perhaps as opposed to sugary confections). It is usefully illustrated later in the Memoranda Book in a note on Henry Nevile's wedding to Dorothy Dawney (and in Sir John's characteristically assertive tone), that various fruits, nuts and desserts such as gingerbread and almond butter were 'neither fflesh nor fish and yet good meat'.[24]

Unless or until more evidence comes to light, details of Elizabeth Nevile's wedding celebrations must inevitably remain speculative; but we know enough of the event (and of comparable celebrations for which more evidence survives) to deduce that Sir John Nevile, although neither royal nor noble himself, was in a position to emulate both the royal court and a great family like the Percies in giving his daughter the most grand and stylish marriage his means could stretch to.

There is a sad and shocking postscript to this account of one of the high points in Sir John Nevile's career. In November 1540, he made the note already quoted from the Memoranda Book, expressing his great satisfaction in the building of his house at Chevet (and, by implication, also in his career):

> and all this haue I done within this 24 yeares Lord I thanke him of his goodnes and at this *pre*sent day *wh*ich is the 28 day of Nov: in the 32 yeare of the Reigne of our Soueraign lord King Henry the eight owes neuer a peny to any man liueing for the said houses or house or any *par*cell belonging therunto.

In February 1541 he was appointed a Commissioner of the Peace for the West Riding of Yorkshire. In April 1541 the King was informed of a planned conspiracy which was intended to start in the West Riding and was thought to be potentially more dangerous than the Pilgrimage of Grace had been in

24. *The Oxford English Dictionary*, under *meat n. I.1.a*, gives the definition: 'food, as nourishment for people and fodder for horses; *esp*. as opposed to drink (but see quots. c1450 and 1575)': the first of these is 'Þi mete schal be mylk, hony, & wiyn' (in F.J. Furnivall *Polit., Relig., & Love Poems* (1903) 185), and the second, 'It is a very good way, to … kill the list and lyking of a Sparhawke, to feede hir … with liquid meates washt in water' (G. Turberville *Book of Faulconrie* 270). The definition seems rather puzzlingly wide, but the emphasis is evidently on nourishment.

PLATE 2: The bride dances? *Percy 'Dancers'* panel, c.1500, from Northumberland house in York. Image courtesy of York Museums Trust [CC BY-SA 4.0], <https://www.yorkmuseumstrust.org.uk/collections/search/item/?id=45009161>

1536–1537. In the same month Sir John Nevile was arrested and taken to the Tower of London on a charge of treason in connection with the abortive rising. In June he was taken back to Yorkshire, where he was executed at York on the 15th. Accounts of the planned rising vary as to numbers, individuals involved and exactly what was planned; it is the French Ambassador, Charles de Marillac (usually a shrewd observer) who, after laconically noting that several people have been arrested, some of them perhaps innocent, reports in a letter to Francis I dated 14 June that the death sentence has been pronounced

> upon one Master Nevel, a gentleman well known in this Court, and of mediocre wit (*faculté*), who, for not revealing the conspiracy lately made in the North which one of the conspirators had disclosed to him, has been led thither [i.e. northward, towards York] to be executed ...[25]

Whether Sir John Nevile's pride in his achievements had gone to his head, leading him to withhold information in order to pursue the conspirators himself, or whether – harder to believe – he had actually intended to join them, the surviving evidence does not reveal. But his fate is a salutary reminder that no amount of loyal court service, building of one's property or gorgeous celebrations of a daughter's marriage guaranteed safety in the volatile world of Henrician politics.

University of Durham

25. Calendared in *Letters and Papers of Henry VIII, Volume 16 (1540–41)* 440 #903. Accessed online at <http://www.british-history.ac.uk/letters-papers-hen8/vol16/pp437-443>, on 27 August 2017.

HEROD'S KILLING OF THE CHILDREN

Peter Happé

This performance on 8 February 2017, by the New College Players and the Frideswide Voices and directed by Elisabeth Dutton, gained much from its setting in the chapel at New College, Oxford.[1] The feeling that this was a place used regularly for worship helped, with certain physical characteristics to enhance it, including an echo. There was a strong musical element, including dancing, in the performance and many of the actors and singers were women or young girls. This accorded with the text which unusually asks for 'virgynes' (line 477). Here women also acted some of the male parts, including an impressive performance of the Poet, who introduced and concluded the play. The slaughtered children were represented by dolls. There was a strong character contrast between Herod who boasted his way to madness and a grotesque destruction, and the virtuous Simeon, who in this production carried a live baby able to sit up and look beneficently at the audience (without needing an understudy). The latter was a fitting part in a play which in performance had a strong emotional appeal, much helped by the music. The episode of the slaughter was disturbing, especially when it came to a frozen pause as one of the Knights held his spear aloft, impaling a dead baby. It was at this point that both modern and late medieval audiences might have anticipated the Crucifixion yet to come, as well as other mass extermination. As a complement the baby in the arms of Simeon might have echoed the many images of the Madonna and Child, as well as the brief appearance of Mary with the child earlier.

Some doubt arises in the text about the order of the two main events, as the Poet in the introduction puts the Presentation first, with the Killing to follow. In this performance the reverse order, as in the text itself, seemed well supported on emotional grounds as the horror of the murders gave way after angelic intervention to the thankful ending centring upon Simeon.

The text is well provided with stage directions and this performance made good use of them. In the chapel, which has a straight central aisle, the wicked

1. Video of the performance can be seen online at <https://www.youtube.com/watch?v=k-uEWUBP6DI>.

end, so to speak, was the west end, while Simeon's episode took place at the east end in front of the altar. This contrast helped to show up well the opposing interests. The dancing took place in the central aisle where the choir was also placed. The references by the Poet to last year's performance showing the joy of the Shepherds, and to the disputation with the Doctors to come next year suggest that the play was part of a longer enterprise, perhaps a lost cycle. If it was, the stage directions seem to point to a *platea* with distinct areas. For example, one of the directions at the end of the episode in which Herod sets up the murders requires the Knights and Watkyn to walk about the place until Mary and Joseph are conveyed into Egypt (sd at 232). This suggests that in one performance, at least, it was intended that they should remain visible, perhaps to strengthen the threat of what was yet come. Another direction says Mary and Joseph are to go out of the place (280), and they do eventually reach the Temple (428).

The play offers different kinds of dramatic style. The Herod episode is rather grotesque, with comedy in the character of Watkyn, who aspires to become a Knight, and is beaten by the mothers. It may be matched in style with other comic episodes in the extant mystery cycles. The Simeon episode also has analogues in some of them. This part of the play has very little action, and in this performance it was sustained by the music, some of which was liturgical.

The performance worked well, particularly on an emotional level. It was given a particularly gentle atmosphere for the most part, and this helped to modify the horror which may be found in the murders. At the same time it promoted reflection upon some of the puzzles in the manuscript. It looks as though the latter is eclectic. While it records many things which are identifiable as typically late medieval, it may be an accumulation of information from different times or performances. The alternative order of episodes may be part of this. The stage direction *Hic occident pueros* (314), which seems rather superfluous, was added in the margin by a different scribe. Another passage of twenty-five lines spoken by Herod and including Watkyn's first entrance is cancelled in the manuscript (separately numbered after line 80). This effectively removes him until he speaks again at line 133.

The programme note interestingly suggested that the play was written for Candlemas when the Presentation was traditionally commemorated, and the overall effect of this production was distinctly appropriate to such an origin.

University of Southampton

EDITORIAL BOARD (2017)

Contributions for consideration should be sent to one of the editors:

Meg Twycross, Department of English and Creative Writing, Lancaster University, LANCASTER LA1 4YD, United Kingdom
E-mail: m.twycross@lancaster.ac.uk

Sarah Carpenter, English Literature, School of Literatures, Languages and Cultures, University of Edinburgh, 50 George Square, EDINBURGH EH8 9LH, United Kingdom. E-mail: Sarah.Carpenter@ed.ac.uk

Gordon Kipling, 3428 Park Avenue, MINNEAPOLIS, MN 55407, USA
E-mail: kipling@humnet.ucla.edu

Articles should usually be sent as e-mail attachments, preferably in a recent version of Word. See website for further information:

<http://www.medievalenglishtheatre.co.uk/submit.html>

Contributors are asked to follow the *METh* house-style (see website: address above). The language of publication is usually English, and translations should be supplied for quotations from all other languages, including French and Latin.

Contributions are not normally returned to the sender. Any photographs or other illustrations should be accompanied, where appropriate, by a copy of the written permission to reproduce from the private individual, library, or other organisation holding the copyright. Payment of copyright fees is the responsibility of the contributor. A form of request to libraries is available on the website.